Major Trends in Modern Hebrew Fiction

ISAIAH RABINOVICH

Major Trends in
Modern Hebrew Fiction

Translated from the Hebrew by M. Roston

THE UNIVERSITY OF CHICAGO PRESS
CHICAGO & LONDON

Library of Congress Catalog Card Number: 68-15035

THE UNIVERSITY OF CHICAGO PRESS, CHICAGO & LONDON

THE UNIVERSITY OF TORONTO PRESS, TORONTO 5, CANADA

For Sara
Sol and Raizel

Preface

This book is the first volume of a study of major trends in modern Hebrew literature. The term "modern" is intended to distinguish recent literature, which regards creative writing as an end in itself, from the literature of the Enlightenment, which employed it for the most part as a vehicle for didacticism or satire in the pursuit of its ideological aims for Jewish society.[1] This initial volume deals with fiction during the modern era; the next volume will examine its poetry.

Modern Hebrew fiction is largely concerned with the task of penetrating the character of the Jew, both as an individual and as a member of the Jewish community; that is, it attempts to express artistically both the realistic setting of the world around the Jew and the spiritual content of his own inner world. The forms of modern Hebrew literature were molded by the great changes that occurred within the traditional atmosphere of the small Jewish town of Eastern Europe as well as by the great national reawakening that spread through the Jewish communities of Russia, Poland, Lithuania, and the rest of Eastern Europe. This reawakening created a tremendous ferment within Jewish society, producing national and social ideologies with accompanying movements whose aims were economic, political, cultural, and educational.[2] But it also opened new sources of inspiration for the individual poet, writer of fiction, and essayist—sources that had long been hidden and completely sealed off or that had sought expression through the mystic symbolism of the Kabbalah and the teachings and legends of Hasidism.[3] Moreover, modern Hebrew fiction, having taken the place of the literature of the Enlightenment, came to be profoundly influenced by the artistic achievements of European literature and turned at the same time to the treasures of

VII

Hebrew writing, both ancient and recent, to find a handhold for its own literary struggles.

The primary purpose of this book is to provide an analysis of those literary struggles as they were expressed in the writings of individual authors and also to view them as part of the organic development of Hebrew fiction during this era. The period begins in the 1880's, when the naturalist writings of Mendelé Mokher Sefarim had reached their artistic peak, and follows in a variegated course to the 1940's, when Hebrew fiction reached its high-water mark in the epic modernism of Haiyim Hazaz and Shmuel Yosef Agnon; the effects of that period are still being felt. This volume, therefore, provides a historical and critical account of modern Hebrew fiction, the material examined forming the backbone of Hebrew fiction during the period which is generally known as the Hebrew Renaissance.

The biographical details of certain authors had, of course, to be examined together with the social and nationalistic trends of the period in which their works were written, since these trends affect the author's presentation of character as well as his choice of themes. No examination of Mendelé Mokher Sefarim, Shalom Aleikhem, or I. L. Peretz would be complete without such investigation, however deep the analysis. Obviously, to adherents of the New Criticism—and there are many in Israel—such investigation is gross heresy.[4] According to the New Critics, a literary work is in no way indebted to the external world of the author, but draws its artistic strength from the self-generating dynamism inherent in the language of the work itself; it gains nothing from the aspirations of the individual and the trends of his society. I am not an adherent of this somewhat extreme school of criticism. Due attention must, of course, be paid to the contextual subtleties of language, but that does not mean we must ignore the historical setting in which the author has placed his character and in which the story unfolds.

The same is true of poetry, the stronghold of the New Critics. All literature, and fiction most of all, must respond to the inner and outer world of man if it is to endure. We have already seen how the leading exponents of New Criticism in Europe and the

Preface

United States—among them T. S. Eliot, Allen Tate, and Cleanth Brooks—by spurning outward realism as a poetic framework and exclusively devoting their poetic and critical talents to linguistic suggestion and connotation eventually turned their backs on the real world and concentrated on the theological implications of Catholicism and transcendental mysticism. They are not concerned with any real "communication" between the work itself and the world that lies beyond the linguistic fence.

My own view is that all literary history must concern itself with the biographical, social, and national background of the period in which a work is written and with the individual literary development of the author himself, who forms a link in the chain of his time. It is the second of these concerns, the literary development of the author, which serves as the primary focus in this study.

The chapters in this book, although they are divided into sections dealing with different authors, do, in fact, form complete and independent units. Some of these sections have appeared in literary journals in Israel but have been rewritten to form organic parts of the present work.

Unfortunately, some of the more important authors examined in this book have had only a small proportion of their work translated into English. Since the reader will therefore have to rely on those passages quoted as illustrations of the critical comments (all of which were translated especially for this book), I have appended at the end of the volume brief notes and biographical sketches for each chapter, including information on available English translations of the author's works.

The system of transliteration of Hebrew words used in this book is based on that of the Library of Congress. As yet, only the first volume of this work has been completed. It is intended for readers with a general interest in literature; if, as I hope, it succeeds in arousing a more specific interest in the development of modern Hebrew fiction, my labors will have been well rewarded.

Contents

Appendix 233
Literary Ingathering/*Ha-Tekufah*

XII

1

Hebrew Fiction
in Search of a Hero

Hebrew Fiction before Mendelé

In discussing the renaissance of Hebrew literature toward the end
of the nineteenth century, critics tend to concentrate on the
poetry of that era, even though the rebirth of modern Hebrew
fiction took place at the same time. Nor is this tendency surprising, for poetry was perhaps more responsive than fiction to the
changing climate of the day—to those factors, whether nationalistic, sociological, or more universal, that were creating an upheaval within the Jewish communities of eastern Europe. At that
time, poetry began to offer new means of artistic expressions, both
intuitive and symbolic, that were nurtured within the individual
psyche of the poet but were expressed through images and symbols drawn from the external world. The poetry of Haiyim Nahman Bialik and his contemporaries is redolent of the nationalist
and humanist ferment of his day. The awakening of the Jewish
people to the idea of nationhood revitalized their poetry, releasing the long pent-up creative forces hidden within. It began to
deal realistically with the problems of the era—the poverty of life
in the Diaspora, assimilation, the Zionist movement—in fact, the
very problems with which Hebrew journalism had been concerned. Poetry, however, remained divorced from journalism because its language had been formed by the accretions of many

generations that combined the old with the new and superimposed apocalyptic visions of the future on nostalgic reminiscences of the ancient past. The poetry of the Hebrew Renaissance was charged with a sense of aesthetic discovery and a deep awareness of the physical world that thrilled the new Hebrew reader. Each of the poets of that era, old and young alike, created his own artistic world, and by means of talents peculiar to himself evoked an enthusiasm among his readers such as had not been seen since the halcyon days of Hasidism. This enthusiasm was aroused not merely by the poets' concern with those social and national problems then vexing the communities of eastern Europe, but to a greater degree by the aesthetic response that this poetry evoked in the individual reader. In the depressing political, social, and economic world of Russia before the 1917 revolution, such poetry produced a mysteriously moving effect. Its aesthetic quality, then, rather than its overt nationalistic theme, made Hebrew poetry a part of a true literary renaissance.

These two aspects, the nationlist and the aesthetic, applied also to Hebew fiction of the nineteenth century, although the treatment there is different. In poetry, the aesthetic effect is immediate and direct, betokening an intuitive grasp involving the realistic plane as well as the aesthetic.[1] Many of Bialik's poems, for example, deal with actual and ideological problems of the day—the physical and spiritual poverty of the community, assimilation, the literary renaissance—in much the same way as the essays of Ahad ha-Am and others like him. Nevertheless, this realistic material, apart from showing the extent to which the poet is rooted in the day-to-day life of his people, in fact becomes little more than a channel for the individual aesthetic forces of the poet himself. This will be examined in greater detail in the second volume, devoted to the poetry of the era, but I have mentioned it here in order to show the contrast that fiction affords. For prose does not offer the artist the same opportunity for intuitive expression as does poetry; it offers it only indirectly, through the more objective aspects of the fictional world.[2] The writer of fiction describes persons and things with a certain detachment, defining the physical setting in which the character is placed and the circumstances of

2

his life. Fiction can never penetrate the inner, psychological, world of a character except by dealing at the same moment with the external world, which is both concrete and objective. Through that external world a number of paths are opened up into the psychological terrain of the hero's mind, making possible the depiction of his real personality isolated from its social setting, or rather, his portrayal as an individual standing within a public domain. The primary purpose of fiction, then, is the depiction of character. Without it, fiction cannot exist—including modernistic fiction that delights in removing all traces of logical development and realism in the stream of thought. Characterization is the yardstick for the success of fiction, even of fiction that denies the possibility of a unified character within the world of art. It is therefore important to examine the development of characterization in Hebrew fiction, which became revitalized at the time of the national awakening.

Characterization, or at least the attempt to characterize, has had a long history in Hebrew literature. The various forms of biblical narrative have this in common, that all the characters are presented as individuals, whether in their day-to-day physical setting or at an inner psychological level, during their triumphs and disasters. No personality in the Scriptures ever knows his complete fate in advance; only as he actually undergoes his physical and spiritual vicissitudes does he perceive his hidden destiny on this earth. Herein lies the profundity of scriptural narrative that gives it its symbolic quality. Only very rarely do we come upon apocalyptic visions in the Scriptures whereby a final and a priori decision robs the individual of his independence of action, of his right to work out his own fate. The biblical narrator invariably aims at creating a human figure growing out of the real soil, a character whose personal traits shape his fate.

This tradition of vivid characterization continued throughout the periods of the Talmud and the midrashic legends. The legal sections of the Talmud and the Midrash are concerned with the community, their purpose being to instruct the people as a whole, and they have no interest in any individual trying to break down the fences and barriers of the law when his own desires clash with

3

those of the accepted commandments. The aggadah or legendary sections, however, even though they are intertwined with the legalistic sections and filled with the biblical passages that they were meant to interpret allegorically, very frequently deviate from their exegetical function to create a lifelike figure credible both externally and internally. Now, while the characters in the Bible and the talmudic halakhah emerge as spiritually whole, in the aggadah they are invested with a tragic significance that illumines their depths, depths that until that time had been hidden both from the scholar and the more general reader.[3] Their inner traits and spiritual struggles apparently had to wait for the fictional form of the aggadah before they could be realized. Obviously, the aggadah could never develop these characters in full; it was far too subordinated to the political, religious, and moral authority of the law. Consequently its stories are always brief, with a blurring of the tragic qualities of the hero, and usually they conclude with a moral epigram that tends to neutralize the artistic merit of the story itself. The characters of Elisha ben Avua, of Bruriah the wife of Rabbi Meir, of Rabbi Meir himself, and of Rabbi Joseph of Yokrat form only a small part of the aggadah's attempt to create individual human beings in all their complexity despite the incompatibility of such characterization with the more communal spirit of the halakhah.

In this respect, the popular Kabbalah was more successful than the aggadah; for in creating fictional characters it could draw upon the imaginative and archetypal legends of the Lurianic Kabbalah.[4] It concentrated on such figures as the false messiahs, on those who battled against Satan and his followers, on those who strove to hasten the coming of the messiah (among them Sabbatai Tzevi and Joseph Dela Reina), and on the figures outstanding in scholarship and mysticism from hasidic folklore.[5] The abstract concepts and the symbolic and allegoric categories of the Kabbalah became clothed in flesh and blood as well as in psychological "husks" that served as an artistic apparatus wherein each character could achieve his own independent existence and, of course, his own eventual downfall and destruction. Each is composed of light and darkness, good and evil, success and failure, blemish and remedy; as the battle between these contrary forces grows within them, so do they become more vividly alive as artistic creations.

The hasidic story is basically different. Although it too was influenced by the demonic dualism of the Kabbalah, it is always deeply aware of the eternal hidden within the dreams of the false messiahs and practical kabbalists. In effect, it always points to the individuality of our subliminal worlds, the source and solution of all man's confusions on earth. The stories of the Baal-Shem-Tov, whether authentic or not, invariably present his struggle with Samael and his followers both before and after his "revelation."[6] And through this struggle emerges an individualized figure filled with the splendor, eagerness, and faith that have always lightened the harsh lot of the Jew throughout history. Similarly, Rabbi Nahman of Braslav is portrayed in all the spiritual agonies that more than once brought him to the depths of despair as well as in his victory, when the power of the "illuminating intelligence" hidden within man helped him fill his existence with real meaning.[7]

Nevertheless, the hasidic story too often chose figures driven by strange impulses who departed from the norm when that norm could not supply their spiritual needs. The Rabbi of Braslav and the Rabbi of Kotzk both possessed an inner mysticism of their own, and hasidic stories seem almost to lower their voices in awe when they speak of them. Yet it was these very figures who bequeathed to hasidic writings a profound sense of characterization, acquired as authors struggled to convey vividly the virtues and traits of these tsaddikim.

The popular Kabbalah, like the various types of hasidic writings, had no small influence on the fiction produced during the modern revival of Hebrew literature, and we shall discuss that influence more fully in the following chapters. Its main effect was felt in the aesthetic sphere, where it far excelled the literary influence of the Enlightenment. The latter opened a number of gateways to the independence of modern Hebrew literature, freeing it from the legalistic and mystical traditions of religious writings.[8] One sign of the independence of modern Hebrew literature is its search for an individualized hero and the means of depicting him in all his complexity as an artistic creation. The literature of the Enlightenment was uninterested in this goal, and never saw its heroes as individuals valid in themselves but rather as representatives of the people as a whole, undistinguished in education or in behavior, whether at home or at work. Modern Hebrew fiction not only rejects the satirical aims of the Enlightenment, but also remains far removed from the artistic perceptiveness and narrative power of that "father" of modern Hebrew language, Mendelé Mokher Sefarim.

Even in the fiction of the Enlightenment it did occasionally happen that a gifted author, while dealing with the more generalized characters of his story, succumbed to the creative power within him and created a real human being. Such was the case with the Galician author Joseph Perl, in his satirical work *The Revealer of Secrets,* wherein he attacks the decadent hasidic movement for its chicanery, its unintelligible jargon, and its cheap imagery.[9] Somehow his artistic powers of depicting atmosphere and character emerge through the satirical attack, almost as if the author had for a moment forgotten that his real purpose was polemical. In other words, his intuition infiltrates the satirical account, endowing it with a far deeper vision than that of mere ideological attack, and it is that vision which brings the hasidic scene and the hasidic characters to life. The result is a certain softening of that bitter mockery which had originally motivated the author. This narrative power is, indeed, inherent in the Enlightenment's concept of social didacticism, and the linguistic apparatus is that of forceful satire. Beneath the satire, however, an ambivalence is created which arouses a certain sympathy for the very objects of satirical attack. On the one hand, Perl identifies himself with the didactic purpose of the Enlightenment, its determination to change the depressing conditions of the Jews in the Galician townships, but on the other hand he unconsciously reveals his secret longing to create a literary epic. As this ambivalent attitude began to spread throughout Hebrew fiction in the nineteenth century, the gulf widened between the trends of modern Hebrew fiction and those that had preceded it. These aesthetic changes within the Hebrew novel go hand in hand with

6

the awakening of Jewish nationalism during the last twenty years of the nineteenth century. As the Jew himself began to perceive the creative forces within him, so did the Hebrew novel.

The Fictional Writings of Mendelé Mokher Sefarim

This duality of didacticism on the one hand and artistic creativity on the other, which gained force toward the end of the nineteenth century, became the cornerstone of Mendelé Mokher Sefarim's success as a narrator. Joseph Klausner has pointed out in his *Two Mendelés* that the "first Mendelé" was a member of the Enlightenment dedicated to improving the conditions of Jewish family and social life and inclined to satire aimed at making the Jewish reader realize what needed correction and encouraging him to set about correcting it himself.[10] This satirical note, however, is frequently drowned by a wave of compassion for the Jews of Batalon, Kisalon, and Kabtziel who are, after all, as their Creator made them. At such points, Mendelé deserts his mockery for a lachrymose sentimentality. Nevertheless, such sympathy never constitutes a serious concern with the individual's personal struggles and suffering. The Jewish community remains the sole hero of his novels, and the individual characters serve solely as types for the community at large. The "second Mendelé," who projects himself as the hero of *The Beggars' Book* and *In Those Days*, sees with a penetrating eye into the body and soul of man, describing both with an artistic and literary power such as had not been seen in Hebrew literature for many generations. These two Mendelés seemed to dwell amicably together, even when the second Mendelé won completely and followed the path of artistic realism in which the "little souls" of Batalon, Kisalon, Kabtziel, and Madmena serve as the materials for his stories. If, however, we examine this second Mendelé more closely, we shall see that even this alter ego is not fully at ease with itself and sometimes splits into two a second time when these two subsections cannot dwell peacefully together.

In the past, critics have stressed Mendelé's representative powers of description.[11] The author is seen as wandering through the Jewish townships of Lithuania and gazing down on all the creatures there one by one, watching their comings and goings and all their comic affairs and then, with his extraordinary literary flair, setting them down on paper and transforming them into stories. Frishman, Klausner, and others were struck by the way he succeeded in integrating Hebrew literature with that of other nations, and they devoted their criticism to analyzing his descriptive flair and his linguistic ability in creating a rich Hebrew, composed of the various strata of biblical, talmudic, and midrashic styles, that was particularly suited to his artistic requirements. In the course of time, however, as Hebrew fiction became dissatisfied with mere fidelity of reproduction and began to explore the depths of the individual Jew, criticism deserted the naturalistic standards set by Mendelé's depiction of the Lithuanian township. That success in the realm of realism which Frishman had eulogized began to be seen in a totally different light, for it placed each of his characters in a vacuum. With the exception of Mendelé himself in *The Beggars' Book* and Shlomo'le of *In Those Days,* each of his characters is utterly rootless, devoid of any personal fate or inner complexity. The scenes of the Jewish townships in Lithuania have a static quality, arising from the author's desire to caricature the people within them. The comic quality of Mendelé's stories does not derive from the specific traits of his central figures, their struggles with a fate which twists and complicates man's life till the comedy of either realistic or non-realistic drama is created. It arises instead from the author's concept of the grotesque, which aims at exaggerating the realistic scene before it. It is therefore doubtful whether Mendelé did depict the Lithuanian township as realistically as was thought. For if Abraham Kariv was wrong in his view that Mendelé was no true lover of Israel, he was right in suggesting that Mendelé did not see the Lithuanian township in its true light, whether in its external, visible form, or in a deeper sense that would enable him to delve into the spiritual and psychological being of the individual Jew within that township.[12]

Perhaps, then, we should not treat Mendelé as a realistic writer in the fullest sense of the term. Perhaps his comic sense of description was not intended to provide an objective and realistic picture

8

of the town and its inhabitants so much as to satisfy the author's own imaginative thirst, a thirst which had needed slaking since his childhood.[13] The grotesque caricature in *The Travels of Benjamin III, In the Vale of Tears,* and *The Beggars' Book* not only failed to fulfil the didactic aim of the Enlightenment, but also failed to provide a truly realistic portrait of the Lithuanian Jewish town. The caricature exists there for its own sake, as if to satisfy an aesthetic impulse on Mendelé's part. As Mendelé the artist becomes divorced from Mendelé the maskil, the imaginative quality of his work increases. The various characters in his stories do not form the realistic novel that aims at objectivity in depicting the outer world of its heroes as well as the inner psychological turmoil of the individual within that world. Mendelé's realism does not depend on any sociological, nationalistic, or psychological concept. It is "pure" comic realism, existing for its aesthetic quality alone, and it forms the only true "hero" of Mendelé's writings.

The problem of the individualized hero, however, did arise in his works, first in *The Beggars' Book,* and much more fully in his last work, the autobiographical *In Those Days.* Until then, he was concerned throughout his writings with a certain approach that suited his artistic needs. He did not commit himself to any specific era in the long history of Judaism as did Shmuel Yoseph Agnon, who concentrated on a kind of Jewish township in Galicia, with its beggars and idlers. Mendelé's stories lack a plot, as well as perceptions from the social, nationalistic, and individualistic viewpoints; he has no character whose fate moves us because of his involvement in a real or visionary world. The realism in which Mendelé's characters are caught is completely static, and they do not develop with the story as do those in the realistic novels of Russia and Europe as a whole. Mendelé's descriptive powers, which are in the ascendancy whenever he portrays the stupidity, laziness, and mendicancy of the Jewish township, prevent him from seeing the inner psychological world of his characters. His magnificent language provides him merely with a surface style, but it is never used as a means of penetrating the depths of the heroes of his stories. Critics are probably right in emphasizing

9

the influence of Charles Dickens on Mendelé,[14] but the Hebrew author lacks Dickens' ability to reach into the heart of his characters. In the final analysis, Mendelé's caricature obscures both the realism within the social life of the Jewish township and the personal struggles and longings of the individual Jew who lived there, so that in the end it serves merely as cardboard stage-scenery behind which there is nothing at all.

This is why Mendelé ignores completely the creative hasidic movement in White Russia and Lithuania, and forgets those working-class Jews who studied, worked, sang, dreamed, yearned, and wrote in the midst of a degenerate Diaspora. Hence the failure of those chapters from *In the Vale of Tears* (so admired by David Frishman) in which a magic ring brings dreams and visions to the Jews of Kabtziel, and in which, on a summer's night, they wish for as many rubles as there are stars and go and take down the gate, until, wearied and empty of all visionary longing, they drag themselves home to their broken-down houses to get a few disturbed hours of sleep.[15] Now this story of a magic ring has real archetypal significance in the legends and folklore of other nations; it is connected with love, with inner struggles, with eternal hope. Yet Mendelé presents the "little people's" dreams as empty of all content, a piece of grotesque nonsense which destroys all the delicate lyricism flowing from the author's pen in these scenes. The same applies to the beggars wandering in groups from town to town, crowding into the communal poorhouses and lording it over everyone. Mendelé knew them very well—their own little world, their trickery, their struggles for a livelihood, their queer leaping and dancing at town festivities, their techniques for squeezing "alms" and "donations" out of people, the cunning they shared—all this is distilled in his superficial caricature, but never does he touch upon the psychological world bubbling and fermenting within each one of them.[16] They serve Mendelé solely as "types" taken from the Jewish community. He is always ready to join the society of these beggars, who lack any real existence whether in the external world or in the inner world of experience. Even from this point of view, Mendelé did not approach the realistic school by delving into the psychological world of the beggars, in whom both Jewish and non-Jewish folklore has always been greatly interested. In the novels of Victor Hugo and Émile Zola, in Shakespearean and modern drama, the crowd of beggars sometimes serves to represent the primitive ferment, whether undeground or overt, of social and national unrest or of the winds of revolt blowing through the universe, while at other times they serve as an expression of the lonely soul torn by inner turmoil who can find no haven in the orderly, rational world. From either angle, Mendelé is far from the creative world of Jewish folklore, whether that of the popular Kabbalah and the hasidic stories, or that of Peretz and Anski.[17] He never dreams that the day may come when these beggars will find their rightful place, as in Agnon's excellent book *The Bridal Canopy*. Mendelé's beggars remain, then, no more than static cardboard scenery for the poor Jewish township.

Mendelé himself recognized this static quality in his characters, although in his view it arose from their own nature and not from his lack of artistic creativity. For whenever he came to depict Jewish children in these towns, the entire atmosphere of his stories undergoes an immediate change. Herschele and Moshé-Yossi from *In the Vale of Tears*, the children in *The Beggars' Book* and Shlomo'le ben Reb Haiyim's children from *In Those Days*, even though he sees them as "little Jews" bearing the yoke of the Diaspora and the burden of Jewish poverty, nonetheless aroused in him a deeper interest that affects his description of the whole atmosphere of the Jewish town. The grotesque vein of comedy no longer serves Mendelé's purpose when he describes children, and the artificial stage setting of his township suddenly comes to life at the sound of the children's voices.[18] It is that which nullifies both Mendelé's didactic satire and his "theatrical" realism. However, in his autobiographical *In Those Days*, there is a true realism which comes through with full force.

Apart from this instance of the children, at times Mendelé makes an effort to leave the grotesque caricature in whose net he has caught this or that Jewish "soul," holding it as it were between finger and thumb for all to see, as he peers at it from every side, amusing himself by playing with it like a puppet. In his

Beggars' Book itself, even though it does contain a good deal of caricature, there is a real attempt on the part of the author to portray his scene with the lively realism of which he is sometimes capable. It is here that we find his description of the landscape and of the Sabbath eve in the ragman's house.[19] But they are rare instances that owe their success to the presence of a new hero who has no parallel in any of Mendelé's other books except *In Those Days*—the narrator himself, Shalom Jacob Abramowitsch, who changed his formal name for the more popular pen name that expresses his love and compassion for all the poor Jews in the townships: Mendelé Mokher Sefarim, Mendelé the Bookseller.

As soon as Mendelé appears in *The Beggars' Book,* the reader at once senses a wonderful change in atmosphere. The central character of the book wanders back and forth between the various towns selling religious appurtenances, and the story opens with one of those journeys that takes place on the fast day, the "17th of Tammuz." He begins to speak as the narrator, and immediately the grotesqueness disappears, as if it has succumbed to the humor flowing from his lips. His conversation is reflective and meditative, yet effervescent with hope and vitality. The enclosed world in which the characters of *The Travels of Benjamin III* and *In the Vale of Tears* are placed opens out somewhat at the beginning of *The Beggars' Book* when Mendelé is seated in his wagon on a fine summer's day, the 17th of Tammuz; as he drives along, he indulges in some self-examination, his introspective monologue sparkling with humor. Light and shade mingle throughout, lending a realism to his spoken thoughts and adding breadth and depth to his lively personality, responsive both to itself and to the world around it. The opening of *The Beggars' Book,* in which Mendelé talks about himself and his travels through the Jewish townships, verges on the epic,[20] but the epic quality is offset when he returns to a more naturalistic, comic vein in his description of Reb Alter Yaknehaz and his anecdote of Fishka the Lame and his fellow professional beggars.[21] The hint of an epic is never fulfilled. The irrepressible humor in parts of the book revitalizes the characters as long as they are in direct contact with the fictional Mendelé Mokher Sefarim, but the moment they are alone, they return to the world of the grotesque. Even the heavily satirized figure of Reb Alter becomes more human in Mendelé's presence—even when the two of them, wearing their tallit and tefillin, are sinking in the mud together with the horse and cart to the scornful jeering of the "uncircumcised" standing around. The humor emanating from Mendelé somehow redeems them both. The moment they part, however, Reb Alter's character becomes emptied of all realism and credibility—a mere caricature.

The "second Mendelé," as Klausner calls him, was thus himself a contradictory figure. When he rid himself of his didactic and satiric tone, he found himself impelled toward the art of fiction, yet without the need of an epic hero rooted in the Jewish environment. A vacuum was thus created in Mendelé's writings, and his naturalism, divorced from the real Jewish life of his time, becomes grotesque. The satire involved, as well as the fictional realism, is nullified by the grotesque portrayal. Yet it was this very naturalism which led Mendelé to create a new Hebrew and a new Yiddish suited to his own style. Accordingly, he delved into the quarries of the Bible, the Talmud, and the midrashic literature until he had created the complete linguistic apparatus without which the modern Hebrew novel would be inconceivable.[22] The real plot of Mendelé's novels prior to *In Those Days* was the creation of a new concept of the Hebrew language, which was to be more fully developed in the writings of subsequent generations, reaching its consummation in our own day in the literary works of Agnon. That language served his purpose in the sole epic that he wrote, *In Those Days*.[23]

This autobiographical novel of Mendelé's is written in a more oblique manner. Reb Shlomo the Elder relates the tale of Shlomo'le, the son of Reb Haiyim; and here Mendelé imposes upon himself a perspective requiring a greater depth and individualization of character. It is this individualization that provides the story with its epic quality, for the hero from his early childhood is sensitive and responsive to the world of his Creator and of himself. The descriptions of the town form an integral part of the boy's private visions and symbolize the imaginative forces stirring within him.[24] The comic vein disappears and is replaced by a symbolic myth overlying the tapestry of Shlomo'le's life; the actual world of the town is interwoven with the imaginative and almost cosmic visions of the boy. *In Those Days* contains the same characters that appeared in Mendelé's previous works, but here a new lyricism permeates his description of the entire township —a lyricism balanced by the profound realism with which the town is treated. The gulf which separates Mendelé from his characters in almost all the previous novels is bridged in this autobiographical work, and a deep bond is formed between the two "sides."

Thus Mendelé's artistic longings reached fulfillment in this final work. The dialogue is clothed in the language of earlier generations and is drawn from the actual township in which he was born and raised, so that it marked a dynamic revitalizing of his powers. Indeed, it was this revitalization which endeared the "Old Man" of Hebrew letters to his literary grandchildren Bialik, S. Chernikhovsky, Shneour, and the other founders of modern Hebrew literature at the turn of the nineteenth and twentieth centuries. All were his adopted offspring, the most remarkable among them being Shalom Nahum Rabinowitz, known more popularly as "Shalom Aleikhem." It was he who paved the way for the Jewish epich in both Yiddish and Hebrew.

Jewish Humanism and Realism in Shalom Aleikhem

By the end of the nineteenth century the walls of the Jewish township in the Ukraine were beginning to crumble. When the failure of the 1905 revolution left the Russian liberals in a mood of despair and disillusionment, the Jewish settlement in Russia seemed about to collapse completely. The reactionary decrees of the government put a stranglehold on the Jewish community and led to pogroms incited by the government and by the Pravoslav church.[25] The government's malevolence, however, kindled within the Jewish population an intense nationalism that inspired both in the Eastern European communities as a whole and in individuals themselves a burst of artistic creativity that could find no outlet in the alien atmosphere of Czarist Russia. Zionism, like socialism, spread through the Jewish masses of the Ukraine, Poland, and Lithuania, offering them the vision of a new future. The man in the street was caught up in a historic movement in a manner unparalleled for centuries. The nationalist and socialist ideals, the mass emigration to America, and the Second Aliyah to Palestine gave Jewish youth a new cultural and ideological image of the Promised Land, prompting them to recreate a literary and artistic heritage in both Yiddish and Hebrew. This entire movement demanded on the one hand a political terminology suited to its specific needs and, on the other, the birth of a new poetry, a new dramatic tradition, and a new type of fiction.

Here, however, the modern Hebrew Renaissance parted company with the Enlightenment. For the former was sympathetic to the spiritual awakening of the common people, those very Jewish "types" that the Enlightenment had always despised and at which it had directed its sharpest satiric barbs. Moreover, the literature of the post-Enlightenment era regarded as its primary task the strengthening of Jewish nationalism and hence the creation in its fiction of an almost epic, individualized hero rising out of the new Jewish community and finding his imagery and symbols within his own inner world. Therefore, Hebrew literature was highly responsive to the shifting winds of the Eastern European community of its day, and from the turn of the century up to World War I, it identified itself almost unreservedly with the historic destiny both of the Jewish community at large and of the individual within it. Hence the surprising fact that the various political parties of that era fostered an interest in the writings of Mendelé, Shalom Aleikhem, Peretz, and Bialik, as well as promoting the literature itself, in both Yiddish and Hebrew. Ideology and intellectualism alone were insufficient for parties struggling to create a new Jew and seeing themselves as fulfilling a new historical imperative. Each party sought an artistic image of the Jew endowed with psychological insight and a breadth of vision which could include the many dimensions of the national concept. "Romantic" Zionism was not alone in its messianic longings, for "scientific" Zionism too, exemplified by Pinsker and Borochov, together with popular Jewish social ideas, saw in the rebirth of Jewish literature a noble artistic phenomenon, bestowing on the Jewish hero a tragic and epic quality in his ideological yearning for a haven for the Jewish people.

In creating this heroic figure, however, Hebrew fiction needed to begin afresh. It had no precedents, either in the Enlightenment literature of Russia and Galicia or in the majority of Mendelé's writings. There were some hints in Mendelé's earlier work and a fuller development in *In Those Days*, but they all ignored the historic changes which had swept through the Jewish communities of that era. The first writers faced with the task of creating the new hero was Shalom Aleikhem and Itzhak Leib Peretz.

As we enter to world of Shalom Aleikhem we become conscious of a tremendous bustle of activity, greater than was necessary for that ironic humor with which the author loved to entertain and amuse his fellow Jews amid the depressing conditions of Eastern Europe. As we read his tales of Tuvia the Milkman, of Menahem Mendel the Dreamer, of Mottel ben Peisi the Cantor, of the Jewish festivals, and of the Jewish children, we are always conscious of historic and artistic undercurrents beneath the amusing surface.[26] Shalom Aleikhem's humor is rooted not in any light-hearted banter about a nonsensical world, but in the most grievous problems of Jewish life—social and economic, communal and individual, cultural and religious. Even his short stories, which give the impression of having been written as merely casual pieces, allude to these problems, while the longer stories are overtly set against the background of the contemporary Jewish scene—a fundamentally tragic background illumined by the luster of the author's Jewish compassion and reflected in the mirror of his humor.

Shalom Aleikhem devoted all his literary powers to creating the characters of his stories, the highly individualized figures of *Tuvia the Milkman, Menahem Mendel the Dreamer, Mottel ben Peisi the Cantor,* and *Children of Israel.* It is as though the contemporary Jewish scene flowed into his characters, became part of them, and found its ultimate expression through them. Shalom Aleikhem's stories, as we have noted, reflect the Jewish world of his day with remarkable clarity: the collapse of family life in the wake of the new winds blowing into the Jewish village from the outside world, the disintegration of class distinction within the towns, the split in religious leadership, the mass emigration to America, and the spiritual confusion created by "the breakdown of boundaries," as Bialik calls it in his poem to Ahad ha-Am.[27] All the realism, however, is woven into the personal tragedy of the individual, and it is this personal note which gives his stories their profundity. The finest instance is, of course, Tuvia himself. Tuvia gazes at the world around him through his own little world, seeing the suffering which the Almighty pours down upon His Chosen People and learning from that what is relevant to himself and his household—Golda his wife, and his six grown-up daughters—and to his own toil and suffering; in fact, to his "all in all." This very perception constitutes Shalom Aleikhem's artistic success. The more Tuvia gazes into himself and his tragic lot, the more vividly does he come to life. Tuvia knows that his own suffering forms part of the suffering of the Jewish community as a whole, yet he still regards his lot as a personal one, a hidden mirror according to which he acts and which gives his life an individual significance. Whatever happens to him is symbolic of the entire community, whether it is his hard struggle for a livelihood, or the fact that his daughters have grown up and that each in her own way is destroying the foundations on which Jewish family life rests; whether it is the loss of his money, which he has invested in the worthless writings of Menahem Mendel the Dreamer, or the expulsion of his family from the village, stripped of all they possessed. And yet he wonderingly treats everything that impinges on him from the outside world as if it reflects some inner meaningful purpose in the very depths of his soul.

Tuvia is endowed by Shalom Aleikhem with a popular "philosophy." What is the sense of all the suffering that the Guardian of Israel heaps upon Israel, and why does He treat Tuvia, a poor milkman, as if he were an enemy by showering worries about his daughters solely on *his* head? The very intensity of his protest against the so-called order of the universe bears a hidden suggestion of his being "chosen," particularly since his protest takes the form of a monologue that, as the story of the daughters develops, pulsates increasingly with a sense of his personal destiny. His suffering when one daughter "shames" him by marrying Fefferl the Tailor[28] is exceeded by his grief when another has an illicit love affair and commits suicide.[29] And his pain in driving out one daughter because of those "forbidden pamphlets," which try to "turn everything upside down and make the good bad and the bad good,"[30] is exceeded by his agony when another becomes a Christian, eventually throwing herself in despair on her father's threshold.[31] But as his sufferings increase, so does Tuvia's self-knowledge and the clarity with which he perceives his lot. This gradual process, based on the author's own tragic vision of reality, gives the story its epic quality, wherein the individualized character of the central figure is set against the historical background of the era.

The plot of *Tuvia the Milkman* contains sufficient humor, history, sociology, and psychology for a full saga of the spiritual crossroads reached by Russian Jewry at the close of the nineteenth century. Tuvia always stands at those crossroads, watching from his own individual viewpoint the changes sweeping over Russian Jewry and their attendant dangers. He had seen them with his own eyes as each of his daughters in turn broke away from the traditions of past generations, emptying her heart of all trust and faith and destroying the Jewishness within her. Tuvia fights valiantly to defend his village, Katriel, and the social and religious traditions it contains, the wealthy Jews of Yehupetz with its Stock Exchange and Menahem Mendel the Dreamer, the summer resort in Boiberek from which he earns his livelihood for the rest of the year. That same Boiberek's summer days shine upon Tuvia too as he follows his horse and cart, pondering on his Creator and the "justice" of the universe. He fights for them all, lest they disappear into the abyss which awaits them, swept there by the ill winds blowing from outside that have already destroyed his own home. Shalom Aleikhem's flow of words, however frivolous and entertaining it may appear on the surface, in fact constitutes a battle for every soul, lest it be isolated in its suffering or lose its sense of the meaning of life. Each of his characters demands from him the existential meaning that lies buried deep within his own heart. They pray for peace of mind even in the worst conditions and remain firm in their faith though everything collapses around them. This is the tragic element in Shalom Aleikhem's writings. Tuvia's response to the catastrophes which rain down upon him as his inner and outer worlds collapse illumines him with the tragic radiance of the Jewish people throughout the generations. In fact, Shalom Aleikhem is the first author of modern Jewish fiction, either in Hebrew or Yiddish, who gave his "little people," drawn from the real, contemporary world, those tragic dimensions that the novel of the non-Jewish world had provided since the early 1820's. It is this achievement that places Shalom Aleikhem among the great figures of the modern Hebrew novel. True, he used the technique of the monologue, which perhaps disqualifies him as a novelist in the technical sense, but it was that very monologue, with its humorous irony, that, in contrast to the modernistic struggles of I. L. Peretz, presaged a great psychological change in the Hebrew literary revival.

Shalom Aleikhem's writings are completely free of the didactic purpose which pervades the prose of the Enlightenment, and are also free of the caricature that fills Mendelé's pages. The fierce satire of the maskilim was always directed at the degenerate members of the community as typical of depressed Jewry as a whole, and consequently it robbed them of all individuality. Shalom Aleikhem did the very reverse by concentrating all his artistic power on the characterization of the complete individual, set against the realistic background of his era. That is why he always refrained from pursuing comedy for its own sake and thus avoided the grotesqueness of Mendelé's writings. His real artistic purpose, for all the irony and humor, was to portray the ordinary Jew, outwardly crushed by his depressing conditions but inwardly glowing with a majestic sense of his past and his future. In this way, his stories marked a historic phase in the history of the Jewish novel, as did the modernistic insights of Peretz. He opened new horizons for the fictional hero—the sure sign of a modern literary revival, whether in prose or verse.

It was Shalom Aleikhem's urge to create a new type of Jewish character, without any literary precedent, that drove him to employ the monologue, with all its psychological possibilities, some of which I noted in the discussion of Mendelé Mokher Sefarim's self-projection into his *Beggars' Book*. We saw previously that whenever Mendelé speaks in his own voice or about himself, the empty world of Kabtziel suddenly comes to life, becoming vividly reflected in the individual instead of being lost in the vague communal atmosphere of Kabtziel, Kisalon, Madmena, and Batalon. In *Tuvia the Milkman, Manahem Mendel the Dreamer, Mottel ben Peisi the Cantor* and *Children of Israel,* the monologue functions as a sensitive psychological mechanism that rectifies all that the satire of the Enlightenment had spoiled. Tuvia is not a scholar, nor is he wealthy; he is not a president of a synagogue, nor even well connected; yet the author gives him a certain inner refinement inherent in his psychological make-up so that Shalom Aleikhem is able to "trust" him to speak in his own name and relate the story. The flow of talk that the author allows his character is not the sole "plot" of the tale, for he offers Tuvia new vantage points from which he can gaze at his own spiritual troubles and find words to express his own personality. The monologue was thus an artistic necessity for Shalom Aleikhem, the source of his irony and humor, allowing him to create the characters of his "little people" and turn them into heroes.

Tuvia keeps chancing upon Shalom Aleikhem, and at once begins to tell him all about himself and his home and about some catastrophe that has happened to one of his daughters. As he thinks aloud he seems to lay the world bare, as if he were saying: "This world is full of blemishes; this is the way the Lord of the Universe treats His mortals, and then He calls it a just universe!" At this level Tuvia's soliloquy serves as an ironic protest liable at any moment to turn into something more than a momentary sense of bitterness. Yet at that very instant there is a marvelous counterbalance; the irony, in the very flow of words, turns into humor. The bitterness of the protest vanishes before Tuvia's response to the heavenly comforts hidden behind bereavement and failure. This is the motive force that gives light and shade to his speech, the technique that so endears Shalom Aleikhem to his readers and that makes him a wonderful Jewish author. The humorous smile, breaking trough the irony directed at the real, everyday world, gives Tuvia his peculiar depth of character.

Of course, it is difficult to illustrate this process by a few brief extracts from *Tuvia the Milkman* or, indeed, from any single work of the author's, since it permeates his writings from beginning to end. Perhaps one of the best known phrases from *Tuvia the Milkman* could illustrate his technique more effectively than odd excerpts—the phrase "as we have learned." Tuvia never ends a soliloquy without quoting a biblical verse or a rabbinical or popular saying to round off his talk. He always quotes the beginning of the phrase verbatim, and it is always directly relevant to his actual situation, buttressing his own thoughts about the trouble which the Holy One, blessed be He, has poured upon him, and about the so-called justice of the universe. The opening of the verse or saying invariably contains a hint of irony, directed for a moment at the "relations" between Tuvia and his Creator, at his meager livelihood, at Golda, his wife, who deprives him of every moment of rest with her stream of complaints, at his daughters' behavior, at Menahem Mendel, who placed Tuvia's last penny on the ram's horn in the Yehupetz Exchange. One verse, for example, reads: "There is no wisdom and no understanding nor counsel against the Lord. . . ." The sensitive reader catches a note of bitterness mingled with a reluctant acceptance of Divine will: that is the way the world was created and man can only cry "The Lord liveth!" Yet, at the very moment of this fatalistic and semi-ironic philosophizing, the second half of the quotation breaks away from the original wording, with its significance for that world Jewry of which Tuvia forms a part, and turns aside to deal with Tuvia's personal problems. "There is no wisdom and no understanding," says Tuvia when he is telling Shalom Aleikhem about a journey through the forest of the Boiberek summer resort on a glorious spring day, "that can deal with a wretched horse." That morning he had been walking behind his horse and cart enjoying the beauty of nature, his heart filled with songs of praise, just as if Golda and his six daughters had melted away in the morning mists that the Holy One, blessed be He, had spread over the world. Then suddenly his horse stopped—the horse which had always been so faithful and trustworthy—and refused to budge. It had eaten nothing all day and its stomach was empty; the wretched beast refused to listen any longer to its master's pleas and promises. The glory of the morning immediately vanished from Tuvia's heart, driven away by thoughts of his troubles and of the worries awaiting him at home. The sudden change in his mood had prompted the words "There is no wisdom and no understanding" to explain God's ways in the world. In a moment, however, the fatalism of the verse is humorously diverted by Tuvia's addition: "There is no wisdom and no understanding that can deal with a wretched horse," as though Tuvia's horse has suddenly chosen to be obstinate. The end of the "quotation," therefore, combines Tuvia's irony with an oblique sense of the affection and companionship he feels for his horse. In a way, then, Tuvia's hidden lyricism modifies the apparent harshness of the opening words, creating the mingling of light and shade that is typical of his speech. The same point could be illustrated over and over again. In effect, this technique gives depth and subtlety to Tuvia's character, and it is fundamental to all the writings of Shalom Aleikhem (except for the novels, which have long been forgotten).

Yet, in the revival of modern Hebrew and Yiddish literature, his use of the monologue is no less important than this mingling of humor and irony. It is only by means of monologue that Tuvia and Mottel ben Peisi the Cantor can achieve knowledge—knowledge of their place in the real world of society and family, and knowledge of their own world, which gives true meaning to their existence. It is in this monologue that the hero is truly himself. He speaks for himself and we come to know him directly, not through the indirect descriptive form of narration usually employed by authors who only rarely let the characters speak. The first-person narrator, however, prevents the other characters from coming to life and speaking for themselves, so that they tend to become mere satellites revolving around the central figure and existing only through him. This is the main drawback of the monologue in general and of Shalom Aleikhem's use of it in particular. For this reason, Tuvia's daughters can never move beyond the orbit of their father's monologue, can never be seen as individual people except through the eyes of Tuvia himself. Their tragic fate forms a central theme of the entire book, but it never becomes dramatized as their personal tragedy. Each phase of the tragedy is in the final analysis related directly to the speaker himself, in terms of his own private world of grief, suffering, complaint, and acceptance. Nevertheless, for all its drawbacks, Shalom Aleikhem's use of the monologue marked an important contribution to the need of post-Enlightenment literature to create individualized characters.

There can be no doubt that this trend towards individualization of character can best be seen in the monologue, as when Shalom Aleikhem devotes his story to Jewish children. The world of light and shadows, of suffering and dreaming, of pain and soothing joys, creates the personality of the Jewish child in a wonderfully realistic setting. Those changes of mood in *Mottel ben Peisi the Cantor* and in *Children of Israel,* which take place in the flow of the monologue, are a mark of that deep intuitive insight for which only Shalom Aleikhem could provide a suitable literary medium. The method of indirect narration could never have revealed with equal effectiveness the inner struggles of the Jew caught in this period of transition. In these stories of children, the basis of his humor comes more clearly to light, for while these children are fully aware of the real suffering and poverty in their city and within their families, they also respond to the joy of simply being alive in the universe, which the Holy One, blessed be He, created. It is they themselves who instinctively bear the glad tidings that all is not dark in the Jewish world. In their harsh surroundings they can always perceive some legend or fairy tale, and in the midst of suffering they can always dream. From this duality of awareness is derived the humor that runs in so many variegated colors through their chatter. Tuvia the Milkman, Menahem Mendel the Dreamer, Mottel's brother, and others like them can only discern the dream from afar, in the midst of struggles that frequently, as in the case of Menahem Mendel, end in total defeat. But the children of Shalom Aleikhem's stories always grasp at once the powerful truth that reality and dreams are indivisible.

Itzhak Leib Peretz: In Search of Modernistic Expression

After the collapse of the 1905 Russian revolution and the growing reactionism of the government prior to the First World War and the 1917 revolution, the Jewish township went into decline. Jewish emigration, both to the larger cities of central Europe and to those of the United States, reached its peak, marking an upheaval within the Jewish community that was to produce enormous changes. One such change was the conversion of the majority of the community into city dwellers, with all that such urbanization implies. The Jewish village and township, with its rich religious and cultural traditions and its specific way of life, was allowed to die in isolation. No realistic writer arose to rescue it from oblivion, to record in epic style the rise and fall of the community, and to depict the characters deeply rooted in its soil. The Jewish intelligentsia was indeed concerned with Yiddish literature at this time, but the intellectuals themselves were situated almost exclusively in the larger cities and regarded the small township as of no real significance for the Jewish world. They therefore ignored it. The few writers who did devote their work to the townships in which their fathers and grandfathers had lived usually did so by gazing at them through rose-colored spectacles in a nostalgic, romantic fashion that conveyed little of the reality they were attempting to describe. Shalom Ash's *The Township* and *Reb Shlomo the Noble* are typical of this school. Alternatively, in the fashion of the period prior to the communist revolution, some of them dedicated their writing to the melancholy of the collapse and disintegration of the township, as did David Bergelson in his *Beside the Railroad Station* and *The End of Everything*.[32]

That sense of Jewish destiny, which in previous years had wonderfully united the communities of the Jewish townships, disappeared. The Jewish intelligentsia in the cities had left behind them the economic and cultural traditions of the towns, and the common people in the cities before the revolution were crushed by poverty and despair. The Jewish intelligentsia was astir with the new ideologies of political Zionism and the socialist Bund, while the writers of this group were torn by dual loyalties. They could not desert the man in the street because, ideologically speaking, it was for his social, cultural, and economic betterment that they were working. At the same time, they were greatly influenced by European Decadent literature, which was revolting against realism and its interest in the day-to-day activities of the man in the street. The main source of this interest among the young school of Yiddish writers in this period, and one that was to have considerable influence on subsequent writers, was Itzhak Leib Peretz.

Even today in certain literary circles Peretz is spoken of as the greatest innovator of Yiddish and Hebrew, the father of *modern* Jewish literature. There is some truth in the statement, provided it is restricted to Yiddish literature and even then qualified with certain reservations that I shall enumerate later. Peretz understood the needs of Polish Jewry very well, as he showed in his survey of the Jewish townships (which appears in a special book written after a tour of Jewish settlements undertaken on behalf of the Warsaw community), and in his enlightening articles discussing educational and cultural problems as well as those connected with the political ideologies that were then engaging the attention of Jewish intellectuals.[33] Sometimes he even devoted fictional writings quite openly to contemporary themes, as he did in *There Once Was a King*, a play in which Jewish workers raise the banner of revolution against an oppressive government and are put down by the Cossacks. Here he stresses the ideological element. But outside the realm of this ideological interest, deep within his own personality, he frequently succumbed to irrational, aesthetic impulses—a secret longing to be borne away by the sounds of some infinite harmony flowing into his soul from the outer universe and carried to a mighty ocean beyond the horizons of human imagination. He was responding to the neo-romanticism inherent in the Impressionism and Symbolism of Polish and European literature.[34] He hoped that the younger men about him, his literary disciples, would one day create a modern Jewish

25

literature similar to that of Poland, Russia, France, and Germany. The complaint that constantly recurred in his conversations with these younger writers was that Jewish literature "always missed the boat," that it always lagged behind contemporary trends.

In saying this, Peretz had no intention of diverting the Jewish writer from the common people, from their past, their future, their problems and visions. For Polish literature had seldom turned its back on the common people, who seemed to spring from the beloved soil like the thick, ancient forests on the banks of the Vistula, which in the late spring and early summer flows majestically into the distant seas and on moonlit nights evokes magical dreams of secret folktales. Yet, at that time Polish literature was wide open to the influence of the individualistic impressionism and mystic symbolism that had spilled over from French poetry in the 1880's and conquered the Slavic literatures of Russia and Poland. In these trends Peretz saw a sure heritage for himself and for the younger generation of Jewish writers nurtured in the cultural centers of Warsaw and Odessa. He introduced these elements first into his own writings and then passed them on to the young writers to whom his home was always open. He thus encouraged them to turn in the same direction, filling them with secret longings for that splendid beauty shimmering on horizons far removed from the world of the Jewish ideologies.[35]

The modernistic element in Peretz's writings is obvious, throughout the various periods of his work, to any sensitive reader. His style tends to be allusive and subtle, with broken phrases ending in a row of dots. The pauses are so carefully modulated that one is almost steeped in profound silences. There is no outside disturbance, no sound from the market place to disturb the reader as he listens to the character's dialogue with himself. Were we to try to illustrate this from each of the various types of Peretz's writings, there would be no end. It will suffice to quote a few lines from "By a Dying Man's Pillow," whose rhythms and style are typical of the majority of his prose work.

> Toward evening, the caretaker of the Garden of Eden—an angel crowned like the others with light emanating from the Almighty—approached one of the windows of heaven and, leaning out, sorrowfully asked the setting sun:

Itzhak Leib Peretz

—Sun, do you know what has happened to our Leibel? . . .
The sun said nothing—nothing; for he did not know. . . .
The angel silently withdrew his head, closed the window, and
sat down in his place even sadder than before.[36]

The artistic purpose of this extract from one of the stories in
The Voice of the People is quite clear. Peretz is attempting to
break up the more direct, concrete style of writing, which seems
to him to have exhausted itself, so that his words can convey
more effectively the subtlety of variegated emotions. The hushed
style of his writing, the musical pause at the close of phrases and
sentences—a pause that seems to be listening to itself as it slows
down the spoken dialogue between the angel seeking Leibel and
the setting sun which knows nothing of his whereabouts—both
suggest to the reader some divine inspiration hovering above and
detaching itself from the question, "Where is Leibel?" It recalls
the reader to himself; he hears it, wonders for a moment, and
then succumbs to emotions that have no questions and no answers
in the silence of the twilight. This impressionistic tendency pervades nearly all of Peretz's work, but it is most striking in this
folktale, which begins as a legend merely retold by the author
but gradually acquires a musicality over and above its folkloristic
source and transcends realism.

In fact, Peretz is here entering the world of symbolism, which
had conquered Russian and Polish literature at the beginning of
the twentieth century, and he does this even more noticeably in
the Yiddish version of his play *The Golden Chain*. Yet even in
some of the stories in *The Voice of the People* this symbolism is
dominant, particularly in "Hear O Israel."[37] It is the tale of a
poor young man who came to Tomashov and kept himself se-
cluded from all his fellow creatures except when hunger drove
him to beg for a crust of bread. Outwardly he gave the appearance
of being an idiot. He could not carry even the simplest message.
His memory failed him, and on the way he would stop to examine
a mouse or a bird that seemed to be calling to him; he would mut-
ter "it has eyes which seem to see into the distance, yet it cannot
see the ground it walks on." He remembered neither his own
name nor that of his father, and simply called himself "Abraham"; his father he referred to as "my father," pointing heaven-

ward as he pronounced the words. The story recounts various incidents in his life until he obtains the position of double-bass player in the town band (the previous player having died in a snow storm); he "plays" with them at weddings both in the town itself and elsewhere. The other members play together in harmony, but he simply draws his bow across the strings of his double bass without paying the slightest attention to the sound produced.

Now it happened that there was a wedding between the families of the Rabbi of Cracow and the synagogue president of Lublin, which took place in Tomashov since it was located halfway between the two cities. Tomashov was agog with excitement. Of course, in addition to bringing the bands of each of the two cities, the celebrants invited the Tomashov band to help entertain the bride and bridegroom, their parents, and all the honored guests from the three towns. Each of the bands in turn played its very best, but the Tomashov band had one advantage—the entertainment provided by its double bass. The band played its gay or nostalgic tunes, while the double bass—the idiot youngster—played independently. He stood facing a corner with his back to the audience, simply drawing the bow back and forth across the strings of the large instrument. There was no connection between him and the band. Moreover, when they finished playing, he ignored them and went on playing, to the great amusement of the audience.

It was nearly midnight when suddenly there rushed into the hall a wild-looking old man dressed as a beggar and followed by a crowd of paupers. To the astonishment of the waiters, he went straight to where the Rabbi of Cracow was sitting at the head of the table, drew himself up to his full height as a hush fell on the hall (except for the sound of the young man's playing), and announced: "Midnight!" Then in a loud voice of mysterious authority he informed the rabbi that the playing of the young man Abraham was the true "music of midnight." In order that the rabbi should hear this holy music "it had been decreed that his family be united in matrimony with that of the president of the Lublin synagogue with Tomashov as the halfway point between the two. . . ." Then he pointed to the ceiling, which at once opened "like the flaps of a sukkah, one half to the right, one to the

28

left." Next the sky split, revealing all the host of heaven bathed in eternal light and listening intently to the glorious playing of young Abraham—"And the world trembled and was afraid." When the sky closed again and, after it, the two halves of the roof, Abraham's instrument suddenly fell from his hand. "Then he rose up, turned to the audience, began singing "Hear O Israel" to a heavenly tune . . . and swooned away. . . ." The next day the lad died. "He had been called to the heavenly host; they needed a double bass there." "The old man and his crowd of beggars disappeared."[38]

I have provided this somewhat detailed summary of "Hear O Israel" because it is typical of Peretz's technique not only in *The Voice of the People,* but in those other collections in which he clothes the "pure" aesthetic form in the garb of Jewish folklore. The theme of the story is not exclusively Jewish, but contains elements from world literature too. An almost primitive character, unable to think clearly, unable to express his thoughts, and driven by his inner confusion to find expression through a primitive musical instrument he finds, frequently appears in world folklore.[39] In folklore, this primitive creature is always inferior to his cultural environment, while in "Hear O Israel" Peretz endows his character with a sublimity that dims his surroundings even though they are culturally superior to him. Moreover, fairy tales relate the magical expression to the magic instrument itself, the player undergoing no recognizable change, while Peretz does the contrary. From the beginning of the story, the author supplies his character with a vivid imagination that, for better or for worse, must find its outlet. The musical instrument is an ordinary double bass with nothing intrinsically remarkable about it other than its deep tone, which on the one hand emphasizes the awkwardness of its player and on the other the heavy weight of personal problems that have accumulated within him. But above all, there is the emotional catharsis itself. Under our very eyes, as it were, the author removes his hero from the category of a creature of flesh and blood in the concrete world of the wedding at Tomashov and magically transforms him into a mysterious figure transcending the world of actuality, transcending the world of lucid thought

29

and expression, transcending even the inner struggles of the hero himself.

The story thus attempts to break away from its original realism to achieve the sense of mysterious beauty that pervades its close. It departs from a normal narrative style aimed at presenting one or two episodes with logic and clarity. Though Peretz does in fact provide us with a detailed account of the course of events, he makes every effort to desert formal realism, giving his prose the conversational tone of an older man reminiscing with friends of his own age. The carefully modulated tone, the rhythmic pauses suggestive of a person listening both to the story and his own soul, the overt and subtle allusions—all these combine the hasidic folklore with a modernistic symbolism similar to that of Maeterlinck, and show how near Peretz was approaching his literary aim.[40] Yet that is the trouble; for this submission to an instinctual, aesthetic sense, devoid of any outwardly realistic goal and ignoring the day-to-day ideological problems of his people and his society, is disturbed by the general course of the story, for it almost always responds to the dictates of an external and rational "morality." In "By a Dying Man's Pillow," which we referred to before dealing with "Hear O Israel," the mystical element culminates in a moral lesson teaching a love of Israel and a more universal humanism, namely: it is better for a man to descend into the fires of Hell to help a fellow man than to ascend to Paradise to enjoy alone the eternal splendor of heaven. Although in "Hear O Israel" the author attempts to break away from a realistic style in order to present his central character more vividly, it remains a mere narrative with a more oblique approach. The author increasingly subordinates the story to his eccentric theory that if a man's inner world is not endowed with conceptual thought purified from the mists of its origin, it is liable to "split the heavens." This idea dominates the story from the beginning, detracting from its intuitive quality and hence spoiling its literary effectiveness.

This point, which we made in connection with the stories in *The Voice of the People,* the high-point of Peretz's artistic achievement, is even more marked in some of the earlier collections of stories, such as *She,* containing "The Dumb Girl," "Melodies of the Day," and "Tales of the Moon," and *In a Vision,* containing "Three Calls," "Thought and the Violin," and "A Mother's Vision," all of which deliberately sacrifice impressionism on the altar of intellectualism.[41] The story is a sort of vignette, and was written quite deliberately for the purpose of conveying an intellectual idea. There the impressionism turns into an ironic allegory, and there is nothing more antagonistic to symbolism than allegory.

The clearest indication that Peretz recognized this subordination to intellectuality and that it served as the source of his tragic awareness is to be found in the desperate intensity that increases throughout his works until it breaks through the barrier of the short story to adopt the drama in its stead—at times the melancholy drama of romanticism, as in *The Collapse of a Rabbi's House* (of which the Yiddish version is superior); at times the expressionist drama with its cry of bereavement, such as *At Night in the Old Market.* But before examining them, we must look more closely at the series of short stories that both his own and the following generation regarded as a sort of neo-Hasidism, and in which his earlier intuitive style reached its full fruition.

In the hope of rescuing the modern Hebrew novel as well as his own works from the burden of allegory, Peretz turned to hasidic themes and styles, particularly to their lilting musicality. Through them, he felt he could realize his dream of achieving an impressionistic style that would eventually be transformed into symbolism. He deliberately imitated the language of the hasidic folktale, especially that of the Polish versions so close to his heart because of their musicality and allusiveness. Apart from listening to these folktales during his travels through the Polish townships, he also collected the moral teachings of the hasidic rabbis. He greatly admired the lively fashion in which they were phrased and modeled his own style on them, both in Yiddish and Hebrew, until it became more flexible, connotative, musically evocative of the inner world of the Jew, and, above all, redolent with allusions to a transcendent reality, to the mystery concealed within the visible world.

His collection entitled *Hasidism* may rightly be regarded as the focal point of this trend, not merely as far as Peretz's own literary efforts were concerned but for the Yiddish novel of his generation.[42] In the same way that Shalom Aleikhem gave to the Jewish novel its literary realism, Peretz in his *Hasidism* provided the Yiddish (as opposed to the Hebrew) novel with a romanticism that deserted the harsh realism of the Jewish township and the urbanized Jews of the Polish cities. His technique in this book deserves particularly close examination, since on the surface it resembles that of Shalom Aleikhem's humorous tales. The stories in *Hasidism* tend to employ the monologue, the soliloquy of a single character through whom the story is told. In effect, the purpose here is the same as we noted in connection with Shalom Aleikhem: the monologue provides a deeper psychological insight into character. In the same way, then, as Shalom Aleikhem's use of the realistic monologue satisfied his aesthetic aims, so the impressionist monologue satisfied those of Peretz.

Not all of the stories in *Hasidism*, however, are written in the form of a monologue. A few, including "A New Melody," and "The Kabbalists," employ a straightforward narrative technique, and it is these that attain full stylistic expression with no extraneous purpose divorcing the plots from their realistic and deeply tragic background.[43] "The Kabbalists" will be examined later, but when, in "A New Melody," the father and son are left in complete isolation and despair after the communal Blessing of the New Moon at the end of the Day of Atonement and the father teaches his son "a new melody" in order to ease his spiritual depression, the realism is so direct and vivid that it approaches Peretz's promised land in its symbolic yearning. Yet, in the impressionist monologue of most of the stories in *Hasidism*, with all the stylistic impression that accompanies them, we find the author struggling desperately to find a suitable mode of expression. For in these stories the intellectual allegory constantly ensnares him.

A closer examination of one of these stories, which is usually regarded by critics as the acme of Peretz's achievement, "The Adventures of a Melody," reveals how little the melody harmonizes with its adventures, how short the author falls of supplying it with any inherent purpose, and how the extraneous moral that gives the melody its allegoric significance destroys the story's effect. The tune's "adventures" merely constitute a metaphor or commentary on the various people who play it and on the vicissitudes of their lives. The melody itself thus has a subsidiary importance; in other words, the artistic work is merely the vehicle for an intellectual idea that has been placed upon it. This was the very technique against which Rabbi Nahman of Braslav fought so fiercely, for he insisted on accepting only such melodies as welled up spontaneously from his own tragic depths, untouched by outside influences which might mar their intuitive origin.[44] If in the realm of realistic fiction this technique is sometimes legitimate, for the modernistic writer it is fatal. Now Peretz, with his remarkable critical perception, clearly recognized how far his didacticism interfered with his instinctive artistic sense, and was afraid that his mystic symbolism would degenerate into mere obscurity. Hence the constant struggle visible throughout his works, the oscillation from an impressionism dappled with light and shade to a gloomy symbolism and from there to an imaginative expressionism with its denial of the creative power of art. Despite all that, his literary aim always seemed to elude his grasp. The most striking instance of this tragic failure occurs in *Hasidism,* in the story called "The Kabbalists."

The technique Peretz uses with restrained dramatic force in this brief story recalls the struggles of the mystical kabbalah to find a suitable form of expression. Abstract allegory never proved satisfactory for popular kabbalah. The early kabbalists had either devoted themselves to "chariot mysticism" and to investigating God's infinity, or had alternatively concentrated on the numerical significance of Hebrew characters as a means of foretelling the date of the messianic era. Then came Rabbi Isaac Luria, with an anthropomorphic symbolism perfectly suited to his abstract and sublime concepts.[45] The "breaking of the Vessels," the "sparks" wandering through space and needing to be "clothed" in various "garments" so they could "ascend" and contribute to the long and difficult "restoration" of the world, the "Right Side" and the "Other Side" in an easily intelligible and highly dramatic imagery, all this was accepted by the popular Kabbalah as literally "true." Moreover, by accepting this imagery as true, the popular kabbalists found an outlet for their suppressed emotions. The popular Kabbalah stories, however, always contained a fatal stumbling block for the "practical" kabbalist, barring his way to the final fiftieth gate that had opened before him, so that "he fell down on the threshold of the abyss."[46] The story entitled "The Kabbalists" takes a stumbling block like this as its central theme, and unconsciously Peretz provides in it the explanation of his own artistic struggles.

The story is about two kabbalists, a teacher and his pupil, who make a pact between them to fast, mortify their flesh, and purify their souls until they break down the fleshly barrier that separates them from the divine melody within their souls. Then the world could be "restored" before the coming of the messiah. The weaker their bodies become from fasting, the more clearly do they feel the splendor of the holy tune beginning to rise from deep within them. But on the third day of their fast, just as they feel the melody they long for at last becoming audible, a poor woman enters the Bet ha-Midrash holding in her hand a bowl of soup for the scholars. Within a second, the younger scholar's intense concentration on his spiritual purpose is completely broken, for he looks at the woman and the soup. At once the gateway to the tune clangs shut, and the two men are left utterly disconsolate.

The story itself is typical of the popular Kabbalah with its tales of "practical" kabbalists who dared to enter the gates and failed because of some external factor lying in ambush for their souls, ready to create a blemish in them and hence frustrate their mission. The way Peretz relates the story, however, reveals such psychological restraint, such withdrawal from the world of reality, that at times the story seems to be raging and roaring beneath the silence he has imposed upon it. The impressionistic effect of the melody playing softly deep within the soul and due eventually to burst forth in all its glory is, as in many other stories in this collection, cancelled out by a strange sense of constraint that was soon to give way to result in a wild, primitive, and almost unintelligible outburst. This story presages his later adoption of expressionist drama, which here is masked by the tradition of kabbalistic folklore, wherein the physical body darkens the soul and delays its redemption. A clearer hint of this change is to be found in another story in this collection, "The Power of a Violin." The theme is again the eternal melody serving as spiritual salvation for the burdened soul. The deathbed confessions of Jonah, the father of the "musicians," contains a lament that really constitutes Peretz's own lament for his artistic anguish:

> I have sinned before You. . . . But You are the cause . . . You gave to me a soul heavy with longing and restlessness, a soul which could never find peace. It sinned through the force of its longing . . . always seeking, but never finding. . . . Do You know whom my poor soul was seeking?—You! You alone!—without You it was cold in the dark world. But You disappeared—You hid yourself from sinful despair . . . and my soul searched for You in the fields and the forests . . . it pursued You over hill and dale. It scoured every corner of the world, searching above the clouds and the mists . . . in every sunbeam, in every color of the rainbow, in every welling spring. . . . Only now have I plumbed the depths . . . so late it has all come clear to me . . . suddenly the truth has flashed upon me, just as I am about to come before You for punishment or mercy. . . .[47]

Peretz's greatest effort, so obvious that it became part of his ideology, was to purify his work into an art form untouched by the external world, and its clearest instance can be seen in his drama *The Collapse of a Rabbi's House* (as previously noted, the Yiddish version *Di Goldené Keyt* ["The Golden Chain"] is superior). The fact that this is a hasidic drama based upon an incident that really occurred is of no concern to us in this discussion of the author's artistic struggles and of his importance for the development of Yiddish literature. A study of literary history attempting to distinguish the influence of Hasidism or the Enlightenment movement on modern Hebrew literature might need to inquire whether Hasidism contained any psychological trend similar to that in *The Collapse of a Rabbi's House*.[48] Such considerations, however, fall outside the scope of this study, which is restricted to the literary trends of a specific era.

35

In this play, the characters are borrowed from Peretz's hasidic stories, in which the symbolic element battles with a more rationalized didacticism. The monologue is replaced by a dramatic dialogue that permits each character to come to life independently and to experience all its longings and suffering. As the monologue is reduced by the pressure of other speakers, each individual personality becomes more distinct. The central problem dealt with in this play is the same as that pulsating throughout the symbolist drama of Europe—how to find a satisfactory vehicle of expression for the individual listening to his own thoughts, absorbed in his intuitive knowledge, striving to uncover the sacred, aesthetic truth within his inner turmoil, and withdrawing from the hubbub of the "real" world outside.

Outwardly, the plot has a hasidic setting. The house is that of Reb Shlomo the tzaddik, and the action takes place late on a Saturday night. The "elders" and selected disciples of the tzaddik, together with the members of his household and a throng of followers who have come to lay their troubles before him and request his advice and blessing, are all waiting for the Rabbi to come out of his study and pronounce the havdalah blessing marking the end of the Sabbath. But the elderly Rabbi does not come out. The older hasidim and the disciples begin to fear that some catastrophe has occurred, and the hasidim outside are filled with dark foreboding. The atmosphere in the play becomes one of ominous pauses, of silences pregnant with emotion like those of Maeterlinck's symbolist plays or the poetic drama of Wyspianski, the Polish romantic.[49] Everything is directed toward some metaphysical event beyond the perceptible world, some mysterious force outside the bounds of reason. The elders in this play guess instinctively what is happening, their silent anxiety growing every moment, and the disciples are filled with increasing fear because of their Rabbi's investigation into the "World of Creation," and because the somber, apocalyptic visions of his daughter Miriam, who foresees the irrevocable doom of her father's house. The elders are terrified of some dreadful, unnameable blemish in the dynastic succession of the tzaddik, while the ordinary hasidim, laboring under their heavy yoke, press forward to the Rabbi's

door in the hope of a drop of comfort from him, a word of blessing, a slight easing of their harsh lives. But the Rabbi remains in
his room, and their melancholy deepens. When he does finally
appear, the dreadful catastrophe is revealed: the Rabbi will not
make havdalah this evening. He no longer recognizes the physical
world and has determined to rise above its petty sphere of action.
When he finds he has to say something to those who are so eagerly
waiting for a word from him, he can only murmur some bitter
satire, heavy with disillusionment and despair—satire recalling
that of the earlier maskilim of the Enlightenment, if somewhat
mystical in its "Here, between death and life, the world trembles."
His words are prompted by a disgust with the petty interests of
his hasidim, who anxiously long for a "spark," a "little gift," "a
minor miracle":

> One sect . . .
> This sect . . .
> Two, three, four . . .
> Four minyanim of little Jews . . .
> All twisted up . . .
> Petty Jews . . .
> Coming . . .
> Knocking on the tzaddik's door . . .
> *(More sadly)* Frozen souls . . .
> To the ever-burning lamp they come . . .
> Stretching out their hands:
> "A spark, a spark!
> A little gift,
> A minor miracle . . .
> A wonder, a sign . . ."
> No—begone!
> Each only worried for himself,
> For his wife and children,
> For his family.
> And here,
> Between death and life
> The world trembles.
> The world drowns in melancholy,
> The universe![50]

Therefore, the Rabbi will not answer his hasidim. He will not
permit the Sabbath to end, even if the whole world of reality in

all its pettiness should perish. He will ascend to the "pure marble" where splendor and glory shine, where one does not use wretched scales to weigh thought against action, good deeds against sins. The world of action is dead for him:

> And we
> The Sabbath Jews
> The Festival Jews,
> The Jews endowed
> With the spirit of the Day of Rest,
> Will walk over its ruins. . . .[51]

Eventually, the Rabbi's beadle, having failed to grasp the threatening catastrophe, rebels against his master and, turning to the mournful, depressed throng, announces in a loud voice: "A pleasant week—the Sabbath is over," thus breaking the spell of the sublime covenant of the "Sabbath Jews." The beauty of the "pure marble" is shattered, the glory dimmed, and the Rabbi expires.

This opening act of the play is sufficient to illustrate Peretz's attempt to bring a modernistic element into Yiddish and Hebrew literature. There can be no doubt that the heavy silences of the play approach the symbolism of Maeterlinck. The sense of something over and beyond the factual termination of the Sabbath and the ominous silence of the elders, the disciples, and the ordinary hasidim—all this suggests a mysterious mingling of life-in-death and death-in-life such as pervades *Pelléas et Mélisande, Les Aveugles,* and other plays by the great symbolist, Maeterlinck. The text of the opening scenes of Peretz's play, before the Rabbi comes out of his study, creates a vivid realism tinged with mystery, the first instance in the history of modern Jewish literature. Yet the climax of the play—the Rabbi's impassioned speech on the sublimity of the "pure marble"—destroys this atmosphere, making it mere pastiche. This fault is inherent in the gulf that the Rabbi creates between the "Sabbath Jews" and those who returned to their mundane tasks as soon as the Sabbath was technically over. This extreme aestheticism, personified by the author in Reb Shlomo, destroys that vital concern with the common people that was the motive force both of modern literature in general and of the symbolist and romantic schools in particular.

What can be deduced from this? Polish literature too turned to romantic symbolism and the lifeline of imagism that French literature had bequeathed to Europe as a whole. But its motive force, whether in its universal or patently individualistic forms, was rooted in the vital realism of the common people, in their sabbaths, their festivals, their myths, and their day-to-day struggles, as well as in the dreams of national independence for the entire people. Even Wyspianski, in his romantic writings, *Redemption, The Wedding, A November Night,* could not find a satisfactory vehicle of expression in the nineteenth-century realistic drama. Instead, he explored the various levels of the popular imagination that had nourished the political, social, economic, and cultural struggles of the people as well as the personal aesthetic longings of the individual. Wyspianski was impelled, therefore, toward mystic symbolism, which enabled him to express with extraordinary vividness the realm of spontaneous creativity immersed in an inner, psychological world. Indeed, he was profoundly influenced by Maeterlinck's responsiveness to a world beyond the physical and the concrete, by his evocation of the profound silences that alone permit man to achieve a wonderful awareness of his own inner depths, and by his cognizance of the music rising from those depths, endowing the dramatis personae with an intuitive spontaneity needing no rational explanation and ignoring logical development in its mingling of life and death.[52]

The Polish poet captured the beautiful originality of Maeterlinck's symbolist prose, and yet this prose was not suited to his own artistic needs. Wyspianski's style had drawn its imagist strength from the ancient myths of the common people, from the heroic epics of the past, and from the people's present struggle for national freedom and independence. That was why he turned to dramatic poetry, in which he could combine the external and inner worlds, the past and the future, the nation and the individual, mythological imagery and modern aesthetic trends. The very opposite is true of Peretz's *The Golden Chain* (as well as *The Collapse of a Rabbi's House*). His play allows no room for the visible world; he accords it no artistic significance and sees no possibility of mystery in it. Thereby he nullifies, in effect, any bond between his play and the symbolism of Wyspianski, which draws its inspiration and strength from the traditions of the common people. The beadle's "A pleasant week!" has in no way been prepared for in the play and forms no organic part of it; the author suddenly thrusts it upon us in the midst of the Rabbi's lofty meditations. If Peretz suddenly took pity on the poor creatures crowding at the Rabbi's door and hence brought in the beadle to cut the "golden chain" which bound them, he did so without any dramatic preparation. In this sense, the play is far inferior to Anski's *The Dibbuk,* with all its pseudo-mythology. The profane conquers the holy Sabbath—and the Rabbi dies. Here author contradicts everything he struggled to achieve in his *The Voice of the People,* and it may well be that his indefinable feeling of despair, which accompanied Peretz in so much of his work, was responsible. Striking evidence of this may be seen in the fact that Peretz did not allow himself to close his play with a scene of the Rabbi's death. He moves from one individualistic extreme ("the pure marble") to another ("the completely innocent"), both of which show how far he was withdrawing from the popular traditions that had supplied him with the themes of his stories, namely the religious myths of the hasidim and their opponents, and how much his art depended on an intellectual didacticism.

Like Ibsen's *Brand,* the second half of Peretz's *Golden Chain* constitutes fierce individualistic morality in one person.[53] Pinhas, the dead Rabbi's son, demands with inflexible cruelty the complete purity of his followers, who know in their hearts that the world does not consist of the absolutely innocent and the absolutely guilty but is a mixture, a mingling of light and shade. Pinhas, however, is fighting the Lord's battles in his determination to ascend to a "sabbatical" purity by despising the "profanity" and "pettiness" of the world of action. In creating the character of Pinhas, the author could not make use of the mystic symbolism of a somewhat vague impressionism, and he now employs violent satire as a steppingstone to expressionism:

Itzhak Leib Peretz

We have parted.
Useless chatter.
You came in terror,
In dread you shall go.
The world needs innocent men![54]

Here the gulf begins to widen between the Rabbi's house and the House of Israel. Noble aesthetic inspiration cannot abide the real physical world. We return to the allegory that Peretz's readers will remember from the opening of "The Three Gifts," the souls wandering naked and bare because both their good deeds and their sins were small and weighed equally in the balance. That is all that is left of this great dramatic force. The last divine spark of the "pure marble," Pinhas' son, the grandson of the old Rabbi, returns to the common world of his simple hasidim, and humbly begs his grandfather's compassion:

The grandson
Is neither of Sabbath nor Festival . . .
We have fallen low,
We have met here
For a crumb of mercy. . . .[55]

After such literary efforts as these, whether in the drama or the short story, Peretz could no longer continue with the dark meditations of *Hasidism*. That form of expression, which he had so yearned for throughout his life and which he demanded from his colleagues and disciples, never found its fruition. Almost in despair, he turned from the beautiful musicality of his earlier writings to an expressionist fury that grew in force throughout the first decade of the twentieth century. This idealistic aesthete now began to prophesy the disintegration of the self. Man was no longer responsible for his actions, as nineteenth-century humanism had taught. Strange winds were blowing from all directions upon the human soul. Atavistic desires welling up from their hidden places were creating an archetypal mythology that burst forth with a comic grotesqueness devoid of past or future and possessing only a confused present, clownish in its absurdity. His drama *At Night in the Old Market Place*, with such characters as "the

41

sinner," "the madman," and "shadows from the world of chaos," becomes enslaved to primitive techniques that contradict his frenzied outburst of strangled desires and frustrated visions. A fatal despair now destroys everything with its satanic beauty; everything mates, grows old, and dies. All the dramatic force disintegrates in a clownish laugh, as if to say that the entire universe is only an evil dream without hope of redemption.

Only in the simpler stories of *The Voice of the People* that are devoid of aesthetic or didactic purpose—such as "Seven Good Years," "The Miracle Worker," "Treasure," and "Golden Shoes"—did Peretz really succeed. There the realism of the stories matched his inner dream, and out of the world of the "little man" is woven vividly realistic tales. These stories are free from all grandiose design, and man's inner beauty provides the motive force. The holy and the profane become combined in a fresh spontaneity that mingles light and shade as in the real world. In these Peretz remained close to his Jewish sources.

2

The Isolation
of the Individual

Mordekhai Ze'ev Feierberg: Wrapped in Shadows

The literary struggles experienced by Peretz lent a certain tragic quality to his figure. Yet those very struggles opened up new horizons for Yiddish prose, poetry, and drama, providing until our own day inspiration for writers of Yiddish in all countries where that literature has any standing.[1] It was through him that Sholem Ash turned to the romantic epic set in ancient and more recent periods of history with its themes of the sanctification of God, of the Sabbath, of maternal love, and of humanity as a whole. In Ash's stories, these themes are veiled in mystery, achieving their impact largely through an erotic treatment of the woman and her sublime beauty.[2] Because of the influence of Peretz, Joseph Opatoshu began retracing the footsteps of the Polish Jewish families of earlier generations, with their noble connections, who used to float timber from the forests of the Polish aristocracy down the broad surface of the Vistula. When Opatoshu began writing *In the Polish Forests*, his style, the heritage of various Jewish eras, began to reflect the mystic folklore of the dark, ancient woods, redolent of love and the mighty river, as well as the mysticism of the Kotzk hasidim and the strange, erotic memories of the Frankists who had lived in that forest setting.[3] The tendency of these two great writers to desert contemporary

43

realism and to seek instead the beauty hidden beyond the contemporary world derived directly from the teachings of Peretz. Where Peretz had failed in writing works of epic dimensions, they succeeded, and hence perhaps softened the sharpness of his tragic fate.

Even Peretz's attempts at extreme modernism saw their fruition in the Yiddish literature of Russia before the descent of the Iron Curtain, and in America in the twenties and thirties. A short time before the October revolution, Bergelson wrote his brief story "Beside the Railroad Station," with its exploration of the area beneath the threshold of consciousness. In its melancholy fatalism and its dark, symbolic longings, this story came close to the Russian and European Symbolist movement of the early twentieth century. It was soon followed by his novel *The End of Everything*, which took as its theme the deterioration and isolation of the Jewish intelligentsia in the cities of the Ukraine. It is charged with a wonderful fatalism; everything seems to flow toward some hidden sea to dissolve and disappear, and human beings lose their individuality in the anonymous waters.

This was the period when Yiddish literature reached its greatest flowering in Russia; even more than poetry, its fiction responded to modern symbolism, which had been the focal point of Peretz's literary ambitions. The most outstanding exponent of this trend was a member of the Yiddish literary circle in Kiev, "Der Nister," whose writings were steeped in Jewish folklore and permeated by mysticism.[4] Similarly, Yiddish poetry and drama in the United States during the twenties and thirties ignored the harsh, grey world of the immigrant Jews, with all their economic and cultural problems, and sought instead the bright butterfly of aestheticism. The young Jewish poet in America yearned for a world of his own in which to fulfill his private artistic longings. Aaron Glantz and Jacob Glatstein took refuge in "In-Zikh" (poetry responsive only to itself, or in which the poet responds solely to his own inner being), and Mané Leib hid himself away to write his marvelous ballads, which were created in a popular Jewish style but were filled with hidden beauty and silent desires.[5] Zisho Landau created a pseudo-hasidic rhythm that recurred through-

44

out his writings to find expression for his literary groping, while Moshé Leib Halperin, with his strange, secret melancholy, wrote poetry about a golden peacock that leads man beyond the hills and the sunset to love. All these writers had in common the wish to express their inner being in the tradition of their teacher, Peretz.

Hebrew fiction, however, was different. The divorce of Hebrew from Yiddish literature did not result only from the decision at the 1907 conference of Yiddish writers in Czernowitz that Yiddish should be the national tongue of the Jewish people. It was also a result of Peretz's insistence on a complete distinction between the techniques of the two literatures. The Hebrew revival had, as we have seen, begun by rejecting the didacticism of the Enlightenment movement, which had employed a bitter, intellectual satire that ignored Jews as individuals.[6] It had never forgotten, however, its aim of dealing with the social and cultural problems of the Jewish people and giving them artistic expression. This proved to be the distinctive trend in all the varied forms of modern Hebrew literature.

One main difference between Hebrew and Yiddish literature of this era is that the former concerned itself with the profound sense of isolation that Russian Jewry experienced as a result of the "Confusion of the Domains" both before World War I and in the subsequent revolution. The buttresses of religion and tradition, like those of the state and the economic and social conditions of the people, had already begun to collapse, filling the world of the Jew with dark foreboding. Bialik, as we have noted, discussed this breakdown of sanctions in his poem to Ahad ha-Am.[7] It may be that Bialik believed at that time that the liberal, humanist philosophy of Ahad ha-Am would eventually serve to repair the broken boundaries—even though Bialik's poetry was in fact dependent upon emotional forces far removed from the rationalist theories of the philosopher. In any event, Hebrew literature in Bialik's generation was in no way inspired by Ahad ha-Am's teachings, but instead drew its strength from its powerful concern with the isolation of man and with the variegated forms that the sense of isolation took in each individual.

The dominant theme of this literature marked an important step in its development, for there can be no literary examination of such isolation without some attempt to convey the collapse of the Jewish world that had prompted it. With the exception of only two or three writers, all Hebrew literature of this period was concerned with the recent history of the Jewish townships in Poland, Lithuania, and the Ukraine. The tragic setting, if not the tragedy itself, in the stories by Feierberg and Gnessin, Berkovitch and Ben-Zion, Brenner and Berdichevsky, is one and the same—the abyss created within the Jew who realizes that where before he was deeply rooted in a firm soil, he is now cut off, deprived of any real significance in the world. His soul wanders naked, hopeless, and meaningless in the world of nostalgic regret to which he has been fated. Usually, this sense of desolation drives the character into some traumatic experience that forms the climax of the story. But this development could never be credibly depicted except against the background of the world from which the central figure has been isolated.

This new trend had enormous potentialities for epic realism. It could provide the setting for great scenes of the rise and fall of the Jewish township, out of which the individual characters grew. But the earnest attempts of the young writers to combine the two worlds, the old and the new, and the fact that they saw as the ultimate purpose of their work the grim depiction of their own solitude and isolation, hampered the development of a fully realistic novel combining at different levels the actual world against which the events took place and the inner world of the individual living in that era. Isolation and the subsequent meaninglessness of existence became the watchwords of the young writers and prevented them from achieving the breadth of vision and depth of insight that are the prerequisites of the epic.

One further point needs to be made here, parallel to the first but of greater importance for the history of Jewish fiction at the turn of the twentieth century. If this concern with isolation lessened the possibility of an epic, the loss was counterbalanced by positive achievements visible in the writings of Feierberg, Gnessin, Berdichevsky, and others, paralleling the literary trends of

contemporary European literature. Since Feierberg's stories illustrate with particular clarity this concern with the author's personal sense of isolation and are also marked by the absence of any
epic realism, I shall discuss them first.

Mordekhai Ze'ev Feierberg was born in 1874 in Novgorad-
Wohlinski. He was from a very pious hasidic family of the extremely ascetic and musar tradition of the Lurianic Kabbalah.
In his biographical notes on Feierberg, Fischel Lakhover remarked: "From various allusions in Feierberg's writings, it may
be deduced that his family venerated the memory of their fore-
fathers who had died martyrs' deaths in the Khmelnitski massacres."[8] Until he came into contact with the rationalism of the
new Jewish philosophy and with modern Hebrew literature itself,
he had been immersed not only in the religious legalism of the
Talmud and commentaries, but also—and far more deeply—in the
homiletical and kabbalistic teachings that had been woven around
them. From his father he learned to respect the authority of the
books of the Talmud, the Kabbalah, and the Musar, which lay
on the table and bookshelves, but from his mother he imbibed
the numerous folktales from the popular Kabbalah and the
Hasidism of the Baal-Shem-Tov and Rabbi Leib Soré's (the son
of Sara),[9] which insisted on the dualism of holiness and impurity
struggling eternally for mastery in the world.

From his childhood, therefore, the author's view of life was
dominated by a sacred dualism, from which he never freed himself. His father's teachings imbued him with a melancholy awareness of the presence of Satan and his followers constantly lying
in wait to catch him in their powerful snares. This solemn feeling
inspired in him, as he stood between the powers of good and evil
in a world caught in the net of Satan, a secret, apocalyptic longing for the messianic era, when the Holy would at last triumph
in all its glory. The Jewish exile became for him a symbol of this
apocalyptic war from the time he was old enough to sit in the
Heder on the bleak winter evenings studying the weekly portion
of the Pentateuch with the other "grown-up" boys. When he
returned home tired, hungry, and depressed, however, his mother
used to tell him folktales till he was caught up in the world of

47

shadows as he nestled in his mother's lap—his mother, who would protect him against all evil. Even his father, despite a harsh discipline and a stern insistence on service to one's Creator and to the sanctification of God, imparted to him a deep sense of belonging, which blossomed with extraordinary beauty out of that very "eternal war" with evil, out of the burning stakes of the Inquisition and the pogroms of "Tah and Tat" instigated by the evil followers of Satan in this world. This sense of belonging was for him the true and sacred reality of life, and to this he dedicated his finest literary work, "The Shadows," a story written shortly before his death, which occurred when he was only twenty-four.

> My father told me that in his youth he used to love to study the Talmud in the Bet ha-Midrash; it was his only pleasure throughout his troubled life. I remember that whenever he reminisced about his youth and described how conscientiously he studied, my eyes used to fill with tears, tears of longing for those wonderful evenings in the Bet ha-Midrash. He would recall that he felt a spirit descending on him from above, a holy flame lighting his heart, and a warm glow suffusing him within—a glow of love for the sad chant, for the night and the stars. . . . Who knows! Perhaps it was the same chant, the same night and stars that I love . . . for that is the heritage I have received from my father.
> . . .
> Then I see the Bet ha-Midrash built in the center of the universe, with bright light radiating from it over all the world. . . .[10]

But before he wrote "The Shadows," describing this complete identification with his father, he had fallen into the abyss of the "breaking of the sanctions," and a wave of anguish had encompassed his ailing body and depressed soul. His father's holy world had not dovetailed with that of Ahad ha-Am, of Berdichevsky, of Zionism, and of the new Hebrew literature, and it was this anguish that prompted him to devote his literary talents to finding some outlet for the personal catastrophe he had suffered as a result of the collapse of the traditional world. His struggle to do so prevented him from producing an epic work either on this sacred dualism or on the historical transition that Jewry was then undergoing; it did, however, lead him to a style of writing that was at times close to that of the Symbolist movement, of which he had certainly never heard.

Mordekhai Ze'ev Feierberg

Like most young writers at the end of the nineteenth century, Feierberg was acquainted with the nationalistic and socialist ideas of his day, and particularly with the secular nationalism of Ahad ha-Am. According to the biographical details provided by Lakhover, the revolution broke through the walls of his sacred world before he was aware of modern Hebrew literature. Among the books of musar and kabbalah in the Bet ha-Midrash, he found some works on philosophy. He was profoundly impressed by *The Book of Faith* of Rabbi Barukh Kossover, by Yehuda ha-Levi's *Kuzari*, by Maimonides' *Guide for the Perplexed*, and Gersonides' *Battles of the Lord*. From there he was attracted to Isaac Hirsch Weiss's *Generations of Scholars*, to Nahman Krokhmal's *Guide for the Perplexed of the Time*, and finally to Ahad ha-Am's essays and modern Hebrew literature in general, both that which preceded the Enlightenment movement and that of his own era, with its search for new forms of expression. The hasidim in his town, suspecting that he was drifting away from his faith, began to hound him, embittering his life and even interfering with his father's livelihood as a ritual slaughterer.

In his twenty-first year he began to write, looking for inspiration to Warsaw and Odessa, the centers of the Hebrew literature of his day. In the three years he devoted to literature, the last years of his life, he produced little. Nevertheless, his writing, which consists entirely of personal reminiscences, illustrates the new trend in modern Hebrew literature, which not only departed from the rational didacticism of Mendelé Mokher Sefarim but explored new paths. Feierberg joined this trend neither deliberately nor even consciously, but because the unique forces that welled up within him deprived him of rest and never left him until he had written his final reminiscences, "The Shadows," in which he achieved his purpose of reconstructing the religious atmosphere of his father's house. By this reconstruction he wished to express all that he had lost when uprooted and spiritually deprived by the breakdown of sanctions.[11]

He used to submit his stories to Ahad ha-Am's *Ha-Shilloah*, and Ahad ha-Am, in the same way that he had failed to understand the battles of Berdichevsky and other younger writers (as I shall examine more fully a little later), failed also to understand the

49

struggles of this young writer from Novgorad-Wohlinski. Feierberg tried to explain to him the new literary approach of his
Hophni the Dreamer. In a letter attached to his story "In the
Evening," he emphasized his desire "to provide in my reminiscences the *complete world* [the italics are his] of the Jew," and
the folktales in the story form an integral part of that "complete
world."[12] The more he struggles to express what is in his heart,
the further he moves away from the intellectualism of Ahad
ha-Am, even though at times he employs the ideological language
of the day: "Many treasures of the human spirit are buried under
the rubble of the dark entrances. We must not remain there—we
cannot remain there. We must remove our possessions into the
'open world' of the younger generation."[13] This language was a
camouflage for the profound lament in his letter to Ahad ha-Am:
"The new way of life is opening out in our midst without the
approval of literature, while the old life, with all its sanctity and
nobility, is dying." Feierberg was filled with the gnawing fear that
man's sense of his own place in the world was dying together
with the old world. His stories, therefore, are not simply reminiscences about "worship" and "midnight study," the musar teachings of his father or the folktales of his mother, or even a conscious
attempt to introduce folkloristic trends into modern Hebrew
literature as Peretz, Berdichevsky, Yehudah Steinberg, and others
had done.[14] Fundamentally, he wanted to recreate the old world
that was dying in order to find an outlet for his sense of isolation
and bereavement.

His desire to recreate the dying world does not mean in this
case an attempt to create an epic work on that theme; rather,
Feierberg wished to allow that world to come alive once again in
order to ease his pain and grief. No objective, epic reconstruction
of the past, even with all due attention to chronology and logic,
would have served his turn, for the literary element would have
barred him from his purpose, dooming him to failure from both
a personal and literary viewpoint. He therefore attacked the
stylistic form of his story with vehemence, in order to remove
from it any trace of the confidence so typical of the epic tradition
wherein the author does not reveal his inner self. His ultimate

Mordekhai Ze'ev Feierberg

aim was to convey by style of the story that religious and imaginative world he had inherited from his father's home. Hence the tension in the stories from *Hophni the Dreamer,* and even more so in his *Whither?*. It is an inner tension that compresses the language until it ceases to be reminiscence and enters the realm of symbol.

Lakhover has noted that something is "wrong" with the story "In the Evening." In effect, it contains three separate folktales, and the attempt to unite them creates ". . . a serious artistic flaw, for we have before us a story within a story, a folktale within a folktale, of which the first cannot serve as the framework for the second, as it does for the smaller tales of the children in the Heder. For the final story is longer than the first, and the first neither contains it nor acts as introduction or preparation for it, particularly since it contains smaller stories of its own."[15] The separate sections are as follows: it is dusk in the Heder as the afternoon service begins, and the children are left on their own in the gathering shadows, until darkness fills the house with fear. The children huddle together for comfort, and Hophni, "who was shivering and whose hair stood on end," comes over to them and begins to tell them stories of ghosts who enter the synagogue and are called up to the reading of the law, and of various demons and spirits. Then the Rabbi returns from prayer, the Rabbi's wife lights the lamp, and the children resume their study of the weekly portion from the Pentateuch. That is the first story. The second is also self-contained; it deals with Hophni's visions of the shades that lie in wait at every corner of the house, filling the children's chanting with sadness such has his father always used to talk of whenever he told him of the evil ways of Satan. So the story "In the Evening" continues until Hophni goes home to his mother, who, seeing that he is sad, tells him a long story that forms the main story within the story. It is the tale of a lonely tax collector in a town run by a squire, a dreadful magician in league with the devil, who steals a new-born child from the tax collector's wife. Rabbi Leib had gathered a minyan of Jews in the room where the woman gave birth, pronounced oaths, laid charms on the child's bed, and formed a circle round about to prevent the demons from

51

entering, but all to no avail. The squire changes himself into a dog, steals the baby, and brings the child up in his home until he reaches the age of thirteen. Then an old man of horrible appearance begins visiting the squire in his dreams, uttering terrible threats until in terror he takes the child and leaves him in a deserted spot to die. But the forces of good overcome the forces of evil, and the boy studies the Torah until he becomes one of the brightest lights of the sad Diaspora. . . . At this point, Hophni feels calmer and falls into a deep sleep.

It is clear that these stories do not form an organic unit; each is self-contained—the artistic fault that Lakhover points out. Lakhover does, however, acknowledge one link in the stories: all are concerned with ghosts "and in the final story . . . the author relates how deeply these ghosts are embedded in his heart."[16]

But here I have reason to differ with Lakhover. For he repeatedly refers to Feierberg's stories as autobiographical, "episodes from his life," and then forgets that the structural rules of literature cannot be applied to autobiography at all. A man may relate all sorts of reminiscences in one evening, without paying the slightest attention to the artistic relationships Lakhover demands. The latter regards the stories as "overflowing" from reminiscence into story, which for Lakhover means the realistic story, constructed with care and unified in form so that all sections constitute organic parts of the whole. He finds a common factor in the concern with ghosts, but he regards it as insufficient to unify the three or four diverse stories within the main story.

In modern criticism, the technique of a story within the overall structure is no longer regarded as a failing. In fact, the reverse is true. For example, any examination of Agnon's merits as a writer must acknowledge that his work contains a number of different structural levels. Feierberg, however, is trying not merely to break up the stratum of reminiscence but to destroy all trace of the old realism in the story as a whole. There is no real distinction between "The Calf," "The Charm," "The First Story," and all the others up to "Nahman the Madman" in *Whither?* except in the intensity of their expression, which was intended to recreate by vicarious experience that world of which the author had been deprived in real life. The purpose of his concern with ghosts, which Lakhover so wisely noted, is to dispense with the "prologues" and "epilogues" of most stories, allowing the reader to plunge straight into the main theme. Hence the increasing imaginative impact of the ghosts as the story progresses, until finally it attains an almost apocalyptic dramatic force, tearing down the cobwebs of ideological or religious moralizing traditional in the short story to reveal the stark realism of the eternal battle between the forces of good and evil. Before the majesty of this battle, the narrative simply disintegrates. The concern with the old order and the new, which dominates so much of contemporary Hebrew writing, is here simply removed from the realm of historical realism into that of the symbolic:

> He had taken a solemn vow to dedicate his life to hastening the coming of the Messiah. And how hard a task it was! To subdue the "husk" in which the "spark" was enclosed, to subdue Samael, to increase the holiness of the world and crown the Messiah as King—and he was still only a youngster. He remembered that terrible moment when he had taken his holy vow; he had felt instantly that a heavy weight had been laid upon him. . . . But the step had been taken, the vow had been pronounced, and there was no going back.[17]

It would be difficult to illustrate this symbolic technique by means of mere quotations from *Whither?* since the entire book is filled with a profound joy in the mystic forces of the world. This mysticism had its roots in the archetypal myths of the Lurianic Kabbalah, which Feierberg had inherited from his father. The "reminiscences" grow increasingly forceful and demanding, becoming a sort of stylistic obsession whereby the author could restore himself to the lost world of his father's home. Not only does this mythological intensity here exceed anything visible in *Hophni the Dreamer,* but it rejects the comforting calm he had found in his mother's tales, which reappears in "In the Evening," in favor of the awesomely majestic image of his father, with its somewhat harsh insistence on service to the Creator and war against the non-believer.[18] To a sensitive reader, some of that deep spiritual joy is visible even in "Nahman the Madman" whenever the theme of the battle between the Messiah and Samael is touched upon. In fact, all of Feierberg's efforts to create a secular literary work culminated in an attempt to discover a dramatic outlet for his own psychological problems. The "breaking down of sanctions" is thus only faintly reflected in this work of self-expression.

After he had found this solace for his sense of isolation and the loss of his childhood world Feierberg produced his finest literary work. His story "The Shadows" is entirely free of psychological meandering among stories within stories. It does indeed employ a narrator speaking in his own name, and it does constitute the young author's final confessions before his death, but above all it provides a vivid portrait of the author himself. After all his crises and agonies, he is able to see himself with complete objectivity, as if from outside. Through the lyricism of "The Shadows" emerges a vivid realism. He sees himself in all his complexity, and the shadows serve as a mirror symbolizing the real world about him.

> I amuse myself with the shadows, my soul consumes them. . . . I love their darkness, and I want them to grow even darker and broader, spreading their sweet fear and pleasing dread over the entire world—as they do over me.
> The Gemara is open before me, and I chant it in a sad and terrifying tune. The shadows hearken, and begin to dance to the tune, while my heart within me pulsates in rhythm. The tune enters my heart and takes its place within against my wishes.
> I, Hophni, do not know what I feel—I do not understand my own soul. I can not fathom the myriad forces that rule over me, making peace between themselves at these rare moments. I gird up my strength and struggle to understand my soul, if only a little; I try to preserve for myself a few fragmentary memories of this holy joy.[19]

The inner struggles of the earlier stories have totally disappeared. The author has uncovered the roots pulling at his soul, and is now sufficiently strengthened to write of them with an almost epic assurance and a harmonious lyricism. In fact, in "The Shadows" Feierberg retraces all the material in his earlier stories, but now he has no need to break up the literary form since he has at last found an outlet for the psychological turmoil within. It is in this last story that he fulfills his impulse to talk about his father, his inner world, and his real self. But these are not mere reminiscences; they constitute a new literary creation of symbolic proportions. In his story "In the Evening," his mother's love and kindness protect him from the apocalyptic fears inspired by his father, but in "The Shadows" it is his father's integrity and holy faith that gently influence the author. The ideological confusion of *Whither?* has melted away, together with all the apocalyptic mythology, and the aim of the story is now entirely artistic—the portrayal of the sacred integrity of man that can be achieved solely through the holy shadows. The return to this spiritual integrity after his great inner struggles was Feierberg's only means of assuaging his sense of isolation, replacing it only a short time before his death with a profound inner calm.

This spiritual integrity and inner calm is not to be found in previous modern Hebrew literature. By his own artistic struggles, the young author rejected the realism of the short story and entered the realm of symbolism above and beyond the "breaking of the sanctions" of his own day—and that achievement is in itself a heritage for coming generations.

Uri Nissan Gnessin: The Search for a Lost Reality

The autobiographical element in Feierberg's work was, as we have seen, the source of his literary power, compelling him to depart from the current realism of Hebrew literature to create new forms of expression. The mythological world of demons he had inherited from his father served as a symbolic vehicle for expressing his own personality more directly, on a number of different levels. Feierberg risked this directness because he was quite certain of the ultimate purpose he had in mind. When we turn to the writings of Uri Nissan Gnessin, a contemporary of Feierberg, Brenner, Berdichevsky, and Ahad ha-Am, we find the same driving force, but with opposite effects. Gnessin, too, had been educated in a religious home firm in its traditions and had left it behind him—not for the clash of the old world with the ideologies of the new, but in search of the hidden meaning of his

55

own existence. Where Feierberg's writings had led him back to his father's house and to the inner calm of a world with religious values, Gnessin's provided his final divorce from the ordered world of his father's house, and the chance of discovering the ultimate significance of his daily life. He also employs autobiography as his literary form (even if it is presented in the third person), but there is no spiritual link between himself and his childhood home. The literary impulse that his writings offered to Hebrew literature as a whole was to be far-reaching.

Only once—in the book *Beforehand*—does Gnessin allow the central character of the story, Uriel, to return home, and then only for a brief visit. All his books (*Aside, Meanwhile, Beforehand,* and *There*) display a progressive movement away, toward the distant horizons of a world in which reality has grown blurred —an empty waste irremediably burdensome to man. Gnessin, unlike Feierberg, has no clearly defined purpose in mind; he wanders back and forth aimlessly, in ever widening circles, until he reaches the edge of the wasteland and is lost forever. The four books form variations on a central theme, treated with increasing depth and perception: the isolation of man from his sense of personal significance. Each of them employs a different literary technique in presenting the problem, but in each case the gateway for man's exit from the old world is the same—physical love.

This use of love as the means of expressing man's isolation is not unique; it is employed by Brenner, Shoffman, and, with far greater success, by Berdichevsky. With them, it had a twofold symbolism: on the one hand the escape from the strict moral discipline of the parental home, and on the other the empty bohemianism of the Jewish intelligentsia, despite all the splendid ideologies to which they subscribed. With Gnessin, however, love has no immoral or bohemian connotations, but serves instead as a symbol of man's search for individual meaning. In this respect, he had much in common with his friend Brenner, whom I shall discuss later. In love Gnessin finds the myth of isolation vividly reflected, and he conveys this vividness more powerfully than almost any other young writer of his day, so that we respond in his work to the subtler vibrations of fate itself.

56

Any serious analysis of this point demands an investigation of all four books in order, not merely from the biographical aspect—the interplay of events in his life and their literary expression in the stories—but also from a stylistic point of view. In the very first of his stories, *Aside,* the style itself is constantly moving toward the wasteland, avoiding any fixed standpoint, coming back to repeat a previous movement, and then moving off elsewhere.[20] There is no trace of the normal narrative structure that starts out from one point, moves in a straight line, and eventually reaches the author's destination. In Gnessin's *Aside* such realistic techniques as a plot to provide a sequence of events and a literary form in which the plot can be housed cannot be separated. It is almost impossible to summarize the story. If one were to try to do so, one would have to say that Hagzar, the central figure, flutters around a number of girls but never approaches close to any one of them. A summary of this kind, however, gives a completely false picture of the story, for the style of the story is not something that serves merely to clothe an idea the author wished to convey before he set pen to paper, but itself constitutes the primary material of the story. The language, then, is not intended to relate the love of Hagzar for this girl or that (a love which is never consummated for reasons that have little to do with the girl herself), but rather to convey the myth of isolation, which has an archetypal force in *Aside.*

Even the despair typical of his generation does not assume here any particularized form; it can not be analyzed, nor does it achieve any tragic expression, for the love theme of the story lacks actuality and serves solely as an isolation myth presented through the various experiences of the central character and the stylistic techniques of Gnessin himself. It is his language that makes excursions, changes direction, flows toward that hidden sea in which it may lose its identity, and then turns back to its starting point to begin its excursions again. Hence the note of fatalism subtly conveyed by the story; for, if the rhythmic movement of Gnessin's language carries the reader over large areas, it must always return to its source and can never move beyond the boundaries that fate has decreed. In this story, however, the effect is not one of despair or of the spiritual paralysis that follows despair, as in the other stories. On the contrary, it creates the deep satisfaction that every artist experiences when he hears his inner voice speaking aloud, and it is that which crowns his work with success. In *Aside* the language responds so accurately to the author's needs that the time factor disappears; we are unaware of the sunrise, the sunset, and the clock which rules our lives—it is as though everything takes place in a vacuum removed from the confines of time. The theme of isolation thus takes on a metaphysical quality to provide the mythological aura of the story.

The very opening paragraph of the story reveals the technique that pervades the whole of *Aside:* there is no concrete identification of objects, places, events, or thoughts, or even any details to suggest to the reader the historical setting or environment of the story, whether by analogy or association. It rejects, then, all the apparatus of the realistic story. If we analyze the four opening sentences one by one, and then re-read them together as a literary unit, we shall discover the technique by which Gnessin achieves his success. We are introduced to the central character, Nahum Hagzar, whose name, "Festival Stranger," symbolizes the fact that he always feels an outsider at festivities.

> For the first time Nahum Hagzar approached the fine house at the end of the quiet street because of some trivial reason that had occasionally occurred to him but was immediately forgotten.

This sentence is intended to introduce us to the story. It is brief and apparently quite clear. It states an important fact: Hagzar's arrival at the house in which the subsequent erotic story will occur. Yet at the very moment the sentence states this fact, it blurs the realistic setting. The phrase "the fine house at the end of the quiet street" is followed at once by "some trivial reason that had occasionally occurred to him but was immediately forgotten"—a generalization that leaves us wondering whose house it was, in what street, what the trivial reason was that occurred to him sometimes but was immediately forgotten. This vagueness is intended to suggest on the author's part that it is not worth going into any details about Hagzar's visit to the fine house.

Then follows the second sentence, which seems to be rectifying the vagueness of the first.

Uri Nissan Gnessin

> To his surprise, he met there his fat neighbor, Hanna Heller, with the artificially loud laugh, and he began talking to her for the first time.

The sentence flows smoothly, describing the young lady and the opening of a conversation. But the realism of the incident is at once offset by the following sentence, which weakens the effect.

> Just then he did not stay long, for he was deep in thought and in a hurry to get home and his coat was flapping and his heart beating, and he was waiting for the next day and for his steady job and the interesting life now beginning for him in the small new town in which he had chosen to live after leaving Vilna.

If this sentence had merely informed us that Hagzar did not spend a long time talking, all would be well; it is understandable that Hagzar should be excited at the prospect of the next day, with a regular job and interesting life beginning. What detracts from the normality of this sentence is the use of one small word, which we would scarcely have noticed in a realistic novel—the word "just." Here it has an ambiguous effect. Does it mean that just at this moment he can not stay long but that later the house will become the focus of events, or is its function to undermine any sense of definiteness implicit in the author's statement? Before we have time to decide, the next sentence has disrupted our inner dialogue. It repeats the little word "just," but this time the point is concluded and the stylistic effect of the sentence introduces a more pleasant note, even though it is merely repeating the information contained in the earlier sentences.

> But the next day just happened to be overcast and rather gloomy; the window panes were damp, the walls dark, and the ceiling low, so that he sat at the table for a long time with his face in his hands, biting his lips, till suddenly he pulled himself together, thought up a pretext, called for his neighbor, and together with her walked to the fine house at the end of the deserted street.[21]

If we go back and re-read these sentences in one breath, as it were, we may receive the false impression that the style is leading the author by the nose rather than the author molding the style. Before the author has made up his mind whether Hagzar is to remain at the house, the language has forestalled him. Moreover,

59

from the very opening phrases, a sensitive reader can perceive something of primary importance for this story: Gnessin dislikes descriptive passages and removes metaphors and images from his writing, as if they might lend the story some realistic immediacy effective at the various levels of his writing.

The further one reads in Gnessin's story *Aside*, the more convinced one becomes that this is no superficial tale, comprehensible at a glance, but a submerged stream sweeping the reader along with a fatalistic certainty of purpose. This fatalism is echoed in the stylistic gyration, in the fascinating monotone that always returns to its own tracks, and it attracts the reader far more than the sequence of events, which never really takes place. One need not be disturbed by the fact that the events do not actually occur, for the plot itself is concerned with the erotic drives of Hagzar, which are never consummated—in fact, with the very isolation that is the motif of the whole story. As I have noted, his isolation is not the divorce from his childhood home, with all the religious and moral values that brought peace of mind to so many generations, but the divorce from himself, from his deepest desires. There is a constant movement toward some destination that Hagzar has yearned for in his heart of hearts—a constant drawing nearer to some great ideal. Whenever anything seems likely to fulfill his hopes, he turns back, as though he has no interest in the ideal, as though everything returns only to its source.

The story *Aside* seems, therefore, to be constantly cancelling itself out. As it moves along a line of forward development, it suddenly turns aside because of some fault in the central figure; and once it has turned aside, it has nothing more to relate and so needs to begin again. No doubt, many readers lose track of the story, for this monotonous circular motion is most demanding. But for others the swirling movement has a mysterious beauty, a fatalism that lends a harmonious musicality to Hebrew literature.

> Eventually there was a sad silence; the lamp burned and the samovar steamed away on its yellow stand and the boiling liquid flowed into the cups, and Hagzar sat there in silence gazing at the other lamp, the one reflected in the window panes steamed over from the cold outside in the street. At ten o'clock at night,

boots began to squelch in the strange dark mud of the street, and he leaned slightly forward, thinking about the fine room and its shadowy beauty, about his friend Carmel with his queer face, about clever Rosa with her lovely eyes, and about the fine life unfolding before him.[22]

The isolation that in Feierberg's writings had expressed itself in outbursts of spiritual agony weighing down the style with apocalytic visions becomes in Gnessin's *Aside* pregnant with a mysterious universality. Hagzar's love always stretches beyond reality, beyond silence, and beyond the night with its steamy windowpanes, in the same way as it stretches beyond Hagzar himself. Hence the mystic brotherhood that exists without prior agreement or condition between Hagzar and those he loves. He stamps each of them with his own temporality, with his sense of being a wave rising and falling, moving away and reappearing, turning aside and returning. Hagzar's complete identification with everything in his world, his entry into the world of reality and his exit into a different reality, itself lacking realism and seeming lost in a mysterious sea—these charge the story with its mythological quality and musicality. The same is true of the special rhythms and syntax within the sentences of *Aside*. The light punctuation, the brief, simple sentences followed by lengthy ones that seem to contain circles winding back upon circles, and the monotonous tempo heavy with emotion all form part of this style.

The language is highly modern, not only in vocabulary but also in flexibility, in its ability to juxtapose clarity and subtlety. Yet at the same time it has something very old about it, a hint of love concealed in the treasure house of time since the world was first created.

> And recently, when the long, thin gossamer began snaking down through the air and yellow leaves began falling and scattering along the garden paths, Hagzar used to tread on them with a wild joy and feverish energy, his shoulders squared, his broad chest expanded, his countenance eager. . . . Another week or two and the nights would be dark, the lonely street lamps shimmering, the rain lashing down, and the mud thick. . . . In the beautiful room it would be light and warm and pleasant, the balcony decked with flowers to appear soft and spacious; the girls' delicate

61

faces will be lovely, their talking eyes will sparkle. Rosa's charming chatter will flow on and Mania's stream of complaints will tear him to pieces, stop in the middle, and then burst out again, while small, pale Ida with her wondering look and soft tresses will refuse to sit on his lap and rest her lovely head on his breast until he catches her by her hair. And he will know that she is no longer a child, and he will catch her by her hair and force her to sit. Then she will snuggle up quietly like a lost sheep, and her beautiful hair will be so smooth, and rich, and obedient to his touch. Then came the autumn, and one day Hagzar went into the library. . . .[23]

This extract, which is typical of the rhythmic movement of Gnessin's prose in *Aside*, is different in only one way. It is richly punctuated, whereas in most of Gnessin's writings he uses commas and full stops very sparingly to create the effect of a free uninterrupted flow of thought. If one reads this excerpt aloud in a suitable tone of voice, with due attention to the pauses and punctuation, the impression is created that one is re-reading something familiar from long ago; or one has the feeling that something like this recently happened and that one is recalling it. The spiritual isolation that plucks these erotic chords seems to emanate from the author's own life, becoming transformed into an obsession, deeply moving in its musicality of language and universal significance, and unifying the work with archetypal force. The provincial Jewish intelligentsia, which formed the subject matter for many Hebrew authors trying to express this sense of isolation, serves in this story only to demonstrate Gnessin's own view of universal isolation. That is why Hagzar identifies himself so completely with the seasons of the year, and why one feels that the entire story has been planned to coincide with the annual cycle of nature. Hagzar's own experiences, expressed in the form of his love affairs and their attendant illusions, are reflected both in the seasonal changes and in Gnessin's language. Hence the scarcity of imagery in Gnessin's writing, since it would merely weaken the personal isolation of Hagzar as well as the universal isolation it signifies.

He was silent. Dusk veiled the deserted fields in the distance, mingling with the cold mist rising above them. Here and there an isolated valley could be vaguely distinguished. They walked on together, treading upon the soft earth and sharing the silence of their surroundings. One of them began humming a quiet, sad tune, and the slight, trembling sound became part of the evening hush. Once on an evening like this Rosa had told him her hands were cold and that she had forgotten to bring her muff. He took one of her hands and told her to put it in the sleeve of his coat. But it was too narrow to contain both their hands, so he held onto the cuff of her sleeve with his. Soon they realized that this was forcing them to take small steps, so she quietly removed her hand and they walked on in silence, a little embarrassed.[24]

In *Aside* Gnessin, as we have noted, introduces no open autobiographical elements into the theme of isolation that forms the basis of the story. The archetypal universality of Hagzar's disillusionment conceals the fact that the author left his parental home in order to be free and unattached both psychologically and in those actions prompted by his psychological needs—although his erotic impulses are never translated into action in the course of the story itself. But the autobiographical element remained deep within the author, waiting for the expression it achieved in *Meanwhile*. That joy in the infinite movement of nature with which Hagzar's unconsummated love affairs are permeated is replaced in *Meanwhile* by the gloomy despair of Naphtali. The universal myth of *Aside* has now become the incurable sense of personal isolation within the heart of the main character. Even in this story, Gnessin's departure from his parental home to seek his own individual world does not become projected as the primary motif of Naphtali's isolation, but is shown to have been inherent in his character from birth. It is the cause of his disappointing love affairs, which are set not in the semi-bohemian world of the decadent intelligentsia in the Jewish townships of Lithuania, but within himself, as part of his fated isolation. In contrast to the sensitivity of his style in *Aside*, Gnessin here offers a descriptive naturalism very similar to Brenner's, whom I shall discuss more fully a little later.

Once he was sitting quietly at the window, as he always did, with his legs crossed as usual, his chin resting on his hand, also as usual, listening to the soft, even voice of his pupil who was, as usual repeating the lessons before him. In an adjoining room a child was crying bitterly for a drink, and in the kitchen Mrs. Hashkis was pouring fire and brimstone on the head of the cook, who was already in tears and calling her names. Just that morning the sky had cleared and the sun had shone through, its rays sparkling in the mud; the scattered rooftops already showed dry patches. Naphtali happened to glance up and suddenly saw the bright sky through the window—a clear, deep blue—and the tree-tops of the orchard beyond the quiet gardens were thick with foliage basking in the sunlight. Then he caught sight of the distant heavens and he trembled, for they seemed to stretch on and on to infinity, beckoning the yearning heart to follow. Then suddenly something strange occurred. The chair he was sitting on jumped back and fell over with a crash of protest and Naphtali somehow found himself standing in the center of the room with his head bowed. The boy, pale with fright, a shadow of fear flickering across his brow, said nothing. Then he was frightened a second time by a sudden sharp command: "Read on!"[25]

This passage, which describes an incident (Naphtali giving a private lesson to Mrs. Hashkis' son), provides a striking example of the way Gnessin rids himself of the archetypal aspects apparent in *Aside*. The style is still partially universalistic in its description of the clear sky and is charged with the visionary lyricism of a man isolated and uprooted from the world that had previously seemed to close him in. But just as the language becomes responsive to his pulsating inner self, something happens by chance, such as the chair falling over with a crash, which reduces the literary level to one of buffoonery. This buffoonery removes all meaning and significance from Naphtali's lonely existence. He now realizes that loneliness is not a matter of independence, of a man's right to his own world, but it is something which imprisons and incarcerates man without hope of escape.

All that day Naphtali sat by the window in Mrs. Hashkis's stuffy room; he felt as if all his wretched flesh was superfluous, burdensome, and irritating, and his mind was sluggish, unable to grasp what was going on. The street was deserted, the gate off its hinges, and the garden dry and withered. A farmer's wife, dressed in a long cotton frock, waddled past with a wicker basket in one hand

and a plate of red berries in the other, her bare feet padding in the dust. Silence, noon, and heat.[26]

A careful reading of this passage reveals a similarity to the rhythms of Gnessin's *Aside*—but with a reversed effect. Everything here is presented with a vivid naturalism intended to adapt the factual description to the gloom of Naphtali's isolation. The first sentence, the longest one in the passage, is almost a parody of those long sentences in *Aside* that seem to be murmuring to themselves about the infinity of things. Each section serves as a further stage in the static bereavement of the world. The second sentence, almost staccato in its effect, seems to close the door on some ominous fate. "The street was deserted, the gate off its hinges, and the garden dry and withered." In the Hebrew, Gnessin does not allow even a comma to separate the various parts of the sentence, which are joined by conjunctions as if all were finished, completed, and unified. The third sentence, as long as the first, which tells us of the farmer's wife waddling along, is so objective, so detached from Naphtali's world, that it presages the complete paralysis of the young man who once left his father's house in search of independence. Then comes the essential truth, the desolation in the world:' "Silence, noon, and heat."

It may be that the very concreteness of language in *Meanwhile* raised it to a higher symbolic level than the impressionist style of *Aside*. However, the concreteness serves merely as a springboard to carry him from one level of isolation to another, namely to that of *Beforehand*. For only by such concreteness could Naphtali learn unequivocally to flee from the town before its silence closed in upon him, leaving him no escape. In other words, *Meanwhile* served a transitionary function—a very extreme transition, incidentally—leading from the outlook of the central figure in *Aside* to that apparent in *Beforehand*. It was only by giving literary expression to his flight that Gnessin could satisfy his sad desire to glance back at his past life and see his isolation in the flesh. Such is the theme of *Beforehand* which marked the high point of Gnessin's writings—for he, like Feierberg, died very young.

If one comes to this story after having read through Gnessin's other works, the difference in atmosphere is remarkable. The universalism of Hagzar's frustrated love affairs and the constantly circling movement, which suggests the ephemerality and continual flux of life as it flows toward some hidden sea, has no place in *Beforehand*,[27] which is concerned instead with halting the amorphous movement of *Aside*. The reason for this halt is quite clear. The central character of the story is still in the process of flight we saw in *Meanwhile*, but here he pauses for a moment to think things out, to discover where he is fleeing to and for what reason. This is perhaps the first time that the author's own life overtly impinges on the story. The young man has come to the town in order to live in complete independence and thus to forget the sense of disillusionment implanted in him in *Aside*. Because of the restrictive pressure of the closed world of the town, he returns to Kiev and from Kiev to Homel and thence to the town in which he was born and his father's home. Nevertheless, like the other stories by Gnessin, *Beforehand* avoids autobiographical reminiscing. The author deliberately resists the temptation to relate his own life story in order to preserve the objective artistic integrity of the work, whereby the hero may achieve self-recognition. It is the distance between the author's personal life and that of the hero that broadens the literary dimensions of the story.

In fact, Gnessin returns here to the focal point of all his stories. Once again the love affairs that are never consummated, or rather, that the hero never wishes to consummate, serve as a vehicle for conveying his sense of isolation. Now, however, the love affairs appear in a form totally different from that of Gnessin's other stories. The dominant concept here is that the more a man regards the object of his eroticism as the symbol of life's true meaning, and the nearer he approaches to that object, the more absurd does that existence seem. Uriel feels an unbridgeable gulf between himself and the real world, and as a result is caught up in a nightmarish despair. All his attempts at escape and return are only an illusion of his own making whereby he hopes to silence the sense of bereavement and loss that gnaws within. *Beforehand* is thus in the main a desperate excursion into the real world in the hope of recreating what was hidden all the time within the heart of the hero. In this respect, Gnessin does much the same as Feierberg—he introduces a certain realism into the narrative in order to go beyond his nightmarish delusions into the real world on which they are based. Hence the enormous energy compressed into the writing of *Beforehand*. Superficially it seems to relate a realistic tale, but below the surface there is a power that bursts through the events described, raising the language to the very threshold of the hero's spiritual struggles.

Uriel Ephrat, a "tallish, pale young man" steeped in the loneliness typical of the intelligentsia of Kiev, is continually prompted by his chronic illness to consider leaving the city and return somewhere, though he does not really know where or why. Some parallel to this illness exists in Hagzar too, but there it produces only a ripple on the surface of his thoughts, adding very little to the sense of life as it flows toward an ocean beyond the horizons of man's real world. In *Beforehand*, Uriel's illness takes on a vividness and clarity such as we have not seen elsewhere in Gnessin's writings.

> That dreadful experience, which had begun to exhaust him when he lay sick in bed, had completely worn her out [i.e., the woman in whose house in Kiev Uriel was then living]. Like a hurricane that snatches up a wheel left lying in a field, scattering its spokes in all directions, so this came and snatched up his frightened soul, sapping it of all energy and throwing it back worn out, depressed, and exhausted—so exhausted and weary! That wild raging had again begun deep within him, the strident roaring that would later drip with blood. . . .[28]

There is something new in the stream of thought here that contradicts all that Gnessin had tried to achieve in *Aside* and *Meanwhile*. First of all, the awareness of a universal beauty inherent in isolation is absent, and the isolation itself is no longer a flux of change flowing into the sea beyond human horizons. Uriel's thoughts, unlike those of Hagzar, are concerned with an entirely realistic isolation wherein man is painfully cut off from his roots, the source of his nourishment, in a fixed time and place. His attempts to find comfort in love affairs with no real hold on his heart make him feel like "a wheel in the wind" deprived of its own force and cast down "exhausted and weary." The descriptions here are so realistic in conveying Uriel's physical environment that there is no room for the majestic fatalism that permeates *Aside,* or for the more troubled fatalism of *Meanwhile.* Here, Gnessin concentrates upon one specific human being and is not interested in a type representing some vaguely generalized idea. This concentration suggests an autobiographical quality in the work, even though Uriel never in fact returns to his father's house. Moreover, the rhythmic movement suggestive of the cyclical pattern of fate has disappeared, and the descriptions aim solely at portraying individual objects in their real setting.

> Over all shone the sun, the fresh, laughing sun of spring; its beams smiled on the many passing carriages, danced on the well-dressed people hurrying by, twinkled from the officers' spurs as they sauntered along, and played over the large, shiny hoardings. Trams clattered by, trailing long blue lines behind them and disappearing into the shadows. The windows of the houses opposite reflected the golden rays, and the blue canopy of the sky above beamed down on the fresh pink flowers peeping out from between the well-trimmed bushes in the gardens and on the green plants on the verandahs. But there, beyond the broad, gleaming street bathed in the calm light of the distance, far far away from the red-brick university, trembled unseen the ideals of his youth, the secret dreams, dreams that were no more, that came and then disappeared, hovering in silence till caught in the treetops shimmering in the blue haze on the horizon. . . .[29]

This description, with all its sharpness and clarity, denotes an important change in Gnessin's technique. Despite the enthusiasm with which he pinpoints each detail of the scene both animate and inanimate, despite the lyrical sadness of "the dreams that were no more, that came and then disappeared," one feels that Uriel is not so overwhelmed by the "blue haze on the horizon" that he loses his individuality in vague, unspecified longings. This somewhat impressionistic realism testifies to an increasingly epic quality in the story. The vacuum in which Naphtali finds himself in *Meanwhile* is filled here by Uriel's clarity of observation. He is, as it were, acquainted both with his own soul and with his world, gazing on them and grasping their significance. This change creates in the first part of the story a wonderful sense of expectancy: Uriel is really regaining his inner strength as he is about to return to one of the sources of nourishment from which he had been cut off. The descriptions of his visit to his friends in Homel on the way home to his father's house, despite the twinges of sorrow they evoke, are marked by a thrilling sense of return, of longing for stability and security in the world. The language rises to literary heights reminiscent of great epic, recalling at times the finest prose of Russian and Western European literature. The streets of Homel

> lightly covered by the night dew, and a little sad, recalled dreams that seemed fresh but had long since grown old and distant, and quietly echoed every sound from afar. The broad sky was calm and thoughtful, and the shutters were closed awry. Uriel breathed in the fresh, silent air, his heart drinking its fill of the peace and calm, his limbs, together with his weary mind, suffused with a sweet joy. Part of his heart seemed suddenly to melt away and in its place blossomed a fresh sensation, heavy with childhood memories, as after a glorious boat trip at night. . . .[30]

If we analyze this vivid passage, whose rhythmic movement is not unlike that of the cyclical sentences in *Aside,* we shall see how the "blue haze," which destroyed the detailed clarity in order to create a beautiful myth of loneliness, has completely disappeared, so that each object exists here in its own right. The nightmares of Uriel have been replaced by an intense realism. Even the plot, which had been so vague in the earlier stories, now moves firmly from one specific point to another. Some of the descriptions in the second chapter, when Uriel reaches Homel on the way to his father's house, come across with extraordinary directness and lucidity, leading the story toward its natural conclusion. Gnessin seems to be approaching the peak of his literary powers in such passages as the following.

> When he had finished washing, Uriel felt himself a new man, and entered the large dining room quietly humming a tune. It was spotlessly clean, its walls gleaming with fresh paint. The samovar was boiling, sending up a translucent cloud of steam that rose to meet the golden sunbeams slanting across the room.

> Merka, who had changed her blouse and put on a clean skirt, was laughing and chattering away as she buttered a piece of bread on her plate, and an old lady was sitting there loudly sipping her tea and munching a piece of buttered bread. Uriel sat down and Merka brought him a cup of tea.[31]

This new style dovetails perfectly with Uriel's return home. When he stops off at Homel on his way there, memories of old friends and acquaintances—in addition to some impulse one cannot quite define—prompt him to remain for a few days. The reader senses from the passages quoted above that Uriel himself has changed, that he is no longer, like Hagzar, swallowed up in the vast universe, indulging a narcissism that will eventually destroy his individualism and empty his erotic drives of all real meaning. Uriel can look on the world about him with a certain detachment, a detachment that proves he is regaining his inner strength and suggests that in this realism he will soon find the cure for his spiritual ills. Uriel's meeting with Merka in Homel and the objectivity with which this meeting is described suggest that something is really taking shape; this "something" is the touchstone of fulfilment for all Gnessin's characters—the consummation of a love affair. Such a consummation removes the narcissistic blemish created by the sense of isolation and uprooting, as well as the excessive aestheticism that tends to cut him off from the real world.

The description of the love affair between Uriel and Merka, despite its emotionalism, leaves Uriel himself with a clear and balanced view of himself and his surroundings, and in it Gnessin achieves a literary intensity that he was never to know again in the rest of his work. Merka lay beside Uriel inflamed by the proximity of their bodies, while Uriel accepted her proximity, her strokings and kisses, as no more than his due. It would be difficult to find anywhere in Gnessin's writings a tone of detachment comparable to Uriel's detailed description of the scene, a detachment that confirms our sense of his complete physical and mental rehabilitation.

> Uriel lay there looking up at the smiling blue sky that seemed from the green treetops to promise the perfect peace of his child-

hood; at the buzzing bees and chirping grasshoppers on the golden grass studded with jewels; at the silent butterflies, white, red, and speckled, which fluttered over the petals of a flower; and the flower itself, which welcomed into its pinkish-green petals a prickly-looking caterpillar crawling quietly alone, lifting its brown nose to sniff at the sun and then lowering it to continue its crawling; and everything seemed so new and strange that his heart was filled with wonder.[32]

Within the objectivity of this scene accumulates a powerful splendor, which eventually bursts forth with a vitality inherent in it from the beginning. Yet even here the splendor is vitiated by the blemish common to all Gnessin's characters. As their passionate embrace subsided, Merka "suddenly grew pale and silent, and lay there like a lost lamb. She became weak and submissive, her face expressionless, and from between her lips her teeth shone palely in the slightly golden glow of the sun." Uriel trembled for a moment, raised his head in wonder, and then "lay stretched out like a log in the hot sun, and by his right ear there crawled along silently that same prickly-looking caterpillar he had seen on the grass, lifting its brown nose to the sun."

From now on the style of *Beforehand* changes, becoming ambivalent. On the surface it seems to be dealing realistically with a specific man and his surroundings, with Uriel's journey home and everything connected with it. But at a deeper level this realism is nullified by Uriel's spiritual hollowness. In a way, this story recalls Kafka's *The Castle*. Uriel sets out in search of something which seems to be awaiting him as his ultimate purpose, but everything he touches on the way to it becomes hollow and empty of meaning. The nearer he gets to his father's house, the clearer this submerged message becomes. It is as though Gnessin states something, thereby creating a certain atmosphere, but at the very moment he does so disturbing winds rush in, creating havoc and leaving everything hollow. The realistic power is destroyed by some demon that leaps on its back and takes control.

During the remaining chapters of *Beforehand,* this process clothes Uriel's journey home in a bitter, pent-up cynicism, despairing of any cure. The love affairs that, in Gnessin's writings, constitute the motive force now suggest the sense of loss that has haunted man's steps from the beginning of creation. The realistic details, which in the earlier part of the book symbolized Uriel's physical and spiritual awakening, are now replaced stylistically by a fatalistic staccato rhythm whose inner melody is man's eternal failure and the sense of isolation inherent in that failure. In effect, the myth of love, which has plucked so many chords in Gnessin's works, concludes with the following passage, which on the surface seems realistic but within responds to the melody of man's destiny, the last balm for the eternal wound of his spiritual isolation. As he enters his home town, he recalls a number of things, among them "Batka, pale Batka, sad Batka, that wonderful little girl he had so loved and held so dear." With fatalistic clarity his thoughts continue to dwell on her.

> Tomorrow she would come again—that lovely, sad, beautiful girl. When the sun set. When the sun set in its reddish glow and the flowers in the churches bowed their heads and wept in grief. She would come silently, pale in the reddish glow of the sun, and would silently pause at the wall of the house and lay a bunch of roses at Uriel's window without his seeing. A bunch of roses trimmed with a spray of green, just as she always did, and with a touch of forget-me-nots and cornflowers here and there. She would quietly leave them there and go in to her sister Linka; soon she would be sitting with him, looking out of the window. The treetops of the nearby orchard would be tinted with gold. The gold would sparkle on the windows. The section of the heavens before them would turn red, then yellow, then pale, breathcatching in its loveliness. It would grow pale, then bright, then silvery in the distance, while the sun would redden and weep as it parted and sank below the horizon. Suddenly, the windows would weep. The shadows would come. It would grow cold. Darkness would descend, and silence. Then she would rise like a shadow, and quietly approach him, and quietly beseech him, "Take me to the mountains, Uriel, to where the sun sets." Uriel looked around him, lit another cigarette, recalled something, and decided that he would die like a dog. . . .[33]

The tone of this passage has no parallel in Gnessin's writings, with its clear exposition of the death of all meaning, its awareness of the uprooting from a parental home, and its recognition that the whole apparatus of the love affair in his works is no more than an illusion. The element of narcissism has been transformed here into an epic detachment, a vivid perceptiveness on the part of the artist himself. There is not the faintest trace of sentimentality in this passage, nor of self-pity, and it has the sureness of touch one finds in the classical prose of the nineteenth century. From this point on, both in this story and in his last story, *There*,[34] the author continues at this peak of perceptiveness and with the mark of his final redemption—his own death.

The point of Uriel's return to his father's house is now clear: it symbolizes, throughout, the young man's advance toward the emptiness that is the focal point of his existence. The scene of Uriel's meeting with his father, the rabbi, is perhaps the only one of its kind in the whole of modern Hebrew literature in which the theme of isolation forms the artistic motif. Every word, every description, is simple and unelaborate, even though permeated with the love and yearning of the parents waiting for the return of their lost son. But it is filled with a certainty of utter waste, such as one finds in the style of Kafka. There can be no doubt that it is this certainty which serves as a link between Gnessin and Brenner. Indeed, Brenner's tone can be felt clearly in the following passages.

> After that, his father returned to his study, and to that same quiet, repetitive chant. Uriel rose and looked around him in desolation and despair. The corners opposite him were empty and dim, and the walls looked down on him with the coldness of strangers. . . .[35]
>
> . . . .
>
> Her cry prevented her—her cry irrevocably prevented her. It was a quiet cry, as if she had been deprived of her life before it ended. And when it ended, she would flutter in death in the same silence. The marks of the weary sun lay there as though suppressing a sigh, and a trapped fly buzzed despairingly.[36]

There are many similar passages in the final love episode of *Beforehand*, as if this were the last despairing effort of the author.

The final paragraph of the story, however, illustrates this better than any other. Each sentence has its own realistic character, the realism of concrete description typical of all Gnessin's stories. But when they are read together, there emerges the rhythm of an inexorable fate which cannot be tempered by the love affairs. This paragraph presents Gnessin's fatalism in its most complete form. The first and comparatively brief sentence has the tone of a man who has at last reached the threshold of his desires, the threshold of destruction. The second, the fairly long final sentence of the story, serves the same function as the chorus in a Euripidean tragedy. It draws to a close the tragic suffering of the hero without asking any questions—such is fate and we can only accept it for what it is. We have only our "suppressed, yellowish" knowledge, and to that alone can we give ear.

> Uriel smiled at her again with such a smile as he would greet death; then he rose and wandered toward his room. There the windows were open and on the leaves in the garden little red sun-beetles were crawling, and the broken-down phonograph playing in the distance, pouring out its weak complaints, seemed in the restrained yellowish silence to be wearily paving a way, wasting its last strength, dying alone for no purpose in the big yellow marshes that surrounded it and stretched into infinity.[37]

The prose writings of Gnessin constitute an important stage in the development of Hebrew literature at the beginning of the twentieth century—a literature impregnated with the sense of isolation of its authors during this historic transition period of Jewry. His work marks one of the most strenuous attempts among the younger writers to break away from the shackles of autobiography and create a type of literature that, for all its surface similarity to the period in which it was written, should bear the stamp of a more universal symbolism. This effort in Gnessin's work was really a desperate struggle between his own tragic personality—his attempt to find expression for his rootlessness and dissatisfaction in love—and his literary purpose in raising that tragic expression to the level of objective symbolism. Without such literary struggles on the part of Gnessin and Brenner, who can tell what future would have been in store for Hebrew literature with the rise of modernism in the countries of Europe. The

Uri Nissan Gnessin

autobiographical element in Gnessin's work may have prevented him from achieving the epic dimensions of the novel, but his universalism drove the author to seek new literary forms for the Hebrew language.

Each of the four stories has a mysteriously dramatic quality, and each forms an organic part of dramatic advance toward an inexorable and preordained fate. However, this mysterious quality appears in different literary forms in each of the stories, forms typical of those employed in Euopean literature at the turn of the century. He begins in *Aside* with impressionistic rhythms, then tends in *Meanwhile* and *Beforehand* to an expressionism that explores the inner world of man, and finally comes to depend on an old-fashioned concrete realism, finding within it the finest symbolic expression for man's spiritual isolation in a predestined universe. This final stage is visible in *Beforehand,* but in *There* it carries the motif of isolation beyond the autobiographical (when Uriel meets his parents in his home town) into the realm of pure tragedy.

None of Gnessin's stories approaches as close to the "objective" epic as *There*. In the opening paragraphs, the story responds only to the external world; the language is filled with sights and sounds, with an awareness of objects, with a firm acknowledgment of the real world that seems to bridge the gulf between most of Gnessin's characters and their environments. All the obstacles have been removed, all problems solved, and the riddle of man's isolation has evaporated in the clear light of day. The world created by Gnessin easily absorbs the simplicity that has entered Ephraim's life.

> In the broad fields, quietly breathing the heavy night air, a bird suddenly chirped harshly and angrily, filling the wide spaces with her cry. The old man, Arkip, whom, together with his son Prokop, Ephraim was accompanying for some night fishing among the ruins, suddenly coughed, removed his pipe, which had gone out, and spat noisily over the side.
> "Has he fallen asleep, that fine young fellow, eh?"
> He began to sit up, and looked around as if in some doubt. Then he looked around a second time, coughed again, this time

75

more deliberately, and began to do up the buttons of his great-coat.[38]

This is perhaps the only time Gnessin begins a story in this way, the opening lines pointing out in epic fashion the psychological change the hero's world has undergone. The sense of isolation is drawing to a close and in its place there comes a different realism, fresher and more confident, free from suffering, and creating a harmonious relationship between the outer and inner worlds of the central character. This epic quality continues for many pages in *There,* occupying an important place in the story, until the reader begins to believe that Gnessin has entered a new phase, that he feels himself bound to the earth, the rivers, the landscape, and the world at large, and that the physical world has served as the means of this spiritual redemption. Ephraim lies stretched out alone under a bush on the bank of the river "gazing at the various floats attached to the fishing rods he had fixed into the ground beside him. He saw them bobbing brightly in the water, sensitive to every swirl of the current." The peacefulness of the scene seeps into Ephraim's mood, producing a profound calm. The sentences here are long, sometimes filling a third or even half of the page, but there are no passionate outbursts about the joy of the changing seasons as in *Aside* or about the growing awareness of death as in *Beforehand.* Each object exists in its own right, each detail helps to create the vivid scene.

> From behind the hills drifted the moon, already a pure bluish-white, and the small clumps of trees scattered over the large plain before the hills seemed to move, as if shrugging off the heavy darkness which had previously obscured them. The darkness leaped off the branches as a child leaps from a man's shoulder, and remained crouching at the foot of the trees whose branches now stood out clearly above the fresh, sparkling mist that had begun slowly creeping its way here and there, displaying every leaf and twig, as clearly and brightly as those imaginary treetops painted by famous artists. . . .[39]

The most striking aspect of this passage from *There* is the close bond between Ephraim, the central figure of the story, and the details of the landscape before him. Somehow, man's isolation in

76

an alien world has disappeared. Even the nostalgia for "the days of childhood that are no more" is only the product of that firm understanding wherewith he gazes at himself and his world. Hence the many descriptive passages in the opening pages of this work, in contrast to *Aside,* and even *Meanwhile* and *Beforehand.* It would appear that Gnessin is no longer afraid of these descriptions, since they only relate to the superficial, external world and not to the inner realism of the person himself. The young author, who had never allowed the slightest trace of sentimentality into the love scenes that form the core of his stories, is no longer afraid that it will spoil such a sentence as: "A plump white-haired boy suddenly picked up his instrument and with his delicate fingers plucked a few sad notes." He apparently regards the plump white-haired boy together with his musical instrument as part of the realistic world that he has now accepted. Sentences such as these, which are very frequent in the early pages of the story, puzzle the sensitive reader until he begins to ask himself whether the author has left the story teetering on the edge of a sentimentality liable to destroy the psychological realism, or whether he is searching for some new viewpoint soon to become apparent that will restore the story to its previous literary level. All the descriptions of the landscapes of his birthplace served Gnessin as an associative framework whereby he could reconstruct all that had happened to his hero, whether the wanderings of Hagzar, Naphtali, and Uriel or the reminiscences of Ephraim.

The realistic description of Ephraim lying under a bush on the bank of a river watching the floats of his fishing rods bobbing in the water is intended solely to prompt him, almost hypnotically, to think back to his childhood and to all the imaginary events of the four stories. "Ephraim began to muse at the foot of the mountain"—and his musings give a new realism to his reminiscing, a sort of tangible firmness. Everything that Gnessin clung to in Homel, Kiev, and the small town where he gave private lessons after he had left his father's home now comes across with a clarity far greater than that of the actual world of his earlier stories. The reminiscences are not an artificial recalling of past events but a revitalization, a determination to relive them with all their longings and illusions. "The wonderful magic of that evening when the bluish-white moon shone so silently has vanished—has completely vanished." The suspicion of sentimentality quickly evaporates before the lyrical, almost epic tone of the story, the clear self-knowledge of the hero.

As this clarity increases, so do the sentences increase in length; but as we have said, they no longer are filled with those outbursts intended to provide an outlet for the pain of passing time and unfulfilled love. The sense of isolation has disappeared both from the hero and from the girls who surround him like satellites of a dying sun. He himself looks boldly ahead, confronting the world of actuality and calmly foreseeing the end for which all is destined. Even the love affairs, which play an important part in this story too, seem to withdraw from the mists and darkness in which they were veiled in the previous stories and are presented lucidly, possibly because this reminiscing about the past places them in their proper perspective, possibly because Ephraim himself, withdrawing from the world of mystery, sees himself, and Zena, Ruhama, and Zilla, in the true light of failure.

> The three girls sitting together in the street he loved by night, the Street of the Annunciation, were laughing a great deal, and that inner light which does not control laughter but nourishes it with its silent beams, was twice as strong. When one of them left to accompany him to the dark corridor, the second stealthily glanced after her, and the third, suddenly remembering something, ran to catch up with him in order to ask him with a shy yet cheeky grin, "Um . . . What did I want to tell you? Oh, I wanted to say . . . ha-ha-ha. . . .⁴⁰

This is what troubles the reader acquainted with Gnessin's works. On the one hand there is a clear lyricism in the descriptions of the landscape, whether it be the landscape in which Ephraim is situated at present on the bank of the river or the landscapes of Kiev buried in his memory. But on the other hand there is a harsh sarcasm whenever he talks of Zena, Ruhama, and Zilla in the Street of the Annunciation in Kiev. In *Beforehand* Gnessin never employed sarcasm so strongly as in his description of the girl from Bobroisk in *There:*

At this point, the girl began laughing, her laughter ringing out loud and clear except that it tended a little too much to the seamy side.[41]

This sarcasm, which is interwoven into most of the story, growing in intensity as the story proceeds, indicates that we are approaching Gnessin's final inference. In effect it is this: that all the love affairs of the previous stories were only pretence, both on the part of the male and the female. The girl's purpose is solely "the seamier side," while for the man all that tragic sense of isolation is expressed in one instance that emerges with extraordinary delicacy and lyricism in Gnessin's writings, but that has hidden within it the strange cynicism of the man who is completely uprooted, knowing neither the reason nor the purpose of his existence.

Thus, for example, a man in his travels will suddenly recall a lovely, delicate white flower that he has once seen but did not have time to look at closely by the side of the long, lonely, flat road leading toward the quiet noonday; the hand of God led him there in his childhood. Now he remembers, but will at once forget it again.[42]

In this respect Gnessin here rejects the literary aims of *Aside*. Now he clearly needs images and descriptions such as "lovely, delicate white flower" in order to present his love scenes effectively, in the same way as he needs them more generally in *There*. This is the clearest proof that Gnessin is not concerned with a universal sense of isolation in which everything disappears into that ocean where all rivers end, but rather with a personal despair, a sense of failure, of having lost one's way. These descriptions, so delicately worked into the fabric of *There* as symbols of his characters, mark the final stage in the myth of isolation that Gnessin handled in a manner unique in his generation. In effect, each of them serves at first in this story as a stifled cry of lament, eventually becoming more audible through the veil of factual description, which is the only type of description Gnessin allows himself; as if to say that such alone is the ultimate realism. The descriptive passages in *There* are not unlike those of K. in Kafka's *The Castle*.

Not far from that spot, a lonely, sad horse munched its hay, a horse tied up and left there to spend the night; a bird in the marsh voiced its lament, and all the noises of night blended together so that it sometimes seemed as if a single dog was barking incessantly in some far-off place.[43]

Throughout Gnessin's literary career, he never once referred to the great reassessment of values that had affected Jewish life in his day. The national and social problems that produced so lasting an effect on modern Hebrew literature never became part of the isolation that forms the motif of his four stories. In this too he came close to the modernism of his age, for, like the Decadent movement of the late nineteenth and early twentieth centuries, he ignored the external changes affecting the wider public. Hence the vacuum that seems to seal off his stories from the outside world. It is as though all the hubbub of the Jewish world in that era had subsided, and all the historic movements of the Jewish community had vanished, devoid of all reality, leaving only Gnessin's heroes isolated and uprooted in their loneliness.

In this respect, Gnessin was unique in his generation. His complete separation from the external Jewish world opened his work to the foreign influence of the Kafkaesque. Nevertheless, this separation also helped him to explore new psychological depths and to inject into the Hebrew language some of the powerful sensitivity of modernistic literature. It is not surprising that the younger critics in Israel have begun to turn their attention to Gnessin. They too feel confused and isolated from the historic trends of their day, and in him they find a heritage they can trust.

Yosef Haiyim Brenner: In the Pangs of the Messiah

The group consisting of Uri Nissan Gnessin, Yosef Haiyim Brenner, Gershon Shoffman, Hillel Zeitlin, and Shalom Sender Baum was closely knit. Deep personal friendships, as well as the sense of isolation they shared, united them. The first three turned to the Hebrew story, where each hewed out a literary form suited to his own needs. Hillel Zeitlin was, through his personal struggles, drawn toward the various crossroads of European culture, eventually devoting himself to the search for God and to the mysticism of the Kabbalah and Hasidism. Shalom Sender Baum began to withdraw into the deep aesthetic silence he had learned from the pessimistic fatalism of Schopenhauer. It seemed to Baum's friends that he possessed within him an intuitive knowledge of the secret of man's existence, and each of them in his own way longed to attain that majestic knowledge. The various literary forms adopted by Gnessin were all straining toward it, and Brenner too was striving in the same direction.

Brenner's stories are based on the sense of isolation that oppressed him throughout his life, until the day in 1920 when he was cut down by an Arab gunman in Jaffa. Although each of Gnessin's stories marked a new stage in the expression of this fatalism, it is sufficient in Brenner's case to concentrate on one of his works, *Around the Point,* in which all his literary struggles find their clearest expression.[44]

In the introduction to the first volume of Brenner's works, Menakhem Poznanski, Brenner's personal friend, colleague, and editor, stresses the autobiographical nature of this story.

> In *Around the Point* Brenner presented, above all, himself. It is he, in the person of Abramson, whose soul is aflame with the Zionist vision, even though he was a non-Zionist; he is the librarian busily astir in the city, becoming involved with "certain persons"—the young revolutionaries; he is the young Hebrew writer, bitterly demanding a change of standards; he is the simple man hating hollow forms and shrewdly observing life around him in general and the life of the Jews in particular.[45]

Poznanski identifies each of the characters in the story, gives them their real names, and assigns to each his place in Brenner's life, with all its contradictions, struggles, and doubts. Throughout Poznanski's comments can be felt the affection in which he held Brenner, an affection that adds much to our understanding of the latter's character and writings. This authoritative account of the autobiographical elements in the story, however, is liable to obscure the more objective literary aspects, for not everything can be interpreted directly in terms of the personal and social environment in which Brenner lived so intensively. An examination of the stylistic techniques he employed leads us beyond the biographical details embedded in his prose and interwoven with the social and the political problems of his age, so that we may identify the less obvious artistic and personal ideals hidden beneath the surface.

Brenner himself would clearly have objected to such an investigation as distracting attention from the actual, everyday world of that generation of Jews. He would certainly have rejected any a priori artistic theory that turned its back on the real lives and suffering of mankind in favor of abstract intellectualization. As far as he was concerned, such intellectualizing was permissible only for "heavenly affairs," where it could frequently achieve noble and sublime success. But he himself explained his inner conflicts as a never-ending struggle to achieve realistic truth within human life and within Hebrew literature, and there can be no doubt of his sincerity. Nevertheless, an objective examination of Brenner's attempt to convey national, social, and cultural realism—that is to say, an analysis of his stylistic techniques and of the powerful inner voice that can be heard through the ideological curtain—will reveal that the problems expressed in his surface realism function also as a means of expressing something hidden, to which Brenner gave the rather mystical name "point."

As long as one approaches this "point" from an autobiographical angle, it seems to be rooted in Brenner's incessant longing to express succinctly the meaning of his own personal life. But if one explores this longing more deeply as it follows its course "around the point," a gulf is seen to exist between it and the author's nationalist and humanist interests, which, as they appear in the story, never satisfy that longing. Beneath all the psychological and ideological searchings, beneath the contradictions displayed in his social and political tendencies, Brenner was yearning to hear his own inner voice and thereby grasp the "point" of his existence.

Brenner knew very well that he would never succeed in his attempt except by faith or art, or both. From the very beginning, however, he took it upon himself never to break away into any individualistic art form, as had become fashionable in European literary circles of his day and as his friends Gnessin, Zeitlin, Shoffman, and Berdichevsky had done. Each of the latter had raised his own voice in isolation from the current ideological trends among the Jewish intelligentsia of the cities. Brenner wandered from one ideology to another, even to the nihilism of despair, but in each case he undertook a messianic role—the cultural heritage of both traditional Judaism and nineteenth century Russian literature. This messianic role affected his physical and mental health, and made his lot harder to bear. Yet all this he accepted readily, for the sake of some wonderful illumination that might one day shine upon his existence. All his desperate literary efforts arose from that struggle to discover someday the means of expressing his "point." The most obvious instance is provided by his story *Around the Point.*

In the opening pages of the story there is a strange undertone, half humorous and half ironic, which runs through the scene of Abramson's parting from his student, Shlomo Frankel. The young Shlomo is expressing his sorrow at being unable to accompany his friend and teacher to the large city of A——, where the "new life" is to be found (that is, the sociological, nationalistic, and ideological ferment of the intelligentsia in those cities with large Jewish populations). Abraham tries to alleviate the somewhat exaggerated and "provincial" sorrow of his pupil, and out of a sense of the mutual trust between teacher and student promises to support him both financially and spiritually. His words, however, sound peculiarly antiquated, for he uses the language of the Bible, the Talmud, and hasidic folklore, which both master and pupil recognize as being somewhat obsolete and musty. The mild irony created by this inner contradiction between subject matter and style seems to cancel out the mutual trust, replacing it with a mood of loneliness and sorrow. All this stimulates the attentive reader.

> "Hearken to me, Shlomo'le, hearken to me," said Abramson in an emotional whisper. "In brief: your life henceforth is empty of value. Not worth a king's glance. . . . In brief, it is incumbent upon you to leave. The main point—to know that there is another life, a new life. Your place, my boy, is away from this world; there is the world of light and creativity. . . .[46]

This irony intensifies enormously Abramson's feelings about leaving the old life for the new; for at the very moment when he is, in an emotional whisper, stressing to the pupil the absolute necessity of leaving, he uses the very language of the world from which he is now parting forever. This technique lends a wonderful power to the opening scene and to many others like it in *Around the Point,* and creates a certain ambivalence in Abramson's conversations. On the one hand, he responds to the external world of the ideological conflicts, while on the other he is attentive to the repressed longings of his own individualistic, inner world, which have no part in the ideological battles outside. The ambivalence indicates that in this autobiographical story Brenner frequently deserts reminiscence for a hidden world that the sensitive reader can only discover by a close examination of the text itself.

With one ear, then, the reader listens to the surface plot of the story, which contains an account of Brenner's wanderings within the framework of his generation's problems and struggles and his fierce and almost fanatical attacks upon an empty Zionism and an empty socialism; hence the reader comes to discern the tragedy of Abramson, who is caught up in a world empty of meaning and purpose, one that will lead him eventually to disillusionment and despair. The reader's other ear, however, catches a hidden note in the story, the sound of some deeper ferment as Brenner withdraws from the disillusioning actuality of the story to devote himself to some other "point" to be found behind the façade of the plot, deep within Abramson, who serves as a projection of Brenner himself. In this way, the reader responds to the real meaning of the story at a deeper level. It is as though the story has been deflected from its main course in order to discover a means of finally expressing the "point" that dominates all, that provides the story with its literary power and yet continually eludes Brenner's grasp. This deflection gives the story its tragic quality, a quality frequently missed by critics looking for non-Jewish influences on his work and by the New Critics, with their somewhat arid aestheticism. It is, in all probability, also the source of the conflicts, contradictions, and struggles that permeate all of Brenner's writings.

Yosef Haiyim Brenner

Abramson's departure for the city of A—— is never fully explained by the author. Unlike the rest of the characters in the story, he never formulates his desire for the large city as the center of all his hopes. Like his pupil Shlomo Frankel, he seems to be escaping from the old life to the new. Yet, as he approaches that new life, he finds it devoid of meaning, lacking in true significance. The empty dialectics and hollow psychologizing of the Jewish intelligentsia sometimes lead Brenner into a satiric vein, as in chapters thirteen and fourteen, which are devoted to Zionism, socialism, and Hebrew literature in the city. Nevertheless, this satire at no time provides us with an insight into Abramson's own attitudes and aims. The two people who had a profound influence on Brenner's own life—represented by the characters Hava Blumen and Uriel Davidowsky in this story—both achieve complete self-knowledge and an understanding of the meaning of their existence. Abramson, on the other hand, falls between these two characters, and shies away from self-definition, from formulating his aims and desires. Even the subject that was for him of fundamental importance, the place of the essay in Hebrew literature, always becomes blurred by the casual tone in which it is presented. It becomes no more than a faint echo, fading away and disappearing, so that it never really comes to life in Brenner's work.

All this suggests that a gulf exists between Abramson and the actual world with which the story deals. He seems to be standing in the very center of this actual world, reacting to its favorably or unfavorably, but his thoughts are really elsewhere, concerned with a world of his own in which others have no part. Stylistically, Brenner is often impressionistic in this story, responding both to the outer and inner world at the same time; but the two worlds never become united. Abramson wanders in and out of the two worlds, but is unable to charge them with a vitality whereby they can respond to each other. This situation creates a serious literary problem for Brenner, and one that taxes him in his other stories too. The author realized very well that he would never be able to turn his back on the Jewish community and all its ideological problems, however badly they might affect him both physically and spiritually; hence he hesitated to create a literary vehicle for expressing his own, individual world, the reality hidden within his despairing artistic efforts. This is the problem that constitutes the central "point" of all Brenner's work, of his tragic struggles and conflicts, and there are many clear indications of this in the ambivalent atmosphere of *Around the Point*.

This atmosphere has a specific literary function, as was hinted earlier, and throughout Brenner's work it recurs with an almost dogged insistence. Its function is to raise the artistic level of the story above the merely biographical, which, in the chapters dealing with Zionism,[47] for example, or the conversations between Abramson and Shmuel Davidowsky, the revolutionary,[48] weakens the story's power. There we find only one level of meaning, and the reader is left uninspired. Brenner himself tried to overcome this deficiency by introducing into the journalistic style a number of more flowery expressions intended to raise the stylistic tone. We find, for example, "Abramson's enthusiasm flamed up like the unextinguished candle of the Lord, and Frankel's arrival further redoubled his strength." Sometimes he adopts a satiric vein reminiscent of the Enlightenment movement: "Tell me, then: who raised this young fellow from wallowing in wealth like a worm in a cabbage and set him on the ladder to a better life?" Such stylistic tricks destroy the irony inherent in Abramson's use of biblical, talmudic, and hasidic language.

The proximity of the story to Brenner's own life imposes this stylistic difficulty upon him. It sometimes forces him into exaggerated psychologizing, which at times swamps the artistic element in the story. Even Abramson's conversation with Uriel Davidowsky suffers from this defect, for it lacks all relevance to the pregnant silence of Uriel, who represents Shalom Sender Baum: "Then in the evening Abramson would visit Uriel and tell him about the difficulty of loving one's neighbor on the one hand and the burdens of loneliness on the other." It would seem that Brenner understands the meaning behind the pessimistic, pregnant silence of his friend yet cannot accept it for himself. All the ideological and social problems are here treated in a tone of insipid jesting. But at the same moment Brenner also shies away from the realism of the man, like a man shying away from

something lurking within himself. It may be inferred that the
figure of Shalom Sender Baum served Brenner as a distorting
mirror for his own art, even though he greatly admired the fascinating pessimism of his friend who knew and understood everything.

Unlike Uriel Davidowsky, Brenner determined to enter the
real world of his day and, again unlike Uriel, he felt impelled to
search for some means of expressing the psychological truth of
his own being within the realm of pure art, rather than in terms
of the various ideologies of the real world about him. Brenner
always fell between these two extremes, and his failure to unify
them is the source of the tragic note that permeates all his writings, as well as their wonderful brilliance. The struggle involved
is visible both in the weakness and strength of *Around the Point,*
and the touchstone is always to be found either between Abramson and Uriel or between Abramson and Hava Blumen. When
Brenner deals with Uriel, the prose is always ineffective and
casual; when Abramson finally rejects his friend's nirvana, with
all its inherent despair, and turns instead to Hava Blumen, the
style suddenly becomes revitalized, as though bearing tidings of
tragic faith.

The character of Hava Blumen in *Around the Point* deter-
mines to a certain degree the depths of Brenner's story. She never
allows any room within her for the dark pessimism of Uriel, yet
she is always responsive to the inner quality of objects and people,
particularly of Abramson, as though she insists on distinguishing
their real and ultimate significance. She too accepts unreservedly
the visible world of actuality and all its ideological and social
problems. In her case, however, the hollowness common to the
Jewish intelligentsia of A—— is replaced by a deeply rooted realism, and through her Brenner's prose too achieves the level of
artistic truth. Her individuality of mood is captured by Brenner
and presented as a symbol of his own artistic longing. The relationship is less a symbol of Brenner's love for a woman called
Hava Blumen than an idealization of his own literary aspirations.

We may deduce from this that any attempt to see in *Around
the Point* an autobiographical account of Brenner's love for Hava

will prove vague, impressionistic, and somewhat sentimental; the result will be that the characters of both Hava and Abramson will emerge hazy and unclear. If, however, we see in it an ambivalent account of his literary strivings, the true meaning comes out with brilliant clarity, since such a viewpoint serves to unify the two levels of meaning. We might put it this way: to some extent Brenner's love resembles that of Dante, the medieval poet who descended into the Inferno, but with this difference: Dante had Virgil as well as his Catholic faith to guide him along the brink of the Abyss. The Hebrew writer of the early twentieth century, struggling with a terrible sense of isolation and deprived of any religious guidance, had to hesitantly carve out his own set of values for his literary work.

If we examine the text of Brenner's *Around the Point,* we shall find numerous meditative echoes. If these echoes do not separate Abramson's grief from the real world surrounding him in the story, they do open before us a deeper, more intuitive understanding of the inner world that Brenner develops in the story. The following passage from the earlier part of the story shows how attentive he was to the artistic aspects of his work, concealed within the various levels of the plot.

> He stood up and swung his haversack over his shoulder. The thick pages and heavy binding of the *Kuzari,* together with the one volume edition of Berdichevsky's five books published by "Tze'irim," which were packed into the top of his haversack, pressed down firmly on his shoulder, sending a pleasant sensation through his body. His quick stride was directed towards Caucasian Street, where Uriel's parents lived; for Abrahamson had heard with sorrow that Uriel Davidowsky was, at the beginning of the winter, going back to live with his parents.[49]

Brenner's language here has a peculiar force all its own, combining the author's personal world with the worlds of the *Kuzari,* of the one volume edition of Berdichevsky's five books published by "Tze'irim" ("the Young Ones," a group of Berdichevsky's followers), of Uriel Davidowsky's silent longing for nirvana, and of the latter's brother, Shmuel Davidowsky, the socialist revolutionary—and over all hovers the splendid spirit of Hava Blumen. At

Yosef Haiyim Brenner

times the language achieves a harmony seemingly directed toward some mighty, hidden meaning about to take shape somewhere and act in its own right. The sense of anticipation opens new vistas in Brenner's mood, revealed through his own intuitive understanding.

One aspect of these vistas is the suppressed sadness that runs through his work and pulsates beyond the veil of reality. It arises from his compassion for his fellow man or from his disgust with his surroundings, and is visible, for example, when Abramson is travelling by train and the various gentile landowners push the poor Jew from place to place until he has nowhere to sit. Here Brenner displays profound psychological insight in describing Abramson's headache as he protects "the holiness in his heart from contact with the profane." Those critics who accord Brenner bouquets for his "secularism" ought to listen for a moment to the following passage.

> Abramson stood in his corner, and everything around him seemed strange. The continual headache, which was reaching its peak just then as his emotion flooded over him, helped him to protect the holiness in his heart from contact with the profane. He placed the palm of his hand on his burning forehead, and screwed up his eyes as if he were trying to concentrate the entire world into his thoughts.[50]

The fierce pain serves Abramson as a refuge from the ugly world about him, for which he feels only disgust and contempt as something profane, and the pain is conveyed with extraordinary intensity in these lines. That other world, however, which Brenner calls "the holy" or "the unconcentrated world," for which the pain and the screwing up of Abramson's eyes are intended, is never described directly in the way that Brenner describes the ugly world of reality. As the narrative progresses, heavy with grief and sorrow, we hear something struggling though his suffering, something expressed in terms of harmonious landscapes flowing out of the individual soul of the author and stretching over the entire universe in all its holiness. Suddenly, the universe seems to be listening to a melody of such beauty that it drives away Abramson's headache; the vision whereby he tries

89

to "concentrate the entire world into his thoughts" has become real. The passage continues:

> Before his eyes a carpet of snow was spread over the landscape; a glorious, pure whiteness filling the world beyond the sides of the cart. Beside him sat a Jew dressed in rags, who kept looking stealthily at the man holding the swinging strings of sausages. Nevertheless, with his long beard the Jew reminded him of his father, Reb Isaac the Shohet, and of the tune with which he devoutly sang the Sabbath morning service. "Glory and splendor . . . to Him Who lives for ever! . . . Ceremony and purity . . . bim-bim-bom to Him Who lives for ever!"
>
> The splendid, warm rays of the setting winter sun penetrated the dusk before completely disappearing, slanting across the cart and touching the forehead of the young man standing there —and illuminating it. . . .[51]

A re-reading of the three sections in this passage reveals two levels of meaning. The first is concerned with the external, squalid world that produces Abramson's headache and makes him lose consciousness. The second, which Brenner refers to as "the entire external world," arouses in Abramson a sense of universality—an emotion on the threshold of the religious devotion that prompted Brenner to introduce the descriptions of landscape. This second level, although it may appear to be dealing primarily with the external natural scene, in fact wells up from within to provide some momentary balm for the sense of loss Abramson experiences wherever he goes in the city of A——. He has turned his back on the ideologies—whether national, social, or literary—to which Brenner seems despairingly to have committed himself, in favor of pure art. Brenner's tragedy is that he can never bring these two separate levels together; they remain sharply divorced, leaving the author torn agonizingly between them, with no hope of release.

The nature descriptions occurring so frequently in *Around the Point* appear at first sight to have no direct, organic connection with the story itself. They seem to be chance additions, thoughts happening to pass through Abramson's mind. But if one pauses for a moment, one can see that in fact they serve in Brenner's writings as a submerged commentary on the action, often exceeding the action itself in realistic intensity. Abramson himself, as the reader discovers in every chapter, can never identify himself in any real sense with the new life awaiting him in A——: not with the empty talk of an intelligentsia lacking any real vision or action; or with Shmuel Davidowsky and his friends, who plan to change the entire structure of Jewish life by means of their socialist doctrines; or with Uriel Davidowsky's fatalistic pessimism, for all its fascination; or with literary criticism, despite its many attractions; or even with Hava Blumen, who serves as the ideal and the source of all nobility in his "point" of existence. "But they did not come any closer," Brenner remarks gloomily after the conversation between Hava and Abramson.

The closer Abramson tries to come to his dreams, his love, and his longings, the more he realizes that he himself lacks something. That is why he so frequently surrenders to a heartrending despair, his comments becoming dull and even his mockery losing its edge. In his sad talk with Hava Blumen, Abramson raises the question of helping his pupil Shlomo Frankel, and he ends with a comment pungent in its fatalistic irony: "Frankel could sit in the Zionist school and prepare a generation of readers for the articles that I am going to write." Yet suddenly, out of this unattractive setting blossom two or three words that create "out of the blue" the quintessential expression of life for which Abramson yearned and at which Brenner's literary efforts were aimed: "Hava Blumen said nothing at all. On the windowpanes, snowflakes began to settle. Without thinking, she pushed a strand of hair back into place." That is all. But "on the windowpanes, snowflakes began to settle" provides a wonderful touch at that moment, raising the reader far above the level of gloomy despair and lifting Abramson into the aesthetic world that alone provides Brenner's characters with any real satisfaction. The few words describing the natural scene provide relief for Abramson's despair, as though something bright has taken shape for him in the wintry landscape. In this atmosphere everything seems to breathe deeper in response to its own being, in response to "the entire external world," which at that moment consists solely of snowflakes falling on the windowpanes, and in response also to the inner world of Abramson-Brenner. The loneliness gnawing at Abramson's heart at last achieves that sublime level to which every creative artist aspires—the quiet seclusion in whose silence man feels himself united with the world at large. This seclusion even contains within it a balm for the mortal wound that opens whenever he is with Hava Blumen. Abramson's love, which in the world of human relationships can never be consummated, seems to be caught up in that meditative harmony of snowflakes on the windowpanes. In this way, Brenner elevates the actual world of *Around the Point* to the realm of natural beauty. As we have remarked, Brenner seems to have achieved this by chance rather than deliberation, but its effect is to throw considerable light on the personality of the author himself.

This inquiry into the ambivalence of *Around the Point* reveals an important facet of Brenner's writing: the sharp individualism of Abramson's character makes him emerge as more real than his nationalistic or social surroundings. Moreover, the author's concern with inner character raises the literary level of the work considerably. On the other hand, his depiction of the social environment, although good journalism, detracts from the story itself. Nevertheless, Brenner cannot ignore that environment, however much it may arouse his disgust because of its hollowness and meaninglessness. He therefore takes it upon himself to deal with both worlds, accepting the resulting agonizing isolation that penetrates so deeply into his weary being. He undertakes to present in his writings the pain of suffering man, his mortal agony, the fear that accompanies him through life, and the despair that haunts his days and nights. Brenner states clearly of Abramson:

> Although he could not always stop himself from participating in those empty debates, he was really very detached from them; he had no need of them or of anything else. One single emotion obsessed him, before which everything else seemed to fade and vanish away. Then he was filled with a bitter anger for those people who lived like mules, sweating out their lives for others without pay.[52]

These "mules" do not form part of an ideology, despite the abstract way in which the sentence is phrased. Each of them is

Yosef Haiyim Brenner

an individual human being with his own troubles and anguish, his own fear, anger, and violence. Each of them lives in his own harsh world, longing despairingly for some meaning in life. This compassion is always apparent in the social aspects of Brenner's twofold stories; similarly, his concern with expressing in literary form the inner world of his characters becomes directed to Bren-ner himself as a prayer for his own existence. His stuggle to find some artistic recompense for the loneliness of wretched man, isolated and forlorn in his dread of the world, is paralleled by his attempt to find an outlet for his own private dreams. The entire story *Around the Point* has this dual quality, and the insight can be applied to his other books, *From Both Sides, Loss and Failure,* and others.

At the opening of the story the duality is casual and subordinate, but by the end it has become the basis of the narrative. On the strength of this, the author moves away completely from a meditative impressionism whenever Abramson withdraws into himself and becomes submerged in the sorrows that beset him on all sides. Instead, the language takes on an almost primitive force, distilling the sorrow of the individual, the weariness that consumes his flesh, and the dread that fills his enclosed world. It exposes the sore spreading over his soul and the constriction that oppresses him day and night. Where the story had been concerned with imaginative thoughts it is now devoted to portraying with direct realism pain, anguish, and fear, dispensing with any ideological intermediary that might, by its abstract intellectualization, detract from the concrete depiction of the individual.

This is the tragic "messianism" that drives the author to convey with all his strength the particularized despair of the individual. In the same way that Brenner's use of landscape, despite its apparent casualness, really provided the lament for man wrapped in his subjective thoughts, so he now concentrates on the cruel pain Abramson finds in the new life wherever he looks, until the story resorts to a primitiveness of language intended to destroy the empty sophistication of the intelligentsia. The element of yearning, with its touch of narcissism, is now replaced by an attempt to depict the suffering of the individual man in the street. The author does so through Abramson.

> It was dying . . . life was ending in the Jewish settlement. . . .
> Abramson knew it beyond a shadow of a doubt. Life was not
> changing, but ending. It was not through longing for salvation,
> not through hope of redemption that life in the Diaspora was
> dying, but through worry about the next day's crust of bread.
> The harshness of their suffering, the weight of their fetters, the
> dreariness of their empty future, was killing life in the Diaspora.[53]

With this knowledge Abramson sets out to destroy the ambivalence, with its impressionistic reflection. He makes up his mind
to stop listening to his own subjective stream of thought in the
same way as he breaks all his connections with those superficial
creatures hanging about Menashé's house, with their absurd bohemianism and the impression they gave of doing something—
making changes, creating revolutions—when in fact all they were
doing was playing about with the emptiness of their souls. All
these, Abramson felt, should be put aside in favor of the "suffering that was stronger than he could bear." The messianic echoes
in this self-dedication can be heard in the passage that concludes
the one previously quoted.

> The suffering was more than he could bear. He ceased reaching
> out for those visions of life from within his own being, from with-
> in the reality of his self, as he had been doing until now. He
> ceased to judge others by himself. The agony of others, their com-
> mon longing to be able to eat to the full just once, all this came
> to teach him something. He and all his actions would henceforth
> be as chaff in his own eyes. So would his feelings for Hava Blumen,
> who had said to him that she was troubled.[54]

Generally speaking, Brenner does not find it difficult to express
Abramson's *conscious* thoughts about the suffering that is too
great for him to bear. The language of the above passage is lucid,
conveying Abramson's feelings aptly and informing us directly of
his plans. The simplicity of diction performs its function admirably. But one aspect of this simplicity is the disappearance of
impressionistic reflections that by their spontaneity burst out of
the narrative as if it has no control over them. All the humor
created at the beginning, all the irony in the introspective parts
of the story, all the satire that appears at various points, he is
determined to remove in favor of an expressionistic and at the

same time naturalistic depiction of Jewish poverty. The latter
style becomes entrenched in the squalor of his isolation, lacking
the wider echoes of irony or the didacticism of satire, and concentrating instead on conveying the external world. That is the
way Brenner describes the father of Shmuel and Uriel Davidowsky, a lost creature immersed in both physical and spiritual despair: "As he was speaking he resembled a wet fly stuck to the
bottom of a jar filled with dirty water."[55] This simile has no ideological or satirical intent, but is simply descriptive. It seems
callous, but it is complete and achieves its full effect. Brenner
appears to be under some unavoidable compulsion to use the
dirtiness and squalor of life, with all the feeling of desolation it
produces, as a means of expressing himself fully and completely.
The same is true when Uriel's mother replies to Abramson's inquiry after her son with the comment, "How much blood flows
from every crust of bread!" Such vague thoughts are unsuited to
the author's attempt to express facts with clarity, but fact becomes
joined to fact until they burst out with a primitive force in which
the discursive no longer satisfies Brenner insofar as it acts as a
barrier between the fact and its literary expression.

For this reason, Brenner began to cultivate a more flexible
imagery to assist the literal description in achieving an effect of
immediacy. When, for example, Abramson recalls his poor, aged
father, who, because of his dire poverty, has been forced to work
on the Sabbath, he himself is filled with "despair, anguish, and
loss of faith" that any Jew should be forced by his poverty to
work on the Sabbath. His grief is only too obvious. He knows
that mankind endures suffering "greater than it can bear." But
here Brenner is attempting the literary experiment of creating
something firm, monolithic, naked, and unadorned in its finality.
He remembers his father sitting in his prayer shawl and phylacteries in his home town "reading over the weekly portion of the
Torah twice in Hebrew and once in Aramaic." His father's poverty on the day before the Sabbath arrives is a fact, but so too is
his father sitting in his prayer shawl and phylacteries. Each of
these facts has its own reality, and together they suggest an existence which does not depend on poverty and desolation.

Perhaps, therefore, the facts of poverty and hunger become less firm and definite when something comes from another level of experience to "redeem" them or offer a Sabbatical "exchange" for them that is totally different in itself and will of itself demand expression from the author. Brenner did, indeed, recognize this difference between facts, but he refused to provide them with the duality of meaning he had supplied for his own introspections throughout much of *Around the Point*. He dedicates himself then to the desire for immediacy of expression of the two facts, the two being mutually exclusive: the despair inherent in his father's poverty and his father's Sabbath joy. From this point of view, the simplicity of language is ineffective since it tends, as it were, to invert the facts. He therefore makes the language dovetail with the immediate physical appearance of the father reading over the weekly portion. He quotes the Hebrew passage, and then the Aramaic translation beside it, and in the Hebrew text includes the cantillation signs as if only by an image of this nature can he convey the immediacy of his father's Sabbath atmosphere—in much the same way that he created the immediacy of poverty by the image of the wet fly to which Shmuel and Uriel Davidowsky's father is compared. In this way he manages to include the two extremes of poverty and Sabbath atmosphere, and, by mingling them, to produce a mixture of grief and irony.

> Reddish-green lines and sparks of white fire danced before his eyes. "And the elder shall serve the younger" he read in Hebrew. "And the elder shall serve the younger" he repeated in Aramaic. Esau, the gentile, will light our fires on the Sabbath, and will chop the firewood, adding warmth in his hatred.[56]

The nightmarish quality of this passage is achieved by the clash of the two worlds that remain sharply divorced in the author's words. The fact that he is hungry on the Sabbath, like the fact that he calmly reads the weekly portion, demands from the author completely separate expression; nor will either suffer the half-and-half ambivalence of impressionism. At this level, Brenner's writing reaches a certain impasse, and takes on an apocalyptic quality such as we have met elsewhere in his writings.

Yosef Haiyim Brenner

The square, pointed letters, together with their cantillation signs, became blurred within the reddish-green lines. Abramson closed his eyes. The letters swam at the edge of the sky in black fire.[57]

In this way, Brenner floundered between the messianic desire to immerse his entire flesh and blood in the suffering of the individual Jew and his personal longing to commune alone with himself. There is no contact between these two worlds. At one extreme, the suffering drove him to a direct immediacy of simple expression that rejected any dressing-up in ideology, whether national or social, since such elaboration would only obscure the individual suffering and the particularization by which it was conveyed. And at the other extreme of psychological introspection, he responded to thoughts coming to him from beyond the horizons of his actual environment. The naturalistic style served his purpose in conveying the suffering, while impressionism answered his introspective needs.

Somewhere between those two extremes was "the point," the style that would suit his artistic requirements and end at last his lonely exile. He was caught between these two "points" throughout his life—in his stories, literary criticism, editorial work, correspondence, and his contacts with the generation of the Second Aliyah in Israel. It is not surprising that this tension led him to create a nightmarish series of symbols to express with striking force his struggles and impulses, as well as the despair always hidden within them.

> The road was long and hard, hard and long. The earth was not far from the heavens—and it was easy, therefore, even for "dreamers" to fall. The traveller's heart was suddenly filled with anticipation, great anticipation. He was waiting, eager; soon the heavens would open and something great, something truly great, would be born. He took long strides, holding his staff with the kerchief attached—the flag of the camp of Judah—and took long, long strides. Suddenly, he was held back. . . . Who was holding him back? "Lift up your eyes and see!" she said. "On the peaks of the hills is a point." Disaster overtook him again. He gathered up his last strength to cross the border, but in vain. There was no passing. The point was tearing at his heart. There was only

97

one—one small point, black and terrible. He decided to go round about, to leave the road and make a magic circle round about it. His lips moved, "Soon, soon. . . ." He seemed to be leaping and jumping after it, but at that moment he knew he had made a mistake: the point was in the sky and not on the earth, so how could he reach it? "Behold, I have not sinned!" he cried bitterly. "It is my white kerchief." But for all his shouting, no sound could be heard. The point remained in its place. He forgot about the road. There was one point and only one point. To the point—but there was no way to reach it.[58]

Such is the conclusion of Brenner's story. Abramson tears his garments in mourning for himself, for the desolation of mankind, for the words the writer yearned for but which never came. The author leaves his hero sitting in mourning, lost in his mad dream, and finally puts a few broken phrases into his mouth—a sort of apocalyptic utterance after the style of biblical and midrashic visions. But in contrast to the opening of the story, where Abramson's use of biblical, talmudic, and hasidic phrases creates the impression of an ambivalence of tradition and a break from tradition, this conclusion, employing the same type of phrases, indicates the loss of all direction and stability. The final sentences of the story are typical of the dark musicality which Brenner develops in his silent pauses.

Abramson sat at rest. His neighbor Haiyim Leib, the maker of yeast, had not yet come. In the house of mourning there was fear and silence. The silence said nothing at all.[59]

Brenner, however, never closes the door completely on his characters, his stories, or on himself as the artist. On the contrary, the greater his suffering, the greater becomes his understanding that man must hew his vision out of himself—out of his heart and soul. Herein lies the dichotomy in his literary work; on the one hand there is disbelief and negation, on the other love and faith. His concern with the ugliness of life and his simultaneous longing for beauty and splendor constitute a dualism that gives his work a majesty overlooked by critics. They have missed the existentialist basis of Brenner's stories, his search for the sanctity of man upon the earth.

Yosef Haiyim Brenner

It is true that all Brenner's stories—and indeed, his life itself —indicate that man can never find the meaning of his existence in this world. That is why he wanted to exchange his atheism for a faith or for an ideology or a definite philosophy that could offer man a vision in the midst of his wretchedness and despair. This vision always comes "to settle all accounts"—to reveal all the deceits and forgeries of religious, social, and national organizations that prevent man from finding the meaning of life. Only the man in the "valley of gloom" does Brenner feel sufficiently positive about to assign him a touch of sanctity. "There is no security, no rise and no fall," proclaims one of Brenner's characters in *Loss and Failure*. "Everything alternates, like links in a chain. What will come next? We don't know. Which link will come last, rise or fall—we don't know."

If every vision becomes blocked and ideals are unfulfilled, then every action must at least have its own vision. Failure and despair await man if he wants foreknowledge of the entire chain, if he dreams in vain, if he deludes himself about prophecy, morals, or history. But the moment he sees each link as a self-contained unit and treats each action in terms of "good" and "humane" criteria applied to it alone, then he becomes master of himself. This is the solution toward which the characters of *Loss and Failure* are striving. Each of them brings tidings that human suffering can break the bounds of despair by means of that link— the action of effort and building. That was how Brenner saw the men of the Second Aliyah, who are represented by the characters in the story. Brenner's "lower self" began to distinguish patches of blue in his life's sky. Beyond the silent, fatalistic pessimism of Uriel Davidowsky in *Around the Point*, Abramson began to catch a glimpse of A. D. Gordon's spendid vision from Kinneret and Deganiah.

Jacob Rabinovich, who knew Brenner personally, wrote of him: "His struggles" (the word appears, in fact, in the title of one of his stories, *The Book of Struggles*) "also formed for him an important basis. He was inclined to wander off to side issues, as if he were afraid of the main point. He sought social, moral, illusory supports . . . but hollowness awaited him everywhere. . . . If the call to build obscures the emptiness, his suffering generally robbed it of any reality. You would meet Brenner when, for example, he was sitting together with strangers who were building a new life (not Arabs, of course), delighting in their simplicity and creativity, their positive attitude to life, and noting how contented they were in their narrower existence, while he was making a little corner for himself there. He was not really a pessimist by nature. No, he loved creating light for others, even for himself, but for himself he never succeeded. He lacked freedom. Some fear or uncertainty accompanied Brenner wherever he went."[60] Nevertheless, through A. D. Gordon the light did begin to shine, as we see in the final confessions of his hero:

> You are standing on the threshold . . . stretch out in joy, stretch out in blessing . . . but don't be afraid, soul, soul of Ezekiel Hefetz. . . . Don't be afraid of tomorrow's mists. . . . Sure, sure . . . troubles will await you . . but snatch the moment and enjoy it. . . . There is no straight highway. There is only a narrow path—narrow and sometimes slippery, sometime crooked. The only rule is the old rule—that it is a joy to wander along this path, a joy to live and to value life, to value every surpise and the infinite pleasure it contains . . . may the Lord be blessed, Amen.[61]

The late critic Dov Arieh Friedman, who was a great enthusiast of the "individual sorrow" in Hebrew literature, made the following comment on Brenner's tragic, creative personality:

> At all events, when we have finished reading *Loss and Failure,* and when we recall the life of that ascetic seer who, throughout his wanderings and suffering called incessantly for creativity, we must close our eyes for a moment in a spirit of reverence and offer up together with Ezekiel Hefetz that short prayer:
> "My Father, Father of light and life, may they be blessed! My Father, Father of Orphans, deal kindly with me and send me Thy beams, and I, an orphan among orphans, will gratefully receive Thy gift in love and hope. I know how to value Thy gift and kindness. My heart will sing and shout in joy O Father of Life, may Thy name be blessed!"[62]

Hillel Zeitlin: Thirsting for God

Hillel Zeitlin too was in search of some ultimate means of expressing the "total sorrow." Unlike Brenner, however, he did not deliberately avoid formal art—indeed, he was unable to avoid it. His entire being was like a taut bowstring ready to play the melody of the ever-changing existence of a life in a constant state of flux. In the midst of this flux was the poet's heart, ever responding to the emotional storms that ceaselessly demanded from him some ultimate expression. There he discovered a deep silence beautiful beyond words, and from there too sprung a primal force never satisfied with the artistic form in which it was expressed, that never achieved final artistic expression. There pain and joy clashed in his desire for this primal force. Isaiah Wolfsberg has remarked of Hillel Zeitlin:

> Zeitlin symbolizes in his work that type of creative artist in whom the primal forces have been preserved. Not all the eternal forces have disappeared from the universe into a tidy, orderly world. Some men preserve within them the primitive powers of Creation, with its mingling of light and dark. They are never governed by an inner harmony, for their longings are not by nature adaptable. Yet they can express life in all its forms. This must never be confused with naturalism, for these writers have no bent for naturalism or realism. In fact, their creativity is never controlled by "bents" or purposes. They never possess any clearly defined plan or path, but instead respond spontaneously to a deep well of inspiration inside them, without any calculation or deliberation. However, both they themselves and their art parallel the real world insofar as the pain within their hearts resembles the pains and troubles of the real world around them. . . .
>
> In Zeitlin's literary work is reflected the heavy burden of the whole of history. In other words, he does not concern himself with the problems of his age, with the conflicts and frictions of his generation, but with the tensions and clashes that have existed since the beginning of the world, when men were first created. He succeeds in grasping the whole universal tragedy of humanity since the days of its birth.[63]

This "universal tragedy of humanity" is also the tragedy of Zeitlin himself, of his relationship to the world at large. The poet in him longed to live together with this world, to become part of the "mighty forces of Creation" with their mingling of light and dark. In this tragic struggle can be perceived a close affinity to those ancient rituals that Nietzsche believed lay at the root of all art. More than all other Hebrew writers of his day, with the sole exception of Berdichevsky, Zeitlin wanted to identify himself completely with the changing seasons of nature, the cycles of life and death within it, and the myths associated with it in art. He wrote songs, meditations, prayers, and poems, as well as some fiction permeated with the ecstasies and despairs of his own soul—and all of these forms of expression serve as an enthusiastic hymn to the great splendor of God that permeates the entire universe, evokes songs of praise from the host of heaven, and renews the face of the earth and man who walks upon it.

Within that hymn, however, can be distinguished a pessimistic dirge for the eternal sunset that leaves the world wrapped in mourning. Zeitlin inherited this tragic strain from his teachers—Schopenhauer, Hartmann, and Nietzsche—as well as from other philosophical and literary sources he came upon in his wanderings. But he himself was, in addition, the heir to an ancient tradition to which Hebrew mysticism had turned at various times. Throughout his life he was influenced by an apocalyptic vision of a final Day of Reckoning, and this he could never make part of his intellectual apparatus, which always needed to know exactly what was before it. In fact, the conflicts and struggles of his soul provided the natural setting for his artistic impulses. The tragic concept of this poet-philosopher arose from numerous conflicts: the contradictions he discovered in the Scriptures, the destructiveness to which he often felt prone, and his despair and lack of faith on the one hand and his desperate search for God and the Messiah on the other. He constantly expected the end of the world, and felt that he stood on the threshold of the shadow of the Almighty. He was pulled in conflicting directions by his great aesthetic love for the beauty of nature, his thirsting for the sublime transcendence of religion, and his deep compassion for the humble man in the street.

Fate gave him an extraordinary responsiveness to that which is hidden within man—hidden but not forgotten, concealed but not lost—and he searched for a full expression of its meaning. Hence Hillel Zeitlin's desperate battle with his own soul, with the "I" of his integral self. His "I" stood at the crossroads of the universe, facing the "extremes," sometimes wandering off into an alien culture and then forcing itself to reject what had been gained with so much spiritual effort in order, at last, to return to the Jewish tradition into which Zeitlin had been born.

The resulting psychological agonies frequently dashed him against all sorts of sandbanks he would at first mistake for solid land. At times he thought of himself as a priest in the temple of a "universal grief" originating in that fatalistic "will whose harmony breathes in the changing seasons of nature and that leads everything to Nirvana." He often held fast to this grief—that is, the sacred experience embracing everything in its infinite mercy—calling it "the sorrow." He used the terms "aesthetic view" and "universal grief" interchangeably until they became almost synonymous. He was attracted to Schopenhauer's pessimism by its individualistic nobility and by the pride it imparted to the man who could hear the breathing of the universe in the roaring of the sea. Yet despite the artistic inspiration provided by Schopenhauer, Zeitlin felt that something was wrong with it. After all his devotion to the "aesthetic view" something deep within the heart of this Jewish author eventually awoke: "That poor philosopher of pessimism failed to understand; he saw beauty only in history and art, but not in man and his deeds." At that point, he deserted the teaching of Schopenhauer and became a fervent disciple of the Nietzschean school.

It should be noted that Zeitlin was not interested in the Nietzsche who had left behind him the Dionysiac ritualism of Wagner and the demonic myths. He seemed to be afraid that he might discover something in his master's teachings which would make him a permanent disciple. He defended Nietzsche against those vulgar critics who spurn human values and, quoting learned sources, quibble with the words and falsify meanings.[64] He was impressed by the purity of the superman concept, whereby any man could, by his own strength, ascend by degrees to the ultimate splendor. In his great loneliness and insecurity, Zeitlin apparently felt that he had found an anchor in the concept of the superman, before whom vast spaces open and whose penetrating vision can reach beyond the narrow horizons.

At the height of this refined individualism, however, lurked a nothingness, and he feared that more than anything. He was terrified of being alone, whether in the cloudy emotionalism of Schopenhauer's pessimism or in the dazzling stratospheres of Nietzsche's superman. Both philosophies hinted at the destruction of the humble humanity living in the valleys, and such destruction constituted for Zeitlin, in contrast to German aesthetes, a terrible crime. Here was the one principle he fled to from all his wanderings, even when he seemed about to take the plunge of denying God. That was why, even at the height of his personal rebellion, he insisted on caring for the simple man struggling for his crust of bread and a decent living. Zeitlin therefore chose a realistic middle way as the anchor of his beliefs, lest he should founder in aesthetic storms.

Such, in fact, was the conflict and spiritual dilemma that united the unique group consisting of Shoffman, Gnessin, Brenner, Shalom Sender Baum, and Hillel Zeitlin. They were held together by a strong bond, tempered in the fire of "despair, atheism, and the song of holiness together." Brenner chose for himself a search for art, while Hillel Zeitlin sailed straight for the clash between a refined, individualist aestheticism and a somewhat duller identity with the masses. He made each of these into an ideal, unifying them by his own form of existentialism.

In his early writings on Ahad ha-Am and Berdichevsky,[65] Zeitlin gave the first indication of his identification with the masses, and from then on it gradually developed into the basis of his philosophy. He could not bear Ahad ha-Am's "rule of the intellect" or his concept of Zion as the "cultural center." Yet he violently attacked Berdichevsky's "broadening of the boundaries" and demand for a change of values. He reacted to the latter's "cries of lament" with a humanist anger in the style of Brenner, as if he himself had never been caught up in the "change of values."

> Unfortunately, I have never found in any of Berdichevsky's cries of lament any sympathy with a real, live Shmuel, Haiyim, or Zalman. He never shares the anguish of the city Jew burdened with a wife and children and not knowing where to find bread for them. He never identifies himself with the sorrow of

a Jewish woman running about all day like a dog in order to bring her children a dry crust of bread in their dark cellar, or with all the starving and desperate sick and crippled who fill the city, or with the young people eager for the light and life of which they are deprived when all doors are shut before them. . . .[66]

This was a harsh charge to level at the romantic Hebrew school of the day. Zeitlin's zealous propagandizing won him a sacred place both in Hebrew literature and in the hearts of those ordinary Jews at whose head he marched into the furnaces of Maidanék. Yet this attack did not release him from his heartsearchings and wanderings in the realm of literature. One thing, however, had become clear to him—that it was wrong for a man to restrict himself to his own inner being, shutting himself off from the suffering of the man in the street. By suppressing part of one's inner world and restraining one's personal desires, even if only the artistic, a man learned to live, particularly if he was a Jew.

This conviction formed the basis of his attack upon Berdichevsky, who "felt much and grasped much, and who wanted to bring it all before our eyes"; "but Mr. Berdichevsky forgets, despite his knowledge of Kabbalah and Hasidism, that the light must be adapted to the ability of the vessels. The vessels were broken because they could not bear the full force of the light." With this criticism, Zeitlin elevates the theory of identity with the common people into a creative force, for he sees it in terms of the "vessels" of the Kabbalah—the artistic application and formative execution shared by both the creative artist and the art lover. Zeitlin's individual search for a form of expression suited to his needs in art and real life becomes here subordinated to his realistic concern for the social and economic welfare of his fellow man. Only thus could his art be of lasting value. Since both light and dark must be tempered for the "vessels," art too must temper its light and shade in order to achieve its purposes of saying something to mankind, of testifying to the meaning of life, of directing men into the paths of creativity. For this purpose, art must restrain its aesthetic and often primitive impulses, and the artist must himself be satisfied with a little less, subordinating his individualistic drives whether he likes to or not. In this way, Zeit-lin began to look back to the paths of his ancient Jewish heritage, and he reached these paths through his constant struggle to moderate his noble pessimism in the name of humanity's suffering, for the sake both of his faith and of the trust that faith brings.

In his own writings, Zeitlin put his theories into practice. Indeed, in his *Intellect and Poetry* he deals with the forces of nature in the expressionist style of Peretz, which reaches its fullest power in the poems produced after this work.[67] But he becomes more self-controlled in his hymns to life, "The Blessings of Rain," and "A Rainbow in the Cloud," as if he were responding to the calm of the universe symbolized by the biblical phrase "and the waters grew tranquil." The quality of Dionysiac tragedy symbolized for him in the movement of nature becomes replaced in "Memories" by associations with stories from the Pentateuch. The noble pessimism of Schopenhauer withdraws before the mingling of joy and sorrow in his view of life's vicissitudes. The poet now directs his affections to "humble Moon, as it walks along full of deep and mighty thoughts, thoughts of the entire universe, thoughts of infinity and eternity . . . as it walks along grieving for the sorrows of the world." Yet it also "walks on air when he is happy, when he is happy and giving happiness, putting aside sorrow and offering comfort." Even in this brief poem can be felt the power of the young writer in tempering Schopenhauer's and Nietzsche's pessimism by means of his humanitarian sympathies. Beauty and morality are integrated here with the personality of the writer himself.

This integration became the cornerstone of his vision in "At the End of Days," but meanwhile he was caught up with his doubts and hesitancies in "On Complacency and Despair." At one moment his heart would throb with a "mighty love," with "the great work of the soul, through his concern with the lot of mankind, until he would be filled with an infinite compassion for them —a compassion that did not die away but turned into a loving bond, an indissoluble bond" leading him to "a profound understanding of the nature of life and of its bitterness." Yet a moment later, he would fall into a gloomy despair about the "exile of God," bemoaning the "wonderful beauty" slowly passing away from the earth, the "life that so depresses and humiliates man, that is so wretched and dull." He thus vacillated between his humanitarian pity for man's social and economic lot and a fatalistic pessimism. It is this vacillation that robs all his writings of a sense of proportion.

Zeitlin believed that somewhere in the realm of metaphysical ideas could be found that which would unify his soul: "Basically there is a fundamental ideal that does not depend upon other fundamental ideals. One can never achieve complete wholeness on the basis of a single ideal if it needs others to support it." Nevertheless, from this very feeling arose his great sadness.

> Because we are not whole . . . we can imagine that there is a complete beauty even if it lacks mercy, that there is true heroism even if it is cruel, short sighted, and humble . . . that there is beauty without sublimity and sublimity without beauty, and wisdom without either.[68]

All this brought Zeitlin to the verge of despair, and it is important to define this despair, since it was basically despair that drove him toward the teachings of Shestov, and toward Hasidism, the Kabbalah, messianism, and traditionalism. His organic dualism was responsible—his search for ultimate beauty and his struggle for ultimate mercy. The blending of the two could be found only in God, but God was "silent." Between God and mankind, whether the latter dwelt in the muddy depths or were climbing up to heavenly glory, there existed an impassable gulf. That gulf was the root of Zeitlin's despair. It was also the despair of Rabbi Nahman of Braslav, of Dostoevsky, of Shestov, and of Brenner. Nor were they alone, for they shared this despair with the whole of mankind. From the depths of this despair, however, burgeoned a new faith, a new religion—man.

Since man is alone and has no one on whom he can rely, he must therefore be independent—the master of himself, the architect of his existence, and the steersman of his life. Each of his acts is a decisive fact, determined by himself and marked by his independence. Beauty is not something he receives as a gift from outside, just as his moral code is not passed on to him by his neighbor. "The beauty we see in another man makes us want to seek the same beauty in ourselves, to search for such beauty, which may be hidden in a corner of our own hearts, and to draw it out from there, to fan the spark within us so that it may shine brightly for us and for others, and may drive out the despicable both within us and outside."

A vital principle of Zeitlin's philosophy is the struggle to rise from the pit of despair lying between the idea of metaphysical unification and the eternal duality of the soul until man reaches the compassion arising from recognition of his responsibility for his actions. The compassion not only redeems man from his loneliness by bringing him close to his fellow man, who is also lonely, but somewhere the gulf between man and God is bridged. This existentialist approach renewed and remolded Zeitlin's faith. Now God was not an idea presented to him as a heritage or something handed down from the past, a discovery of previous generations; Zeitlin now recognized the validity of a personal search for God, an eternal movement toward him, a constant struggle to climb up toward his habitation. That is "the thirst by whose power man extracts from the world around him the nobility of God," and it was this nobility he imparted to his own "beauty" and "mercy."

After that realization, this thirst for God became the focal point of all Zeitlin's writing, nor did he withdraw from the severe test such thirst imposed. Indeed, in the chapter entitled "The Almighty," he begins by "wandering in the orchard of the Kabbalah" and becomes immersed in the theme of divine love it contains.[69] The attempt to convey this love is visible in Zeitlin's own religious poetry as well as in the Jewish legends with which he frequently deals. Yet he always appeared restrained in this work, for he knew what "the tragic Messiah did not know, that the world was still full of pollution . . . that the days of redemption were far off, very far off, that the world still needed laws, Torah, fences around the law, that not everything was yet permitted since not everything was yet pure, and that the world still needed time to achieve the innocence of childhood, inner beauty, and everlasting purity. . . ." He therefore "withdrew" from the Kabbalah and the battle against temptation it involved to the "great purifier and cleanser," the Baal-Shem-Tov and the hasidic movement.

In Hasidism he found the wonderful discipline of joy and compassion capable of satisfying man's great thirst. There the joy is a joy in God and man, as is the compassion. Only in Hasidism could Zeitlin catch a glimpse of the inner quality of despair and draw from it a new vitality he called "faith." In the chapter entitled "The Almighty," devoted to thoughts about Habad Hasidism, one can catch echoes of his own identification with the movement and with the teachings of Shneour Zalman of Lyady, whose influence on Zeitlin was enormous.

> Since the basis of this joy is the desire, the longing, the wish, the yearning for holiness, it goes hand in hand with a feeling of everlasting loss; for one only longs for what one lacks. . . .
> Therefore, even though joy and a sadness are opposites, joy and a deep, inner, and constant grief join and intertwine as one within the soul.

Later, Zeitlin stresses Shneour Zalman's definition of despair.

> I once heard my late father say that no man could accept the truth of biblical mystery, and that the profound thoughts bathed in eternal light could never really penetrate into his soul unless he suffered from a powerful, natural melancholy, rooted in him since his youth, so that he detests life every day and at every hour. . . .

Zeitlin then adds the following comment:

> The melancholy he refers to here is the eternal longing for what ought to be but is not; the everlasting grief that knows no rest, so that when your heart rejoices, your eyes weep; the grief that yearns and craves, and knows not for what.[70]

Zeitlin believed that this synthesis of joy and melancholy was the product of Jewish history. He proceeded to analyze the joy and sorrow, as he was again to do later when he began to interest himself in the teachings of Rabbi Nahman of Braslav, investigating their sources, drives, and contradictions in his *Readings from Rebbe Nahman,* in his biographical works on Rabbi Nathan, the pupil of Rabbi Nahman, and in his *Legendary Stories.* The prayers he composed and all his excursions into the Kabbalah and Hasidism were really devoted to this joy and sorrow. True, he suffered from the oppressive realization that every man is alone, that he is responsible for his own soul and way of life, and that he molds what fate has given him; but within this responsibility, composed of the two opposites, joy and sadness, was a constant awareness of something hidden, for which the joy and sadness mingled sublimely—the thirst for God.

This thirst was characteristic of the last stage in the first group of Zeitlin's writings, a group that in general reflected his full literary development. In it, he made full reckoning of his philosophical and aesthetic wanderings, and throughout he regards kindness as the final redemption in man's struggle for the "end of days." That kindness enables the universe to find its "lost time" in Rabbi Nahman's "The Story of the Seven Beggars." At that time the "heart of the universe" will again meet the "heart of the Fountain," and the man who is listening to the magnificently beautiful sounds in his own heart will enter into the metaphysical "memory" of the experience that touches the light of God.

His concern with "kindness" and "thirst" led Zeitlin to Lev Shestov.[71] He was attracted by the common bond between Shestov and Rabbi Nahman of Braslav. "Shestov has a harmony of his own, the music of complete despair, through which is seen a distant, strange hope."[72] His despair, like that of Rabbi Nahman, is noble and majestic in its universality, and its breathes the breath of Creation. Zeitlin offered numerous explanations of this despair; "As the heart becomes emptied of human values, it is slowly filled with a different hope that can never be named, neither metaphysical nor mystic—the hope of him who descends into the abyss, and from that abyss calls to God for a miracle."[73] It is the same as Rabbi Nahman's cry "Do not despair, my fellow Jews!"[74] a cry to the heart of the Jew, even to the Jews who accompanied Zeitlin into the furnace in a final testimony to God.

Thus Zeitlin reached the shores of his existence. His temple is "the temple of dejected man," a term he applied to Shestov. In this temple "there will suddenly be revealed to man a distant, far horizon, wonderfully strange, a star not from this world, a spring that has been stopped up. Somewhere in the corner of his soul the spring will suddenly open and irrigate the whole wilderness that despair has parched." This, for Zeitlin, was the Jewish basis—the messianic and Jobian basis in the philosophy of Shestov.

During his final years, Zeitlin was caught up in strange dreams and visions, messianic in quality, as though there had suddenly been revealed to him the wells of "memory" the beggars spoke of in Rabbi Nahman's "The Story of the Seven Beggars."[75] He seems to have reached the "fiftieth gate" and to be standing by the primal abyss from which shone that "special kindness" given to him who is saved from those depths. That gift was the "wonderful point from which one could pass to the new world"—the guarantee of life for the man who wishes to pass from his great loneliness to "Our Father in Heaven."[76]

Gershon Shoffman: Man's Place in the Universe

Each member of the extraordinary group consisting of Gnessin, Brenner, and Hillel Zeitlin was ravaged by pessimism and loneliness; each of them struggled with his personal isolation and strove to find some literary expression in which to convey it with the objectivity demanded by art. A close friend of the group was Gershon Shoffman.[77] In contrast to his friends, however, he never needed to be torn between the autobiographical elements in his writings and their literary form. This is clearly a result of the fact that his childhood was very different from that of his friends, and he was therefore unaffected by those changes in traditional values that were discussed in connection with the previous authors.

There is, however, an additional fact connected with Shoffman's literary qualities: his immediate and complete grasp of the isolation of each character in his stories. The material from which Gnessin and Brenner wove their stories was the constant search for a suitable means of expressing that isolation adequately, and from this arose their hesitancy over which style to employ—naturalism, realism, impressionism, or symbolism. Shoffman's style is always direct and wonderfully lucid, going straight to the heart of the isolation. At the very beginning of his stories the reader senses the immediacy of his style as well as the objective firmness of presentation. When it reaches its full stylistic force it becomes a pure crystal through which the reader can see directly into the depths of the lonely soul deprived of its roots in the world. This is not the language of Gnessin's *Aside, Meanwhile, Beforehand,* or *There,* or of Brenner's *Around the Point.*

Shoffman himself did not share in his own life the sense of loneliness his characters suffer, and consequently he never projects himself into them, although his stories, without exception, evoke the reader's fullest empathy for the sorrows described. This detachment makes his stories epic achievements filled with a profound and at the same time vivid realism. Yet at no time does his work manage, or indeed attempt, to cover a broad canvas. The tragic element is not supplied by numerous spontaneous psychological associations but has a firm, well-defined structure.

The narrative in Shoffman's work is directed from the beginning at the very heart of his character, with a concentrated focus that does not allow any distractions, either on the surface or in deeper levels of the story. The central point of his writing is thus the focussing only upon what is relevant, and that focus dominates the language from beginning to end, compelling it to strike unerringly at the existentialist nucleus of the hero's isolation. This is the reason for Shoffman's concern with immediacy. This tendency does, in fact, turn his stories into miniatures in which the various traits of the character become crystallized.

A glance at the first volume produced by Shoffman shows at once that there is something here that is very rare in early twentieth century Hebrew literature: the isolation, unlike that of Feierberg, Gnessin, and Brenner, is presented without any specifically Jewish qualities, as if to say that man, by virtue of his being man, is subject to an isolation that, through its infinite channels, affects him either consciously or unconsciously and make him realize the truth about his life.[78] One such channel, which appears and reappears as a dominant motif throughout Shoffman's work, is the barrier existing between man and his neighbor, his world, his Creator, and his hidden desires.

Indeed, one of the first stories in this initial volume is entitled

"The Barrier."[79] In this story a student returns home from the city where he attends a university in the hope that he will be able at last to recover from an illness. By chance, he finds no one at home, and he stands there alone, lost in thought about something "that he lacks," about a "desolate emptiness" that accompanies his every step, about the feeling that he is in an alien universe, and about his habit of "continually withdrawing into himself," a habit whose origins he does not know. But in the course of his pondering, an idea suddenly flashes upon him with tragic certainty: it is not the world at large that is at fault, or his hometown, or the city in which he studies; the sense of isolation comes from his inner self and is inherent in his own nature.

This certainty directs Shoffman's story into the paths of clarity, leading it to its ultimate fulfillment. The student stands alone inside the house for a few moments, but the barrier between him and the furniture and other inanimate objects in the room forces him to realize that he will never be able to free himself from his constant sense of loneliness, either at the university where he fell ill or at home where he was born.

> The candle burning on the table began to flicker and die. Part of it was already surrounded by shadows and its appearance reminded him of a man's face when he is about to sneeze. . . . Light filtered into the room from the frost-covered windows, illuminating the greenish-white plants set in large earthenware pots filled with black soil. . . .
> He always withdrew deep into himself, like a tortoise into its shell. A thick, dark veil seemed to hang over his eyes, preventing any contact between him and the outside world. He never looked outside—it never occurred to him to look.[80]

This passage illustrates the importance Shoffman attached to the environment in all his stories—even the briefest, of one page or less in length. Frequently, the nature descriptions form an organic part of the story, serving as a mirror in which the hero recognizes his psychological image and the irremediable loneliness within him. These descriptions touch upon the gloomy destiny of such isolation, and, as a result, many of Shoffman's stories have an atmosphere of fatalism. Loneliness spreads like a plague

through the speech, the silences, the actions, and the thought—
and the nature descriptions cover and enclose everything. The
setting of "By the Way" is a Jewish home. A widow is sitting together with her son, a scribe; toward evening the beggars gather
there, each bearing the marks of loneliness on his mind and body,
but they do not complain or ask her for help or show anxiety at
the decay that is consuming them. Each accepts the isolation imposed upon him by fate as part of the unchanging pattern of the
world, so that he does not attempt to break through it toward
any meaningful life. The descriptions of nature balance this acceptance and alleviate their seclusion. Their hearing and vision
are directed to nature alone and they focus on it with all their
power, for it is the echo and reflection of their own silent depths.

> Outside the walls, the trunks of trees and the sides of the
> granaries were splitting with cold, and the wind was howling as
> it scattered the dry snow. The stars twinkled merrily but coldly
> from the dark sky, dogs were barking both near and far, and
> wolves padded across the empty garden lots, their tracks criss-
> crossing the deep snow that covered it.[81]

The same is true of most of the stories written before he came
to Palestine. Frequently, the story comes to a complete stop, as
happened to Brenner whenever he tried to write about the suffering of the lonely Jew in his ugly poverty. But Shoffman's attitude
to his characters is very different from Brenner's. Brenner responds to their suffering with an intensely pesonal identification,
as if he himself were responsible for the way life had treated Uriel
Davidowsky's father. Shoffman remains calmly objective, never
becoming part of his characters' fate, never feeling any personal
responsibility. This epic objectivity, even in the shortest story
Shoffman ever wrote, not only lacks the messianic fervor of Brenner but is also free of the irony that shows author's personal stand
in regard to the events related. It is only Shoffman's profound understanding of life that, with quiet serenity, burgeons out of the
story.

> Toward evening a warm mist descended, through which the
> church spires could be vaguely seen, deprived of their crosses.
> The gaslights were transformed into huge, hazy balls of light

illuminating the leaves of the trees nearest to them. Above the treetops in the park, the crescent moon glowed dimly like a coal among dying embers.

He could not sleep. Through the upper panes of the window he could see occasional falling stars, slowly falling and leaving a fiery trail behind them.

Toward morning he fell into a sweet sleep. In the narrow crooked paths behind the green hill, the wild orgy had died down, and the inhabitants began to smile in their sleep at absurd dreams. Early in the morning a repeated cry awakened them, a cry with a touch of pleasure in it, as if suited to the shocking message it conveyed.

"A man has been found hanged!"[82]

The fatalism is not theatrical or ostentatious, but is set in the everyday world of man. All the events are separate episodes, each depicting isolation and bereavement in the life of this or that man. Sometimes it suffices for Shoffman to relate one tendency—frequently connected with the motifs of love within the framework of isolation—that forces upon the hero the absolute certainty that the foundation of life is missing. Shoffman's stories always move toward such episodes, and the more the author compresses his stories the greater is the emerging certainty and the artistic perception that penetrates like light into the calm interior of a valuable jewel.

One such story is "No," which is less than a page and a half in length, and contains a single episode dealing with an unsuccessful love affair between a musician and a girl, Mania. Mania's body is exhausted, and in fact the street musician loved hearing her say "No more!" But when he began to make love to her forcibly as she lay by his side "her answer 'No!' rang through the dark."

> A little later, he began playing on his instrument through the courtyards of the fine houses beside the park, and girls ran out onto the porches looking with half-closed eyes at the sleepy young musician. The unforgettable melodies sent their sweetness through the air, which had been so strange that day, almost as if it were bending over at an angle....
>
> The park was now damp, deserted, and cold, the falling leaves rustled as though searching for that fundament that was missing. The half-naked trees raised their thin crooked branches to

the cloudy sky, which had turned into another "No!"—cold, eternal, abysmal.

"... No!"[83]

I have quoted the concluding section of the story in order to illustrate one psychological factor common to all Shoffman's writings: a man may remain closed in his own loneliness without the language of the story remaining within that confined space. Indeed, it can impose some of its own certainty on the natural environment of the individual. Thus the natural description with which Shoffman usually ends his stories is not merely a peroration to the episode but also counterbalances the isolation of the individual by a cosmic inspiration in which everything attains a mighty unity—the unity to be found on the razor's edge between the ultimate sorrow of the individual and the sense of comfort to be derived from the community of man with his universe. In this respect, Shoffman brings his natural descriptions to the threshold of symbolism without ever letting them become really symbolic, for he will not allow his wonderful stories to move out of the realm of the realistic world. Realism remains the dominant note of his stories, with the sole exception of "Deep Within," where he allows his profound and lucid understanding to take command.

From all that has been said, we may see how different Shoffman was from Brenner and other expressionists in portraying the sorrow of man. Moreover, the themes he employed are far more varied than Brenner's. One central theme, as we have noted, is love and the sense of isolation it inevitably involves—the same theme that runs through Gnessin's work. A comparison of the two shows the literary opposition, as it were, of Shoffman.

In all the stories he devotes to the erotic impulse arising from the human sense of isolation, Shoffman's approach is diametrically opposed to Gnessin's. There is none of the beautiful mistiness that in Gnessin's work, particularly in "Aside," often acts as a sort of cosmic compensation for Hagzar's unsuccessful love affairs. Shoffman always penetrates the "blue mist" of Gnessin's impressionistic writing, with all its unique harmonies, and reaches with startling clarity to the very core and essence of the heroes' tragic love. Things no longer seem to exist in a state of flux in which they become blurred in the cosmic beauty of the world and in which the individual loses his significance, becomes formless, and finally commits suicide. Shoffman removes all the mistiness, together with all traces of narcissistic delight, as when he depicts the meeting of two friends through whom he introduces the love motif in his story "Love":

> The distant past of their youth, a period filled with dreams that the two friends shared hung oppressively over them, and they sought the forceful phrase that could fittingly rid them of it. But the words they uttered, however heartfelt, seemed to miss the point. Just as in the open country, sometimes, one wants to sing a wonderful tune suited to the beautiful harmony round about—undulating fields of corn, the whispering of the trees, the chirping of crickets—but the free wind snatches the human tune as it emerges and it becomes lost, powerless, and faint.[84]

The same is true of all the variations in which Shoffman presents the psychological aspects of love. He never shies away from the fatalistic elements involved—life and echoes of death, physical embrace and the fatal despair inherent within it, dreams and the reality that so cruelly profanes them. Yet these problems never become a "breakdown of barriers" in which the figure of the sufferer withdraws from reality. The sublime tragedy arising from those problems is conveyed by Shoffman with deft skill and with the sureness of a craftsman who knows in advance what he wishes to portray.

> The passing of five months left their mark and succeeded in enslaving Julie to her husband completely, obstinately. Her figure now testified with terrible certainty to that secret, noctural happiness wherewith she had satiated Obskorov, so that Schmidt, even in his imagination, surrendered to her infinite beauty, and made little effort to deal with him.[85]

In contrast, when Julie dies, Shoffman knows how to describe Schmidt.

> But in the empty universe there was comfort!
> With a profound sense of gratitude, Schmidt gazed at the gaping yellow hole that greedily swallowed up the newly planed coffin containing such beauty within it—a beauty the like of which

did not exist among mortals. A deep calm spread through his limbs, a calm which prompted him to smile; and he smiled as one smiles when sinking wearily into a soft bed, surrendering to sleep.[86]

As the reader follows Shoffman's progress from one story to the next, it becomes clear that he constantly strives to pare down all superfluous matter, leaving only those aspects necessary for a lucid depiction of his material. The process continues until he passes from a more complex story, with a number of different characters, with variations on the theme of isolation, and numerous nature descriptions reflecting the inner moods of these characters, to a vignette containing only one character in which the theme is conveyed through a single episode. Parallel to this trend is a movement away from the theme of isolation on which Shoffman's earlier writings depend. It would seem that the intense concentration of his artistic vision upon one aspect of a single human character opened a hidden door that led beyond this isolation—the a priori motif that prompted him before he set pen to paper—toward a vision of wonderful unity glowing within the jewel-like vignette. At this point, the prose becomes elevated until it is almost poetry. The strictly epic objectivity changes into a vividly personal lyricism.

In many of his vignettes, then, the author becomes more concerned with himself, with episodes that reflect his own life; and all of the episodes record some unique, startling experience that reveals a wonderful vision of the unity of man and nature. This development is particularly noticeable if, following Shoffman's literary progress chronologically, one suddenly comes upon a story such as "My Little Daughter."

> She is not yet eight months old and there is no end to her suffering—one blow follows another. Those nights! Why did I have to raise her from the abyss? Why? I am afraid to look into her future. There she is, sitting orphaned on the stool, wearing last year's straw hat.
> My sorrow is greater than I can bear!
> Only this morning, as dawn rose, our eyes met and I had a

sudden insight: eyes . . . eyes . . . ! Out of its sad blindness nature has slowly gained its vision—surely that is a victory for which it is worth bearing and suffering all!

Then I bent down and kissed her on her cheek, from which arose a divine scent. She smiled and patted my face with the palm of her little hand as if to say, "I forgive you!"[87]

This vignette begins with Shoffman's grim view of man's lot, born into isolation with regard to both the external world of society and his own inner world; but then the author introduces a note of relief and hope. Within the episode there is a glimmer of comfort perceptible through the darker vision of despair that never took sufficient note of man's "open eyes." It may be that the new subjective element was responsible for the change—a use of autobiography totally different from that of Feierberg, Brenner, and Gnessin, who turned it into a cult of irrevocable isolation. Another vignette by Shoffman, in which there is no direct allusion to the events of the author's own life, seems to rectify all that was lacking in his previous use of the themes of love and the sense of isolation it involves. It is called "The Ticket," and in it the language achieves such consummate simplicity, the story is so subtle in its approach, that it seems to summarize all "young couples" and the way the world regards them.

Parting was hard for the young lovers. He was already standing on the tram's platform and she stood below on the ground. Another kiss . . . yet another . . . until the tram moved he kept on waving goodbye with his back to the other passengers, until the conductor's hand touched him from behind.

"Ticket!"

The young man started as though from sleep, and turning around, began rummaging in his purse. Everyone was secretly amused.[88]

Perhaps it is only in these scenes from the everyday, mundane world that the author can convey his deeper existentialist understanding of life. This understanding, revealing the visionary element concealed within the real world, casts some of its creative force over the landscape that, as we have said, always serves as a mirror to reflect the inner world of the character. These descriptions of nature in Shoffman are so saturated with hopelessness that sometimes nature itself seems to be suffering from an incurable melancholy, despairing of any comfort liable to come from the world of light and splendor beyond the horizon. Yet even nature is in due course elevated from despair in these episodes, as if responding to the author's own new vision.

> It is autumn. The fields have been harvested and in the evening, as it grows dark, black patches can be seen on the trees' bare branches—either rooks or the last remnants of foliage.[89]

There is a sharpness of vision here that becomes more compressed in each story, serving as a point of truth reflecting the profundity of life. An excellent instance is to be found in one of the briefest vignettes Shoffman wrote, "God." Here one can see why Shoffman gradually deserted the type of story that relies on amplification in favor of the vignette, with all its dangers of becoming static through excessive compression. This story, like all the vignettes of approximately the same length written after it, seems to hold its breath until the last sentence, usually briefer than any preceding it. This last sentence suddenly throws light not only on the material of the story but also on the human view of life as a whole, which never ceases unless man is blind to it.

> One afternoon in May, the two of us were walking through meadows, fields, and groves.
> "Daddy, I can see God in the sky!"
> "Where?"
> "There, there. . . that white shape. . . ."
> "Where?"
> "Look . . . over there . . . can't you see?"
> "No, my boy, I can't see."
> "You can never see anything!"[90]

This spirit of the story is, in effect, the same as the "white longing" that runs through the poetic struggles of Uri Zvi Greenberg and that never finds sufficient breadth and depth for its needs. In Shoffman, however, it achieves fulfillment despite the stylistic compression. It would seem that the simplicity of language required in a vignette succeeds in conveying the essence of meaning.

Gershon Shoffman

These short stories, free from the struggling of modernistic literature, achieve a realistic immediacy far exceeding that of the
younger Hebrew writers of our day.

In the preceding pages, I have noted more than once that
Shoffman's view of man's lot was basically different from that of
the rest of his circle, Brenner, Gnessin, Zeitlin, and others. For
him, it dominated the moods of man and nature and also the
more hopeful conclusion. His sensitive response to the pulse of his
characters formed part of this outlook. In his third volume, the
sensitivity is greater than in anything he had written previously.
He still tends to compress everything into brief episodes, but the
episode no longer reflects a single level of a character at a specific
moment. Instead, it responds at numerous interacting levels, and
the author himself, either directly or indirectly, becomes part and
parcel of the characters he has created.

The change occurs in this third volume because of the new
material with which the author deals: the Jew working in Eretz-
Israel with the pioneer settlers, fulfilling the ideal to which he
had looked forward for so long. Perhaps as a contrast to this new
material, Shoffman included at the beginning of this volume two
or three stories describing Jewish life in the Tyrol during World
War I and the Russian revolution. The stories "Man and the
Earth," "Eyes and Rivers," and "A New Light" are filled with
a fatalistic terror and are closer in style to those written during
the period of Shoffman's own suffering in the Tyrol. For this
reason, they are much longer than the rest of the stories in this
volume. Yet even in them a "new light" shines whenever they deal
with the Jew within this dark atmosphere. From then on, the
stories become more compressed, a sure sign that the light is shining with greater force, penetrating into the inner world of man
laboring in that dreadful time in the Tyrol. How much more so
in the stories of Palestine, in which all the themes of despair find
their ultimate solution!

All these themes in the Palestine vignettes have a new dimen-

121

sion—the Jewish longing for redemption, either national or individual, insofar as the individual benefits from the communal redemption. Everything takes on a vital significance—the loneliness bereft of vision, the always-frustrated love, the anticipation leading only to despair and depression. Yet the stories never turn to any mystical or symbolic solution; they continue to deal in careful detail with the plot, and never take refuge in any secret world. With extraordinary clarity, Shoffman writes of one young man:

> He had come from a different world, from different landscapes. Yet as he set foot on this soil he remembered that there were men, among them that great poet, who had bent down and kissed the stones. Could he himself do it?[91]

In this passage Shoffman concentrates everything on the revitalizing hope. The young Jew is depicted as lonely, but within his loneliness glimmers some great light reflecting both hope and despair, both love and sorrow. Hence the musicality of the prose in "The Kiss." From the two opening sentences it is clear that the author has no intention of telling a story "about" the young man or of describing him externally. The character must come to life by himself, revealing his own inner world. Thus, Shoffman presents the story in two scenes. The young refugee, with his mingling of hope and despair, is placed between them, so that he must search for some point of existence where his own character, as well as the destiny which awaits him, will shine more clearly.

The young man travels by bus to a communal settlement. "It was the period of Arab rioting at its worst," and the windows were covered with netting. The fields flowing by on either side were "a dry, parched brown," and there was "an unpleasant atmosphere among the passengers crowded together." It is clear that this scene will not answer the young man's question of whether he too will be able to love the soil and "bend down to kiss its stones." But in a moment another scene counteracts this one—the kibbutz itself, the group of youngsters, work, a strong feeling of being in his motherland. Yet the young man is shy, hesitant about the necessity imposed upon him, and these two levels would undoubtedly have neutralized each other were it not that Shoffman instinctively introduces the erotic aspect, which he works into the character's individual world. Among the group of youngsters who have come to the kibbutz is Yael, a girl filled with the joy of living, in whose singing sorrow, awe, and hope are mingled, and the young man feels suddenly at home. In their mutual love is found the real meaning of life whose powerful roots stretch deep down. His innate shyness, however, prevents him from simply approaching her and kissing her. Shoffman does not actually state that his hesitancy represents the human isolation that can never strike roots into the earth, nor does he tell us that the young man will never kiss Yael. But word by word the story does suggest that irremediable sense of isolation.

Shoffman has here employed a literary technique that only the greatest writers of the nineteenth century knew how to use. He utilizes the young man's arrival in the country as a means of sublimating in a literary form his own profound psychological experience. It could not exist solely on the nationalistic or social level, as did the characterization of the members of the Second Aliyah. The young man is searching for a home in the external world and, far more deeply, within his inner world; his discovery of a homeland must affect the spiritual obstacles within him. This accounts for the surface level—his negative response while travelling in the bus where each individual is on guard against his neighbor. The transformation is so startling in its realism and so beautifully intensified that it affects the young man in his entirety, redeeming him from his weakness. By the same road that the young man had travelled to the kibbutz, Yael later returns to the kibbutz to settle in it permanently, but she is shot dead by an Arab bullet. The soil is sanctified both by Yael's blood and by her love, and at once the young man feels that his roots have struck in the soil of the land. Now, like the great medieval poet and many others with him, he falls upon the earth before everyone's eyes and kisses it. All this is accomplished in only a few brief lines, but with a profound immediacy of effect and with an epic tonality never obscured by the lyricism of the story.

3

Two Central Pillars

Mikha Yosef Berdichevsky: In Search of the Hidden

Feierberg, Gnessin, Brenner, and Hillel Zeitlin were like satellites orbiting around the central figure of Berdichevsky, even
though each of them also revolved on his own axis and was concerned with working out his own literary destiny. They all kept
a watchful eye upon him since there was a real bond between
them despite the fact that Berdichevsky never suffered from the
sense of personal isolation that affected the others. In this respect,
he obviously appeared to them as a completely integrated person.
The childhood he spent in a deeply religious home and the education he received in the Bet ha-Midrash, where his studies were
devoted exclusively to Talmud and Jewish law, created no inner
conflicts in later life as they did in his younger contemporaries.
Even his rebellion against the accepted standards of Ahad ha-Am's
school, Bialik's poetry, the social and nationalist ideologies of the
day, and modern Hebrew literature, was not prompted by personal factors. On the contrary, Berdichevsky remained faithful to
that small Jewish shtetl even when he was far from it geograph-
ically. In fact, he tried to embody his own change of values in
stories about the shtetl and in his work on Jewish legend and
folklore.

It is clear, then, that Berdichevsky's literary work did not arise
from an attempt to transfer his own subjective problems from
autobiography into a literary possession shared by all. His stories,

124

like his legends, are completely objective, and their artistic merit lies in the vividness of characterization and atmosphere. It was for this reason that the younger writers regarded him as their teacher and guide.[1] Contemporary critics, however, as well as those Hebrew readers supporting the historical teachings of Ahad ha-Am, nicknamed Berdichevsky "The Outcast"—a term not far removed from the cruelty of excommunication.

The use of the term *aher*, "outcast," has a specially tragic connotation in Jewish history. Any deviation from such conventions and accepted ideas as had become traditional was sufficient reason to drive men out of the community, and such exclusion brought with it considerable suffering, particularly at times of great change in Jewish life. Yet the person excommunicated, whether willingly or unwillingly, had an aura of splendor about him that accompanied him into exile, prophesied his recompense, and thus sweetened his lot. Popular tradition, which goes back much further than the ideological fashions in the "outcast's" own day, never rejects him completely. He is never altogether cut off from the deep roots of his people, and even in his loneliness he draws succor from its ancient vitality, hearkening to an antiquity hidden within the people's consciousness. The "outcast" is thus both an exile and an heir, deserting his parental home and yet cleaving to it in his exile, following his own lonely path but listening to the echoes reaching him from the people's ancient past. Even those books by scholars and writers banned or proclaimed apocryphal because they did not conform to the official authoritative view seemed to "cry out against their disgrace," nurturing, as it were, some distant hope of eventual redemption, of someone who would, in the course of generations, cast a benevolent eye upon them and at last bring them back within the fold. To this day we still recall the "outcasts" of the Talmud and midrashim,[2] of the Kabbalah and of Hasidism,[3] and they still appear as characters in modern Hebrew literature.[4] They pain us by their alienation and amaze us by their voluntary exile. Even today they arouse in us a sense of beauty woven in an ancient and strangely wonderful past, of lives closed in behind a fence, of experiences distant and yet close. We still punish the "outcast" who kicks against the sanctified fences of our day, while at the same time we sympathize with him as he follows the paths of suffering and beauty. Deep within our hearts we wish him well, as if to say, "You are our brother!"

Berdichevsky, too, was an "outcast." He objected to the "historical spirit" and denied the "historical account" of Ahad ha-Am, whom Bialik regarded as his teacher and whom that generation had accepted as the true exponent of all that was happening within the Jewish nation at that time. Berdichevsky could not bear the intellectualism that Ahad ha-Am had borrowed from nineteenth-century European liberalism and from which he deduced his moral teachings and constructed a sort of master plan for his people's future. This "history" Berdichevsky regarded as mere petrifaction, and he refused to accept the concept of "national evolution" whereby moral, social, or religious ideas ascend side by side with intellectual development. In this aesthetic and instinctive response he was unique in his generation. It was not that he withdrew from the mundane world of Jewish life, donning some romantic cloak to take upon himself an artistic isolation of inspiration or despair. On the contrary, his stories deal realistically with the everyday life of the small Jewish town. However, his harsh realism served to break down the barrier that blocked his keen and perceptive eye, revealing the primitive realism of the Jewish shtetl, releasing it from the silent mists that, to an outsider, seemed to be quietly engulfing it as it sank into desolation.

Berdichevsky drew much of his inspiration from this primitivism and seemed proud of his sensitive response to it, of the way his narrative stripped off the imagined calm of the Jew, destroyed his drowsy complacency, and presented the day-to-day life of the village in an aura of ancient destiny expressed with an inexorable sense of fatalism in word and deed. He can surprise us with a sudden leap into the inner world of his characters, or digress to discuss the "breaking of the vessels" in a historical, moral, or literary context. He was interested in stripping bare the intuitive impulses of his characters, calling this technique "suddenness," "surprise," "constant revelation," "creative revolution," "return

Mikha Yosef Berdichevsky

to nature," and so forth. He never lost his desire to grasp reality with a certain immediacy on all its levels, ignoring social barriers, moral fences, and intellectual fashions, all of which were liable to conceal the true nature of man, even though he knew only too well that his approach was likely to place him on the threshold of primitivism. Fischel Lakhover has described this aspect of Berdichevsky's work with remarkable simplicity and directness.

> The basic innovation in his writings is that he always begins afresh. His wonder is that of a newly born child. He always tends to search for origins, for the roots rather than the branches. Throughout history people had been accustomed to explain, to add commentaries to commentaries, to connect ideas, but they never reached the cool waters of the fresh spring. His approach, however, is to look for these sources, and what was customary among other people was never his custom. On the contrary because it has become customary, he regards it as our duty to investigate further, to examine the custom anew, to find its roots, its earliest beginnings.[5]

This "innovation" of Berdichevsky was clearly the result of his ceaseless search for a suitable means of expressing his aesthetic sensitivity, which was, for the most part, at odds with the intellectualism of Ahad ha-Am and the realism of contemporary Hebrew literature.[6] It is his sensitivity that distinguishes Berdichevsky from the other Hebrew writers of his day. We alluded earlier to Peretz's unfulfilled yearning to hear the mystical primeval melody hidden within man's soul, and how thin he thought the partition that separates man from his melody. In Berdichevsky's works, however, the melody is inherent within the narrative. It permeates the story of its own accord, bubbles up from within some particle of speech, and through various channels comes either overtly or more subtly to the fore. Nature flows through the narrative with wonderful ease. At one moment it is visible in a description or a thought, veiled in various forms, and at the next it becomes the main current, surging forward with a primitive harmony that anticipates every word and thought.

The great difference between Berdichevsky and Ahad ha-Am lies in the fact that the latter bases his concept of the "spiritual

127

center" on a liberal intellectualism that pretends it has already conquered the archetypical primitivism in man, both as individual and society. The idea of individualism in art, which is so prominent in folklore, ballad, and story, was entirely foreign to Ahad ha-Am, since from his point of view it detracted from that national philosophy expressed in a people's social and moral code. Both Berdichevsky and Ahad ha-Am utilized elements borrowed from European philosophy, Berdichevsky employing the aesthetic ideas of Schopenhauer and Nietzsche and Ahad ha-Am the "spiritual revival" of nineteenth-century liberalism; both hoped to achieve by their borrowings a revival of Jewish nationalism. Ahad ha-Am was the one who "added commentary to commentary, linking point to point" in Jewish history, examining each era within that history to deduce from it predictions for the future. Berdichevsky, however, was opposed to the system of eras, of dividing history into past, present, and future according to ideological patterns. In his view, the world was not given to man—particularly to the Jew—in a series of separate compartments, but as a unified present with infinite notes playing together in a mighty harmony. Nothing in the world of this present moment is isolated from its past and its future; nothing exists without an inner self beyond the horizons of reality. "True" reality, according to Berdichevsky, is that instinctive grasp prompted by natural impulse.

In an essay on Berdichevsky, Jacob Rabinovich wrote: "Ahad ha-Am, who startled everyone by his revival of the heart, seemed then to close by himself the horizons he had opened up."[7] Berdichevsky, on the other hand, spent his life tearing down the curtains in front of those horizons, and revealing what was hidden behind them. Who can tell what Ahad ha-Am feared more—the "hidden light" of creation that might dazzle him, or the gloomy darkness before creation? It may even be that he did not distinguish between the two because of his lack of aesthetic sense. Haiyim Nahman Bialik certainly was afraid, and he tells us specifically that he feared the "glowering man," the "areas of desolation," and the "deep black waters" as he describes them in his *Scroll of Fire* and other poems.[8] Bialik shied away from the apocalyptic myths bursting through his poem and took refuge in a nationalism which offered an intellectual outlet for this "man of the soil." But Berdichevsky penetrated into the heart of these myths and legends as if they were part of himself, adopting them into his philosophy and writings without the slightest fear that the winds he had released might harm him. For in the very environment of the Jewish shtetl in the Ukraine, which even in his day was silently beginning its spiritual and physical disintegration, he revealed in his stories something hidden since the distant past, and expressed what was forbidden—the erotic myth which he perceived "beyond the veil" screening the Heart of the Jew within that Ukrainian shtetl. As he entered these Jewish homes, treasures of terrible beauty "poured out at his feet," the pristine beauty to be found in man's primitive instincts. He believed that these instincts are unable to suffer a history that cramps them into some intellectual framework or embalms them within national "accounts" or nullifies them in the name of a culture divorcing man from "nature."

Such was Berdichevsky's primary quarrel with "history," "writings," and "books."[9] For him, these serve merely to silence the heart of the Jew, to imprison him behind the barriers and fences of a false spirituality that cuts him off from his true nature by means of realistic illusions. In Berdichevsky's comments on "nature" and "books," there are many echoes of the new schools of art and literature and of their concern with a new aestheticism.

> Nature transcends all the welter of words written about it. The soul exceeds all philosophies about the soul. Every phase, every thought, every statement, is only the offspring of the soul. Man cannot express the emotions within his heart nor make their echoes heard. Writing cannot serve as the currency for the world's treasure house.
>
> Only a small fraction of what is within our hearts is ever expressed in books, only the tiniest fraction. And even this fraction is mere words—empty words without real shape or existence.
>
> On the contrary, what exists within us, deep within us, is without speech and without words, without expression and incommunicable. . . .
>
> It has been said that writing was created at twilight; but writing

is limited, and God is unlimited, without beginning and without end.[10]

These extracts indicate the reasons for the pessimism embedded in Berdichevsky's philosophy of art. It is the pessimism of Schopenhauer, nourished by the intuitive subconscious and never achieving its aim within the limits of conscious art. The true artist is always driven to express himself directly, with an immediacy that includes all levels, while "bookish writing," in its attempt to express "life" and "nature" serves merely to transform these into barriers between the artist and reality. The particularization of objects and events in this literary art form simply presents them in a frozen or petrified form, so that art has been transmogrified into a "book." What had previously existed in a dynamic present involving both past and future becomes by its embodiment in art a static past event.

He believed the same to be true of the epic writer who ignores the primitive forces always at work in life and who describes his characters in the light of some ideological purpose that he imposes upon them. Such a writer immerses his art in an aesthetic ideal fixed in the past and weakens its sense of the future, for the moment about which he is writing is really a moment in the present that corresponds to both past and future. Berdichevsky saw in had ha-Am's philosophy, as he frequently did in Bialik's poetry, a constriction of the real Jewish present, a violation of the bond between modern Hebrew literature and the primitive sources at work in mankind from the ancient past until the end of days. That was why Schopenhauer's pessimism attracted him so strongly. Like Schopenhauer, he was fascinated by the magical power of music, which could draw man unconsciously into the heart of nature without that static particularization to be found in literature. Berdichevsky was of the opinion that intellectualism, "historical necessity," moral didacticism, and the contemporary cult of realism were destroying the soul of Hebrew literature, and that the guilty parties were the periodical *Ha-Shilloah* and its editors. The result, as we have noted, was that contemporary critics labeled Berdichevsky an outcast, while he himself demanded that all Jewish authors and poets become "outcasts" like him.

Mikha Yosef Berdichevsky

As long as Berdichevsky was involved in theoretical arguments with his fellow writers, he could wave the flag of aestheticism. However, when he settled down to write and struggled toward that ultimate reality for whose sake he had launched his attack upon the school of Ahad ha-Am and the prevalent realism of his day, he met with a number of problems that forced him to slow down a little on his way to the inner mystery and in his breaking down of barriers on the path to the "hidden."[11] The outcast then appears to be pausing to think things out—and his thoughts are then not very different from those of the "bookish" school he attacked.

In Berdichevsky's writings one can discern a number of styles typical of European literature at the turn of the century, particularly in his impressionistic stories about the Jewish town such as "From the Mists of Boyhood," "Out of Bounds," and "Over the River."[12] They still show an awareness of the visible world, but the realism is weakened, as though flowing toward some eternal deep to which all the channels of time inevitably lead. Grief and loneliness form the harmonic theme of these stories. Many of Berdichevsky's stories, such as "The Bargain," "A Piece of Bread," and "One Beside the Other," are impressionistic descriptions of the real world and not of the "ultimate reality"—mere glimpses and echoes of what Berdichevsky called "nature."[13] In some of them we can hear echoes of the author's aesthetic pessimism, for a mere glimpse into life's reality never satisfied him. He uncovered one inch and at once the doors slammed shut and he was left with a literary thirst burning within him, driving him to seek the springs of "form" and "image" without which a writer can never achieve his aim.

As a result, a rift occurred within him between the author and the polemicist, for that harmonious bond he demanded of writers was always violated by his own need to clothe the impression in verbal form. This inner clash between artistic concept and literary form produced a constant tension and drove him to experiment with modernistic alternatives. Even in "Over the River" objects seem to sink by their own weight, and all that happens there seems to withdraw into the innermost chambers of his heart. They separate from their external "shells," becoming veiled in some hidden significance that cannot be named outside the realms of mysticism. From this point the impressionism of Berdichevsky's stories changes into a veiled symbolism on one hand and a naked expressionism on the other, visible in such tales as "Kalonymus and Naomi," "The Red Heifer,"[14] and particularly in his novelettes *In the Heart of the Thunder, Thou Shalt Build a House,* and, last but not least, *Miriam.* Yet none of these deserts the setting of the Jewish shtetl. It would appear that every one of his stories is motivated by the shtetl and by his desire to tear off its covering, even in a story like "The Departure," which describes the old shohet leaving his town in order to set out for the Holy Land and be buried in its sacred soil.[15]

This desire lends a certain sense of wonder to his writing. The author always seems to be listening for some change to make itself apparent in his narrative. Whoever looks at his shtetl from without must be impressed by it: the daylight dies away and silence encompasses it with the quiet grief of desolation; yet the narrative opens up within it a profound bustle of activity, as if the town is wearing a mask of silence for outsiders while within there is enormous movement liable at any moment to overwhelm the channels of style. From this viewpoint, the "verbalization" is no longer an external husk over the inner reality of things but a symbol of that wonderfully primitive dynamism raging within the garb of silence and grief that clothes the town. This expressionist desire to penetrate into the inner world of experience paved the way for Berdichevsky's tendency to Hasidism. Hasidism provided for him, as it had for Peretz, a means of expressing his literary impulses spontaneously. He too saw in dance and song an outlet for his own musical interests, but in contrast to Peretz he succeeded in absorbing the hasidic dance and song into his own literary style. He never needed any literary apparatus such as the monologue of broken phrases or the allusiveness whereby Peretz attempted to achieve his effects. In Berdichevsky, the expressionism itself answered his needs as if it were tailor-made for him.

In his essays on Hasidism and the Kabbalah he explains the

purpose of this expressionism, and his entire "natural" aestheticism is contained in his "Study of Hasidism."

> During the periods of the Kabbalah and of Hasidism the out-
> look of the Jews too began to broaden. The Jew began to realize
> that it is insufficient to take as his motto in life: "Turn aside from
> evil and do good!" This time he recognized that the unity of the
> Holy One was above all such forms. . . . Moreover, man ceased to
> search for spiritual life in this world and began to turn his atten-
> tion to mundane matters. In the worlds of Kabbalah and Hasidism
> man welcomed the world with open arms in his search for the mys-
> teries of life. By means of the many laws and commandments, in-
> structions and directions, opinions and philosophies that the kab-
> balist or hasid found before him as things passed on by word of
> mouth or fixed permanently in written and unchanging form, he
> now found in the world around him new aspects and new life. . . .
> He kept feeling within him a divine reawakening, "the trumpet
> call of God"; it was a call from a God who creates and renews the
> universe and its creatures by pouring his compassion upon them.[16]

Berdichevsky maintained that all his artistic longings were summarized in this concept of the "trumpet call of God." The trumpet call symbolizes the soul that is once again impelled by its
original "nature"; it marks the redemption of man, whose inner
psychological world has been opened and whose soul has been
revitalized. The hasidic traits of reawakening, enthusiasm, and
devotion mark stages in the ascent of a man whose soul has again
been touched by beauty. The majesty of creation, which clothes
the universe in its harmony, clothes the individual Jew as well
with the aesthetic splendor of Hasidism.

> Sometimes we feel a divine spirit within us, a spirit that rages
> with the force of the ocean's breakers, roaring and thundering.
> The storm impels us with a force we have never known till now,
> eternal life wells up within us. The boundary separating us from
> the universe around is broken so that we want to break out our-
> selves—and we dance.
> These dances form a mighty yet tangible song, an exalted song.
> It comes not from joyful lips but is expressed solely in movement,
> movement originating from the hosts of heaven. . . . Not the
> mouth alone, but all the limbs of the body burst into song, the
> heart too beating time in joy and devotion. The dance does not

simply consist of feet moving in a circular or straight pattern, but of the entire body with all its members. All of our vital frame participates in the shout of prayer and song, everything becoming united in a mighty movement, a gesture of freedom. A man feels then that he is not alone. . . .

He feels his connection with the light above, the infinite light revealed in all the treasures of the universe. He feels the mystery of all life, including the universal experience, and his heart is elevated. He wishes to become unified with creation, to cling fast to his Creator, to cling with all his heart and soul. Everything within him rages and pulsates as he dances. . . . and that is the secret of becoming united with God. . . .

The rhetorical theorizing of this essay was obviously not sufficient to satisfy Berdichevsky's craving for an artistic expression that would be direct and spontaneous—the "particularized" expression of Hasidism. What Peretz put into the mouths of his hasidic characters served Berdichevsky simply as subjects for essays and for moral dicta. He strove to embody the beauty of Hasidism at a realistic level in his stories without that philosophizing and psychologizing that obscured the vitality of the hasid. Berdichevsky's hasidic stories are free from any monologue aspiring to dramatic profundity, and even that dialogue, typical in its movement of the hasidic tradition, is used only rarely. Nearly everything is in the form of depiction or description, with all the attendant danger of becoming static, and is the very opposite of the "freedom" and "all-my-bones-shall-speak" that Berdichevsky comments on in his *Study of Hasidism.*

At this very point the artistic merit of the author's work becomes most apparent. Indeed, the story is dominated by the realistic description of the hasidic environment, but in it is revealed an instantaneous and direct grasp of the universal dynamism mentioned in the *Study of Hasidism.* For this reason, Berdichevsky took particular pains lest he fall into the trap of the artificial stylization that spoiled Peretz's hasidic stories. A striking example of his caution is to be found in his hasidic tale "The Interval." He begins by raising his gaze heavenward and talking of subjects such as divine exaltation and the profundity of melody, but while talking he senses that his very language has distorted the real enthusiasm and devotion of Hasidism. He at once drops the stylized form and slips into an utter simplicity of language that conveys by itself the enthusiasm and devotion as the Rebbe enters the town:

> The path from the ritual bath to the Bet ha-Midrash was filled with a procession of people. The glowing faces, dripping sidelocks, and white collars gave an impression of contentment. Each man grasped his neighbor's girdle with one hand. The more critical among them stroked their beards as if to say: "Who should lead the *shaharit* service today? Who the *musaph* service? The *Lekhu Neranenah* was not well sung last night. The *Kegavna* was not up to standard. . . ."[17]

This simple, unadorned description is highly responsive to the extraordinary revitalization of the atmosphere of the Jewish village. This revitalization grows stronger and stronger, but it never transgresses the bounds the author has set. The dancing at the Rebbe's house is filled with the "freedom" created by the "shout of prayer and song" and the "breaking of the boundary between us and the universe." The artistic expression in this hasidic dance seems to "go mad" and become primitive in its turmoil, but the author's tone restrains the orgiastic element. He offsets the passion of the hasidic story with the everyday elements without which life cannot exist.

> "Almighty in passion!" Menashe the good-for-nothing jumps up from his place and grasps Yeruham by the hand, Yeruham pulls Shim'on after him, Shim'on catches Benjamin by the wrist, and Benjamin grabs Kalman by the girdle. Then Kalman suddenly begins to sing. They dance, at first as a joke, but then with enthusiasm, with passion, and finally with every fiber of their being. The men standing around join hands and widen the circle, dancing swiftly around, and one man, lifting the hem of his gaberdine, begins leaping in the center of the circle with astonishing energy as the others race round, their eyes rolling, mouths grimacing and dripping saliva. One of them tears his shirt, baring his breast. Wild abandon! Thy nation Israel is dancing!
>
> They dance in the large hall of the Rebbe's house, in the rooms round about; they dance out of that house into another, then from one quarter to another within the town. They dance in all the important houses, in the house of Rabbi Dimta, in the houses of

135

the *shohetim* and cantors. Even the tailors and ordinary people who are normally remote from such affairs join the hasidim and dance joyfully with them. The scholars forget their private researches into Kimhi and Malbim and join in too. Voices grow louder and louder. Mouths utter incomprehensible words. Hearts pound, feet prance, bodies twirl. Wild abandon! Thy nation Israel is removing its outer clothing and dancing. The soul has opened its mouth. . . . Everyone has sevenfold strength, everyone is in the grip of some revitalization, some reawakening, some indefinable passion. A primeval sense of the joy of living is flowing into them, wave upon wave. Objects lose their physical significance —walls no longer divide, ceilings no longer separate. . . . Everyone can make himself taller, reach to the roof, spread himself wide, go wild, shake the foundations, penetrate into the secrets of life, shout and sing without end. . . . Give them rivers of wine, give them a riot of hugging and embracing, of mighty, unimaginable enthusiasm, of unity with God to the very essence of their being . . . give them what they have been owed throughout all generations of all time. . . .[18]

A certain restraint accompanies the bacchanalian description of the dance, lest it produce a "breaking of the vessels" or the licentiousness of complete abandonment. In fact, the very "verbalization" and "bookishness" that Berdichevsky attacked in his essays and in his disputes with Ahad ha-Am helped him in his hasidic story "Lest His Own Self Be Destroyed" in the same way they had helped Rabbi Nahman of Braslav in his stories.[19] The simple diction, the logical sentence structure, the chaste style—all these are the traits of an accomplished artist; they restrain the primitive aesthetic impulses and allow them to achieve a realistic grasp. At the same time, they channel those impulses into creative forces, protecting them from the "ever present danger." This technique accompanies Berdichevsky from the stories about the Jewish village to the hasidic and kabbalistic stories, and from there to the myths, legends, and folkloristic tales of the distant and more recent past, and from there to the novelettes that mark the highpoint of his artistic struggle.[20]

In this literary technique, Berdichevsky was alone throughout his era. It is very doubtful whether he ever came close to the psychoanalytical schools, yet he perceived in the characters living in

poverty in his silent towns the inner turmoil of an ancient demonic myth. They take no part in adventures or epic deeds, yet
they share those primeval spirits that have always been hidden
deep within man. In contrast to the intuitive element in his own
stories, Berdichevsky objected to the concept of national intellect
in Ahad ha-Am's writings as being bloodless, inanimate, and lean-
ing upon the broken reed of on artificial morality coupled with
a false and dogmatic prophecy. When Berdichevsky touched even
lightly upon the silent characters of the Jewish town the veneer of
traditional morality dropped off, and he showed them to be
caught up in an inner turmoil inspired by ancient myth. Berdichevsky perceived this ancient Jewish nobility, which "writers and
pen pushers" had hidden away beneath a mound of obedience to
ritual law, and determined to embody it in his stories—to reveal
the psychological depths that writers had previously ignored. It
was this desire that turned his pen toward legends in a manner
entirely different from that of Bialik and Ravnitsky in their *The
Book of the Aggadah* ("Sefer ha-Aggadah").

It is clear what fascinated Berdichevsky in these legends. When
he was still in his parents' home, studying the rigid laws of Judaism, he must frequently have been attracted to those strange
legends neglected for generations by the Hebrew reader. He had
the courage to look at them closely, to leave the morality of talmudic law and glimpse the impassioned apocalyptic myth within
them. An examination of one instance of such a legend, dealt
with by Bialik and Ravnitsky on the one hand and by Berdichevsky on the other, reveals the contrast between the two approaches.
Bialik is concerned, as usual, with the traditional aspects of the
legend, with its conciseness of expression, its stylistic unity, and
its moral setting.

> Rabbi Shim'on ben Yehotzadak inquired of Rabbi Shmuel bar
> Nahman, saying, "Since I have heard you are a master of leg-
> ends, tell me how light was created." He replied, "The Holy One,
> blessed be He, wrapped Himself in a white prayer shawl and His
> glorious splendor shone from one end of the universe to the
> other." . . . Rabbi El'azar said, "The light which the Holy One,
> blessed be He, created on the first day, man looked through it from

one end of the universe to the other. When the Holy One gazed down on the evil men and saw their crooked ways, He hid it away from mankind. For whom did He keep it? For the righteous in the world to come."21

Clearly, this legend, quoted at the beginning of the *Book of Aggadah,* has no intention of setting itself up in opposition to the scriptural account of creation in Genesis. Not only does it leave unquestioned the biblical account, with its freedom from ancient myth, but even strengthens it by its vision of the Holy One wrapped in a white prayer shawl. The legend catches the moment of Creation with all the magnificence of a monotheism attributing complete power to a single and sole God, and obviously reflects the author's unwavering belief in the world to come. The second section, relating how the light is stored away for the righteous, is entirely devoted to the moral lesson that the Almighty "gazed down and saw the crooked ways" of the wicked; it turns its back on any aesthetic considerations concerning the first outpouring of light.

Berdichevsky, on the other hand, deliberately ignores the moral intent of the legend, breaks through its conciseness of language and infuses it with an epic quality derived from pre-biblical folklore. Although the story seems on the surface to be objective, restrained, and harmonious in its expanded form, in fact it reveals apocalyptic visions symbolizing the author's own inner turmoil.

> In the beginning, the earth was waste and void, and eternal darkness was on the surface of the abyss, a darkness which all could feel as belonging to the dominion of the Prince of Darkness, who resembled an ox casting its shadow over all. When the Almighty wanted to create the universe, He called out to the Prince of Darkness, "Leave Me, for I wish to create the universe in light!" So He rebuked him and he went. Then reddish rays began to penetrate the darkness, and God, calling aloud, shook His prayer shawl and the universe shone from end to end, and there was light instead of darkness.22

In this synthetic form of the legend, Berdichevsky seems almost to be rebelling against the accepted account, modifying its monotheistic element and replacing it by an artistic quality. He gathers a number of legends from various sources, producing from them a story illuminated by demonology. Gods once more walk among mortals and those spirits with which the Kabbalah had struggled unceasingly again come to rest within the human soul and are accepted as "part of nature." Figures that Jewish history had veiled in cultural and national character are laid bare, stripped of their covering, their primitive instincts and impulses visible to all; and among them the author wanders quite at home, as if it were all perfectly natural to him. The mighty struggles of passion and lust in early Jewish legend do not oppress him. On the contrary, Berdichevsky gives the impression that only now has he found what he was searching for. His eye, always searching out the primitive element hidden away in myths, now seems at rest, recognizing what lies before it and gazing confidently at the inner world of the ancient Jew, whether it be Adam, the first man, created as the reddish rays appeared through the darkness, or Enoch of the Apocalypse, or Moses, or Yosi of Yokrat,[23] or Nathan of Zuzita,[24] or the sainted kabbalist Isaac Luria, or Sabbatai Tsevi the false messiah, or the popular heroes of later legends, or even the characters of modern Hebrew literature. For him, no fundamental change had occurred in these people from the ancient past to our own day, and this constituted the real unity of the people—their outbursts of erotic passion, the blood rising with the pride of the ocean toward the startling beauty of human experience, that infinite majesty in which can be heard an eternal mingling of past, present, and future.

There is a universality unifying all things even within their independent existence. Everything symbolizes everything else and is typified in everything else. It represents the whole of mankind, even though each nation follows its own path in giving expression to human experience. Jewish literature, like that of other nations, originates in myth, develops into legend, becomes stormier within the Kabbalah, stronger with Hasidism, hides away for a few generations, and finally bursts forth in modern literature. Modern Hebrew literature, both poetry and prose alike, will succeed only if it penetrates the cultural husks of centuries to the kernel of primeval myth within. Berdichevsky took up this search for the kernel as his personal task and ideology. His pursuit of the "ancient secrets" and later of "hidden legends" was only intended to provide a bridge between myth and those of his own stories, such as "My Sacrifice,"[25] "The Fruit of the Soil," and "Kalonymus and Naomi," which are foreign to the spirit of Hebrew literature. But above all he was attracted by the erotic element in mythology, which served as the motive force for his shorter novels *In the Heart of the Thunder* and *Miriam*.

In the Heart of the Thunder surprises the reader by its short chapters and tends to startle him by its plot and sequence of events. The atmosphere here is the same silent atmosphere as that of the Jewish town, the grief-laden silence of isolation. Yet within these short chapters something apparently forgotten or neglected within the soul has begun to ferment and is now trying to leap beyond the bounds of the story. Within the events related something is at work that, if only empowered by the author's pen, would burst forth with a primitive roar such as the author has described elsewhere in his legendary tales. In fact, *In the Heart of the Thunder* contains certain passages that in both style and spirit may be compared to those wonder tales of demons with their "sons of the gods," Shamhazai, Aza'el, and the giants and mighty heroes, who are all to be found in the Bible and legends.

> Solomon the Red saddled his horse and rode slowly along till he reached his son's castle. There he alighted, opened the gate, led his horse into the courtyard, and placed a sack of oats in front of it. He took a few steps forward and hesitantly tapped on the window of his daughter-in-law's room. Ten minutes passed and then a lady dressed in white opened the door and quietly let the visitor in. A watchdog awoke and belatedly began to bark furiously. A sound of cascading water could be heard rising to the clouds, where it was swallowed up. . . .
> Suddenly, the world trembled. Two mountains were torn up from their places and met to become one. A living shriek rose from the bowels of the earth, a cry of suffering, a sound of thunder as abyss called to abyss. The order of creation was inverted and lightning leaped and flashed through the night.
> Pleiades and Orion changed places in the heavens.[26]

Mikha Yosef Berdichevsky

In this way Berdichevsky describes the strange love of Solomon
the Red for his son's wife. The myth breaks away from its ancient
setting and enters the world of the Jewish town. It leaves behind
all allusiveness and, rejecting subtlety of expression, chooses a
direct forcefulness. The whole world trembles at their demonic
love and is swept up in the eroticism of the myth; the colossal
scale serves to convey the effect vividly and starkly. Yet the story
is imbued with a certain calm, as if it exists within the eye of a
primitive storm that foretells a change in the order of creation.
At times the realistic setting of the story can no longer contain
the psychological power of the myth, and the author has to employ techniques that break over the bounds of realism, as he does
in *Miriam*.

> Deborah was drunk, longing to lift every door off its hinges, to
> leap out of one window and back through another. The birds were
> flying in the sky. From the chimneys of the houses in the street
> rose columns of smoke, ascending higher and higher until they dis-
> appeared from sight.[27]

In this extract the reader perceives a quality that places Berdichevsky's writings on the threshold of modernism. The movement
from sentence to sentence does not follow any logical or chronological order. The veil placed over events by tradition and literary
discipline has been rent, and echoes can be heard of suppressed
passions, driven by deep impulses, which permeate the narrative
itself. Berdichevsky's language becomes heavy with a desire to
express a number of levels of experience at one fell swoop and
to stamp them with the mark of externality as the ancient myth
had done. The silent cry of man, suppressed from of old, when
he first began to wander over the surface of the earth, forces its
primeval terror upon the surface narrative. The short novels *In the
Heart of the Thunder* and *Miriam* have flashes of naked eroticism
that lend to Berdichevsky's literary visions an oppressively tragic
quality from which he could not escape.

> One speaks of marriages made in heaven, of right and wrong in
> this world, of a watchful eye in heaven and of the straight way.
> One asks and answers, answers and asks. If we lift the curtain,
> no hidden hand writes. A heavy weight presses down on us all.

The poet wishes to tell his tale of Devorah seven times. I shall tell about little Devorah for my daughter Sarah. Sarah is the mother of the character in my story *Miriam*. Who shall write the story of Devorah?[28]

It is as if the characters of his stories come together to demand from the author that he give expression to the particular spiritual problems of each (in much to same way as in Luigi Pirandello's play *Six Characters in Search of an Author*), and the author responds to their request, dealing with all their psychological complexes. In doing so, he relies upon certain ideas and visions from the Kabbalah and Jewish legend as if the characters of his novelettes were only extensions of those described by the Kabbalah as wandering "naked" in eternal exile. He does this in *Miriam* most clearly of all. This short novel is broken up into brief sections, each of which serves as a sort of separate mythic unit in addition to forming part of the story as a whole. The dull atmosphere of the town, overcast with silence and loneliness, is ready for some psychological surprises such as that of the Rebbe who comes to Ledina and decides to bless Miriam together with the rest of her family. "The leader rose from his chair, laid his hand on her head and blessed her. As he went out, he remembered a young girl from the days of Shamhazai and Aza'el and thought to himself, 'Place my home too among the stars. . . .' " Berdichevsky becomes involved in the character of this Rebbe and strips him to reveal all the strange longings within him; he will not leave him until he has marked those longings with the stamp of the erotic legends of the Kabbalah.

Even in his youth he had felt an inclination to the fairer sex, being particularly attracted to the Shekhinah, the merciful mother living in heaven. The world is really divided into only two parts—male and female. The lesser light was larger than its brother, the sun; Eve preceded Adam, the first man. His imagination prompted him to write a third book of the *Zohar* while secretly his heart was praying to the faithful shepherd. The nations and Israel in those days worshipped the sun, but he burnt incense to the moon . . . the god of the month excelled the gods of the week. Whoever succeeds in sanctifying the moon's countenance unclothed, merits eternity. . . . On the eve of the New Moon he fasted as usual, confessed, bathed, and lit a candle in his room. On that day the women also purified themselves and made themselves attractive to their husbands, just as the moon had renewed itself. The day of the New Moon was sacred to God, and sanctified by songs of praise. When the moon revealed its countenance, he tried to become one with it as at the time of conjugal union. Had he blessed Miriam and touched her hair, then the sun, who had displaced its mistress, would fall into shame and the beginning of the Redemption would have arrived.

For twelve months after this Nathan sat locked in his room in self-affliction, worshipping God alone and devoting himself to the ancient goddess. . . .[29]

The "merits of the fathers," it would seem, helped this extraordinary author prevent the expressionism of his writing from destroying the structure of the novelettes. From within the stream of tragic myth can be heard the voice of the author himself, in the same way that the voice of the biblical author can be heard in the narratives of the Creation, of the Flood, of the wanderings of the patriarchs, and of the dreams and adventures of Joseph. Something restrains the author from venturing into teleological writing, from being swept away by the current of his visions, from being storm tossed beyond the "fiftieth gate" in the psychological complexes of his characters. As it draws to a close, each section of *In the Heart of the Thunder* and *Miriam* is vividly marked by this restraint. It would seem that initially the author determined to carry his investigations to the bitter end, but a heavenly hand restrains him. Instead, he compromises with some proverb, saying, or allusion such as "And the matter was sinful for the congregation" or "Enough of this." Or, alternatively, the author hints at some prohibition he must abide by, of which we hear some faint echo of his sorrow at this game of life and death played by his characters.

These literary obstacles to his final revelation of the "characters in search of an author" also formed the source of Berdichevsky's own tragic feeling. Throughout his life he clearly longed to write a great novel of world literature, but he managed no more than a novelette. He seemed to shrink back from the enormous range of the great novel lest he founder in aesthetic storms. He was compelled, therefore, to cultivate brevity, to cut down his stories to fit the bounds dictated to him by his literary sense. The brevity in his writings did not arise from any literary weakness but rather from the richness of his psychological insights into mankind. Had his writing submitted unconditionally to this insight, the latter would have restricted the artistic value of the work as a whole by destroying all realism with the force of the characters' inner drives. The brevity in his novels was an extension of the "bookish" veiling in literature that he himself had attacked so violently in his essays.

Perhaps here may be found the solution to the problem of Berdichevsky. Eventually he too admitted the validity of a certain "bookishness" in writing. He delved, peeped in, and was not harmed. He looked at the Jewish world and saw that its future depended largely upon its moral thinking, whereby its aesthetic sense could be raised to the level of artistic creativity. He set this morality as a watchdog for his own literary work to ensure that it should not break through its natural bounds. In this way he succeeded in integrating his literary struggles with the ancient cultural heritage of the Jewish people.

Itzhak Dov Berkovitz: A Vivid Realism

Berdichevsky's nickname, "the outcast," was employed not only by his rivals in the school of Ahad ha-Am; he himself used to insist upon it as symbolizing the difference of outlook that led him to oppose the ideologies accepted among Jews during this period of social and national reawakening. In his critical writings he dealt harshly with the "new way" in Hebrew literature of the late eighties and early nineties. It is true that Berdichevsky himself published important stories and articles through the publishing house of Tushia owned by Ben-Avigdor, the leading writer of this new trend, which had departed from the traditions of Mendelé to create a new realism tending at times to naturalism. The term "new trend" was coined by Reuben Brainin, who was at that time involved in the general European Decadent movement and was trying to introduce its aesthetic ideals into Hebrew literature. In his concern for flowery superficialities, he showed clearly how little he understood the needs of contemporary Jewry. Certainly Brainin was justified in his desire to rid the Hebrew poet and author of the didacticism inherited from the Enlightenment, for his generation was experiencing a cultural ferment that could no longer bear the yoke of the Enlightenment. Various phenomena of Jewish history that the Enlightenment had regarded as culturally inferior, including the Kabbalah and Hasidism, had been taken up by such writers as Peretz, Berdichevsky, and Yehudah Steinberg as noble sources of literary inspiration. Moreover, the Jew had begun to be aware of a new sense of importance in private and public life, a new sense of individuality, so that the prose of Mendelé Mokher Sefarim, for all the flexibility of its satirical sentimentality, could no longer suffice for him.

Brainin was so impressed by his idea of introducing "the beauty of Japhet into the tents of Shem" and was so devoted an admirer of the new Aesthetic movement of European literature that he simply piled exaggeration upon exaggeration in his lavish praise of the movement, until he lost all touch with the real state of contemporary Jewish art and his influence as a critic rapidly waned. He tried to open the Jewish reader's eyes to the inner world of the writer in his search for a literary form that would satisfy his needs and to show that the writer, like any other artist, suffers from psychological complexes demanding a literary outlet; at times, therefore, there would be contradictions in his attitude to man, to life, and to nature.[30] In the course of this effort, however, Brainin employs such exaggerations as the following: "A great author releases mankind or, at least, his countrymen from the manacles of tradition and custom, while on the other hand he enslaves them, robbing them of their freedom of thought and feeling so that all have to pay him a mental tax whether they are aware of it or not."[31] This is an inversion of the view of the Enlightenment; Brainin is here substituting art for everyday utility, a tendency that became increasingly marked in his writings. He described how the artist "compels" men "to see the world through his eyes, to hear everything with his ears, to write and speak in a style similar to his own. If every man is a little world in himself, then the creative writer is a universe containing heavens above and abysses beneath and an infinite number of riddles." Nevertheless, the "new trend" of Hebrew literature in the final decade of the nineteenth century did not follow Brainin. On the contrary, the ordinary man in the street and his "little world" became the hero of Hebrew prose. Berdichevsky regarded Brainin's autocratic approach, together with all the realism of Ben-Avigdor, as a serious threat to the development of Hebrew literature, and he attacked them vigorously.[32]

Yet neither Berdichevsky nor his younger colleagues were the ones to decide the future direction of Hebrew literature at the beginning of the twentieth century. Their work has only been truly recognized in our own day, when modern criticism has paid them their due, most of all in Israel. The turbulent generation of Jews at the end of the nineteenth century needed a literature infused with the everyday realism of the Jewish world, and at the same time penetrating into the very depths of the individual. Ben-Avigdor, the founder of Tushia, which did so much for the development of Hebrew prose, poetry, and essays, was the first writer to put this trend into effect. Unlike Berdichevsky, in whose writings the Jewish shtetl is always depicted as clothed in silence and deep in self-contemplation, Ben-Avigdor offered a naturalistic description of the market place of the Jewish shtetl, whose spiritual squalor and ineradicable poverty are expressed with intense realism. Within this world the author picks out this or that character to reveal the individual light hidden within him. Ben-Avigdor does this with Leah the Fishwife and the other characters who people his short stories.[33] This literary technique, which found many imitators among contemporary writers and those of the following generation, rejected the naturalistic style of Mendelé—a style delightful for its own sake, without any psychological insights into the characters as individuals and hence lacking in tragic implications. At the same time, it was far removed from the somewhat exaggerated emotionalism and pessimistic fatalism of Berdichevsky.

Ben-Avigdor's naturalism is sometimes harsh, creating a rift between the ugliness of Jewish life in the town on the one hand and the complete beauty of the individual's world on the other. Then the style seems to desert the atmosphere of mingled light and shade that pervades the rest of his literary work. This harsh naturalism, however, began to soften until it approached a realism infusing the external details of the characters' microcosms with a deeply tragic anticipation, lending an epic quality to the leading figures. In the history of Hebrew literature during that era one can identify as followers of Ben-Avigdor such writers as Y. Goida, with his idealization of the love of the Torah in his realistic writings, and Alexander Siskind Rabinowitz, who responded sensitively to the social aspects of the various "classes" within the Jewish town. F. Lakhover has described very successfully what distinguished Rabinowitz from his colleagues at the close of the nineteenth century.

> Rabinowitz, more than any other member of the "new trend," offered in certain of his stories written during that period a new type of hero, and the new spirit within society. His stories do not contain the realism they had announced as their aim, but they do possess a healthy simplicity of observation which at times reaches the level of great art. In "The Rich Man's Daughter" Rabinowitz created a delicate and lifelike character; if he did not present all her psychological conflicts, he did describe the clash between her and her environment, between her and her parents—in fact, between the younger generation and the old. This too was one of the aims of the "new trend"—to highlight the contrast between the old and the new, to describe the new hero battling with the past, and to describe the new fashions of society.[34]

If we combine Ben-Avigdor's naturalistic description of the market place in all its ugliness and his somewhat exaggerated idealization of the rather dull, poverty-stricken individuals in it with Rabinowitz's attempt to depict the clash between the generations at the close of the nineteenth century, we shall understand the new vitality in Hebrew literature that Mendelé had never known and that was certainly unknown to the satirical school of Joseph Perl, Itzhak Erter, Abraham Mapu, and Peretz Smolenskin. In fact, Hebrew literature had moved toward the realism that had dominated Russian literature during the second half of the nineteenth century. In the latter we meet vivid descriptions of the social background and all the economic, religious, and cultural problems that constituted the world of the day. The individual character emerges from this environment as the focal point of the story. Although his entire existence depends upon his environment, each character fights against it, is influenced by it, is raised to the peak of his individuality by it, or else fails in his struggle and is destroyed by it. Yet Ben-Avigdor failed to achieve a sufficiently high artistic level to compete with Berdichevsky's description of the Jewish town. Indeed, his failure was shared by others, including Rabinowitz, I. L. Katznelson ("Buki ben Yogli") in his visionary tales,[35] Reuben Asher Broides, I. Levontin in his Zionist stories, and Bershadsky in his realistic novels. It was not long, however, before a second pillar of literature rose next to Berdichevsky—Itzhak Dov Berkovitz, the son-in-law of Shalom Aleikhem and an author of extraordinary realistic powers.

The theme of Berkovitz's finest stories was the same as that of Berdichevsky and his satellites, Gnessin, Feierberg, Shoffman, Brenner, and Hillel Zeitlin: a sense of isolation. In Berkovitz's case, however, the subjective element was completely lacking; the author had no need to find an outlet for his own inner pressures and his writing is less highly charged than that of Feierberg and Gnessin, or of Zeitlin with his religious yearnings. The exception, of course, is Shoffman, whose writings were entirely unique in Hebrew literature at the beginning of the century. Berkovitz was not given to those raging inner conflicts that beset the other young writers, nor did he follow the same literary technique as Berdichevsky, who employed myth to introduce into Hebrew literature the new trends of European writing. Berkovitz concentrates exclusively on the reality of society and the accurate depiction of the environment from which his central characters grow, and there is no connection between his subject matter and his own biography. Not one of his stories of isolation can be interpreted as ambivalent, as concealing within its plot a reconstruction of the author's own life. He does not play the general game of literary hide and seek. The historical, social, and psychological background of the story is brought out vividly in Berkovitz's writings, as is the tragic condition of the hero and his relations to those around him. In other words, Berkovitz's intense realism is rooted

148

in the great literature of the nineteenth century. This distinguishes him not only from such writers as Feierberg and Gnessin (although he is in some ways close to Shoffman), but also from Brenner, who regarded himself, or was regarded by critics, as a complete realist.

In fact, the sense of isolation in Berkovitz's stories is really to be compared with that of Berdichevsky. For Berdichevsky had chosen the Jewish town in the Ukraine as the subject matter most suited to his literary needs, while Berkovitz was drawn to his own Jewish town in Lithuania. Moreover, Berkovitz saw the Jew as cut off from his roots in much the same way as did Berdichevsky. Yet where Berdichevsky ignored the traditional "bookishness" Judaism had accumulated through the ages, and hence did not acknowledge the artistic realism of the Jewish cultural environment, Berkovitz used this environment as the background for his literary work. Berdichevsky regarded it as his task to strip his characters of their social, economic, and cultural problems in order to highlight their longings for the archetypal roots obscured by literary "bookishness." Berkovitz, however, saw the inner struggles of the individual Jew as part of the changes occurring in his social condition, and he devoted his stories to illuminating these struggles. The two were alike in wanting modern Hebrew literature to depict the Jewish world as it really was, and both raised Hebrew prose to the peak of its achievement in the short story. The one who came closest to the epic tradition was Berkovitz.

An analysis of Berkovitz's prose style reveals at once a quality typical of his epic intent—the language of the narrator makes no attempt to convey the actual experience of the isolation of the character as Berdichevsky had tried to do in his novelettes. Berkovitz is not interested in freeing his writing of its indirect form, of the fact that it "relates" past events and that the narrator himself gives the motif of isolation its literary form. His style makes abundantly clear from the very beginning that the experiences of his hero and the literary form of the narration are two entirely separate things. The emotions of Dr. Winik in "The Uprooted" and the literary presentation of these emotions remain legitimately independent. The narrator informs us of Winik's suffering, but the language in which he does so is not itself marked by that suffering. The author recognizes the suffering and knows how to relate it, and the objectivity that results from this dichotomy lends to Berkovitz's writing an epic quality.

One of the outstanding achievements in Berkovitz's work is his creation of individualized characters marked by a deep tragic quality, although, unlike Berdichevsky, he does not depart from the historical context of Judaism, which Berdichevsky's followers had attacked. The hero in Berkovitz's stories is always subject to a tragic struggle with the social, economic, and religious problems that beset him in the market place, at home, and in the synagogue of the Jewish village, and yet his individual tragedy is no less intense than that of Berdichevsky's characters. On the contrary, the very realism of the Jewish scene, which Berdichevsky had regarded as superficial, obscuring the primitive, archetypal element beneath and creating mere illusions of reality, served Berkovitz as a means of depicting the various levels of tragedy within that spiritual isolation, and provided him with the basis for his best stories. Furthermore, by stressing the artistic significance of this everyday reality, Berkovitz succeeded in dispensing with the exaggerated naturalism whereby Ben-Avigdor and his colleagues had contrasted the ugly, squalid market place with the nobility of the individual within it.

In every one of Berkovitz's stories of isolation the private and public domain have equal force and there is always a mingling of light and dark in the "history" of the individual within his social setting. In this, Berkovitz was an innovator, revealing the spiritual depths of his characters within the everyday world of Jewry at the beginning of the twentieth century and finding in it artistic material that did not need the digressions so typical of the writings of Berdichevsky, Feierberg, Gnessin, and even Brenner. Where Berdichevsky's digressions from the Jewish scene tended toward erotic mythology alone, in Berkovitz's work the tragic isolation of his heroes takes a number of different forms, dependent upon various social movements in the Jewish world. I need cite only three or four instances, which are to be found in "Feivka's Day of Judgment," "Cut Off," and "The Uprooted."[36]

Itzhak Dov Berkovitz

In "Feivka's Day of Judgment" one can sense Berkovitz's struggle to free himself from the neo-romanticism of Peretz's school (particularly visible in the latter's "Hasidism"), and to base his writing on the firmly realistic depiction of the Jewish shtetl without ignoring the inner struggles of the individual. The plot of this story is reminiscent of the opening of Sholem Ash's "The Country Tzaddik," and its main idea recalls a number of stories by Peretz; in addition, the style frequently adopts the tone of the aggadah as used by Peretz and Ash. The opening of the story relates the history of a country lad named Feivka, the son of Matit the blacksmith, who, although he did not even know how to recite his prayers, longed for God and yearned to approach him and speak to him, particularly during the High Holy Days, when God's presence seemed to be near him in every breath of the wind. Berkovitz is extremely cautious about the literary problem he set himself in this story—how this primitive character, with no ability for expressing his religious longings, would cope with yearnings greater than he could bear. The author struggles to avoid underplaying the cruel circumstances of the youngster as had Sholem Ash in his pseudo-hasidic "Country Tzaddik" or Peretz in his "Hear O Israel."

> Feivka used to spend most of the summer and autumn in the forest near the village together with other young scamps, gathering mushrooms and truffles, climbing the tall trees, and shooing away the storks quietly nesting in the topmost branches. Or he would spend his time in the ditches, wading up to his knees in water and searching for black slippery eels and other such creatures. He would race back and forth like a colt across the meadows at harvest time beneath the hot summer sky, scramble up a cart laden with fodder, and leap from the top, yelling hoarsely to his friends in wild exultation.[37]

This descriptive prose is much closer to Shalom Aleikhem's story of Mottel ben Peisi the Cantor than to the style of Peretz. Yet it is much weightier than Shalom Aleikhem's since it cannot break out into humor as his does. Nevertheless, this realism creates its own momentum, making sentence surge after sentence in the description of the primitivism in Feivka until it achieves of itself a certain solemnity; and then a striking change occurs which echoes Peretz's *The Voice of the People*.

151

Sometimes it happened that Feivka disappeared from sight, so that even at night his whereabouts were not known. But his father and mother, the blacksmith Matit and his wife, took no notice and did not reprove him. For the curse of God rested on the lad, as wild and unruly as a desert pony, growing up without religion or teaching.[38]

This more solemn tone occurs a number of times in the first two chapters of the story. The realistic, everyday description of Feivka, filled with almost naturalistic details of this primitive character, hides the narrator from the reader until the beginning of the third chapter, when the youngster longs to join the congregation and stand for judgment before God in the synagogue. Perhaps it is because the narrator effaces himself during the realistic descriptions that he deserts the descriptive style for a more solemn tone, to draw the reader's attention to a tragic quality audible within. In effect, the more solemn tone functions similarly to that of the chorus in Greek tragedy, which interprets the action to the spectator by means of its foreknowledge of what is hidden in the future. In the same way that the classical chorus "volunteers" from time to time to explain to the audience the tragic destiny of the actors upon the stage, so does Berkovitz in passages such as the following, from the opening of the second chapter of the story.

Days and years passed, summer followed winter and winter summer. Feivka grew up and was a lad of nine, his face marked and scratched, a red scar slashing his upper lip, his bare feet coarsened and torn, unlike the feet of other children—a wild, unruly youngster with the curse of God upon him. So passed the last summer, and autumn arrived.[39]

The second chapter moves more slowly, filled with the wonder beginning to stir in Feivka's heart and with a vague sense of some terrible approaching change. Anyone interested in investigating psychological implications would find sufficient material in this chapter to show that Berkovitz was struggling to free himself from the artificialities of Peretz's neo-romanticism and from the melodrama of his disciple Sholem Ash. If one analyzes a further passage from this chapter, the point at which the author almost removes the outward primitivism of Feivka and endows him for the first time with a deep response to his inner longings, one finds above all that the basic theme typical of Berkovitz's stories and the source of their vitality is the motif of isolation: "Feivka said nothing and again followed his father submissively, like a dumb lamb."

His submission, the acceptance of his punishment, is characteristic of other stories in which Berkovitz speaks in his own voice, such as "Cut Off" and "The Uprooted." Berkovitz provides Feivka with an insight he would never have been able to express had he not sensed that he was about to appear before God: "Feivka gazed ahead and guessed that they were going toward that distant place where the pale edge of the sky meets the earth, bathed in a pure radiance." In this vision we again hear echoes of Peretz's "Hasidism" and of Ash's "Country Tzaddik": "There, on a high mountain, sits God, a gray-haired old man wearing a large, broad sheepskin, and everyone approaches Him, and He asks. . . ." Yet at that very moment, Berkovitz realizes that he is tending to the melodramatic; accordingly he introduces the restraint of mundane realism and thereby draws the second chapter to its close. From that point on he presents his hero in terms of an isolation that overcomes the primitive elements within Feivka, an irremediable and total isolation. Here Berkovitz achieves his artistic triumph, finding within this psychological realism a new literary independence.

After the third chapter, "Feivka's Day of Judgment" concentrates on Kol Nidré and the following Yom Kippur, the Day of Atonement, in the small synagogue Feivka attends. At this point Berkovitz is faced by an artistic problem far more difficult than those of "Cut Off" and "The Uprooted," which will be dealt with later. In these two stories, the theme of isolation arises spontaneously from the realistic setting. In the story of Feivka, however, there is a certain monolithic primitivism that remains untouched by any mingling of the outer and inner worlds. The purpose of the realism here is to place a restraining hand on the story lest it fall into the more vague impressionism of the earlier chapters; the author wants to depict instead the true quality of Feivka's experience. Therefore, the realism is intended to highlight the desperate inner struggle in the synagogue (which eventually leads to his suicide) between Feivka's primitivism and the spark of spiritual light deep in his soul that lends to his character the tragic nobility shared by most of Berkovitz's heroes. For this purpose the author provides the opening of this section with a descriptive and detailed realism that, taken out of its context, clearly echoes the humor by which Shalom Aleikhem conveys his love of Jewry.

> Each of the worshippers was trying to raise his voice above the level of those around him and to outdo them all in the task of praying. The Jews living in the outlying villages are simple people who do not understand the efficacy of silent prayer. They are not accustomed to praying together with a congregation during the rest of the year; they are remote from the Holy One and from sacred affairs. Consequently, when Yom Kippur comes round in all its solemnity, they gird up their loins and prepare to accomplish in one fell swoop what they missed during the remainder of the year. They make a frontal attack on the Almighty, each for himself and yet in a concerted drive in order to force Him to notice them, and their prayer storms heavenward.[40]

Yet the realism is not inserted here to be enjoyed for its own sake. Berkovitz uses it as a means of making Feivka's inner struggle audible, of removing the inarticulateness that hampers him on this Day of Judgment. Detached from the prayers offered up by the Jews around him, which satisfy their spiritual needs, and driven inward by the response these prayers arouse in his inner world, Feivka suddenly becomes transformed into a tempest that could sweep aside everything in its path. No other story by Berkovitz achieves this staccato effect, the reflection in language of the emotional experience of the central figure.

> Feivka stood among these enthusiastic worshippers alone, a stranger. The stormy prayers, chanting, wailing, and lament swept over him in waves. An oppressive heaviness pulled at his heart and spots of fire flashed before his darkened eyes.

As the description proceeds, Berkovitz succeeds in arousing a sense of great expectancy, and the stormy raging gradually subsides as he prepares for the great revelation that will break the dam of Feivka's primitivism. Within the tense staccato, which makes the reader almost hold his breath, can suddenly be discerned a delicate lyricism presaging the revelation—a revelation that illumines Feivka's soul for one brief moment and then disappears, leaving an infinitely more depressing sense of isolation. Berkovitz was perhaps the first modern Hebrew writer who had the ability to achieve the wonderful flexibility of style necessary to accelerate or restrain the movement of his prose without those literary mannerisms employed by Peretz in his *Hasidism,* the melodrama of Sholem Ash, or the techniques employed by Berdichevsky in his novelettes and folkloristic writings, as well as by his younger colleagues.

The realism in Berkovitz's writings never attempts to rise above the day-to-day world of his heroes or to disappear beyond the horizons of the Jewish environment. Nevertheless, it does in its own peculiar way penetrate into the inner world of Feivka, still obscured beneath his primitive qualities. This inarticulate soul has never grasped what is oppressing and disturbing him and consequently is torn by an inner turmoil as he stands among the country Jews, all of whom know quite definitely what is theirs "by right" and forcefully demand from God that He grant them their "rights." Then Feivka's soul is suddenly illumined by a revelation, described in the direct language of Berkovitz as the opening of something tremendously significant in his life, even if he has not yet found words to express it. But the vision disappears, and again his soul is shut in and imprisoned. The feeling of hopeless isolation on which the splendid light of great tragedy has shone for a moment grows stronger as the passage continues.

> He remained standing there lost and confused among the worshippers, waiting for something extraordinary to happen, when there was a movement in a corner of the synagogue. The white curtain in front of the Ark was drawn aside, and a majestic, white-haired old man moved forward, taking from it a white, round object draped in a garment embroidered with gold thread and resembling a baby in swaddling clothes. The gold thread sparkled in the light of the candles, reflecting its color onto the silvery beard of the venerable old man. A thrill ran through Feivka: "At last the hour has come!" . . . But all this he saw through a whitish mist, as

though from a great distance, as he stood amidst the strange hubbub of shouting and singing. In that whitish mist the wonderful
white object suddenly vanished, even the venerable old man moving away and disappearing into the rest of the crowd. Feivka's
cheeks were aflame, his flesh tingled, and only his hands and feet
were icy cold, as if they had shed their skin.[41]

If, while reading Berkovitz's stories, one takes note of the style
he employs, it becomes clear that, with the exception of "Feivka's
Day of Judgment," the narrator generally finds a satisfactory
means of expressing himself. Berkovitz has no urge to remove
himself from the story and to convey the hero's life with vivid
directness instead of providing a narrator to relate the events at
second hand. The truth is that Berkovitz's voice can always be
heard in the story, for the style whereby he informs us of what
happens to the primitive Feivka lends his character an epic quality. In this way he individualizes Feivka, distinguishing him from
the many other Feivkas in the Jewish towns of Lithuania. In all
Berkovitz's stories dealing with the isolation of the individual, the
style of the story looks over the characters' shoulders, as it were,
gazing at their lives, examining the different levels of their existence, intelligently appraising all they possess, and identifying the
tragic quality of each and every one. Sometimes Berkovitz lifts
them up to peer at them, as if they were very amusing, with a
humor that either bubbles up from within him or echoes that of
Shalom Aleikhem's writings. In the case of the young Feivka,
there was some danger of Berkovitz's identifying himself with his
character and consequently he needed to make a special effort to
achieve his artistic success. In a story such as "Cut Off," however,
the realism comes across in its full and independent force.

The subject matter of this story is perhaps the most "historical"
of all his writings. It is set against the background of the large-
scale Jewish emigration to the United States at the beginning of
the twentieth century, and the economic, religious, and cultural
change that, for better or worse, affected the Jewish community
as a whole and the outlook of the individuals within it. Obviously, Berkovitz was not the only Hebrew author to write on this sub-

Itzhak Dov Berkovitz

ject, nor was realism the only effective means used to express it. In the following pages I shall try to discuss, however briefly, a group of writers who began to write with an impressionistic nostalgia about the Jewish shtetl, which was already seriously deteriorating and showing signs of its approaching end. Nevertheless, "Cut Off" provides a striking illustration of the historical basis of Berkovitz's realism and of the Hebrew style he uses to convey it. The opening paragraph describes the train journey of an old lady on her way to the ship that will take her to America, where her son Reuben is waiting for her, and it illustrates the epic breadth of vision and the integration of various psychological levels in Berkovitz's writings.

> The events of the journey from her peaceful village in Lithuania to distant New York were for the elderly Deborah like one long nightmare. The swift journey along the railroad tracks for days and nights on end, the tall busy stations over the border, filled with the babble of foreigners, the changing views, faces, countries, and strange tongues, the desperate rushing back and forth of the fellow Jews in her party—all this seemed like some fascinating pageant, like some tale vaguely remembered from childhood, now magically reenacted before her eyes. In her elderly imagination there flashed scenes from the past of which she had read in *Tsena-Ure'ena:* the Tower of Babel with men and women who no longer understood each other's tongue, the journey of Jacob and his sons to Egypt and their entry into the gates of a foreign city, the camps of Jewish exiles in fetters, starving with their wives and children and being led away by that butcher Nebuchadnezzar. . . .
> At night, as the dark fields sped past, there would appear on the dark windows of the carriage a vision of Rachel weeping for her mother, a picture of her dead daughter running to the rhythm of the train's wheels, her arms outstretched, her wailing blending with the screeching of the engine. . . . In the distance rose up all five of her sons and daughters who had died before her, each of them just as they had been in life. Her husband, too, rose from his grave accompanied by a host of shadowy figures, dead neighbors and friends, gazing at her from the quiet graveyard on the hill with its low white tombstones. They peeped through the green trees, nodding to her as if to say "where? Where are you running to, away from us all?" . . . Outside, beyond the ship's hull, the

157

ocean roared in its fury, and during the silence of the night the old lady lifted her spinning head like one awakening from another world, sat up, and stared at her sleeping neighbors, unable to grasp who they were, unable to understand what was happening and where fate was leading her in these closing years of her life. The only knowledge that glimmered before her in the future like a spark gleaming through the dark—her live son in America—became blurred in her mind, losing its shape and outline.[42]

This passage is probably the first in the entire compass of the Hebrew short story—and indeed in most of the rest of Hebrew prose—which arouses in the reader the feeling that here is a work of art within whose broad dimensions the tragic conflicts stretch to distant horizons. In fact, the reader's hopes are not fulfilled. The theme of "Cut Off" is superimposed on the story. The elderly lady reaches the home of her rich son in America only to find an atmosphere empty of all cultural heritage and Jewish tradition; she sees herself living a meaningless and senseless life, and realizes as each day passes that she has been irrevocably cut off, "excommunicated," from her roots. There the story ends, because it has nowhere to go—a sad omen for the future of Hebrew prose. Perhaps for that reason, whether he knew it or not, Berkovitz, like many other Hebrew authors, turned to Yiddish literature, with its more broadly epic qualities, and later, after he had settled in Palestine, deserted the theme of isolation and consequently deprived his writings of their tragic significance. At any rate, in its psychological insights and its epic realism this story presaged what heights Hebrew literature could have achieved had its future in Eastern Europe not been cut off by World War I and by the revolutions and civil wars that followed. Yet the peak of Berkovitz's literary success is to be seen in the longest of his short stories, "The Uprooted."[43]

Any serious discussion of this story must examine a fact that also applies to Berdichevsky's stories: the author never leaves the Jewish town for the larger city and its loneliness as did Gnessin, Nomberg, Brenner, and Shoffman in their writings. The central character of this story is the young Winik, who has managed to fulfill his dream of studying medicine at a university in a large city, has qualified as a doctor, and has returned to settle in his town. He regards himself as head and shoulders above his fellow villagers, who are wasting their lives in the small town. By returning to it he wishes to prove to himself how much fuller and more varied his own life is than that of all his relatives still wallowing in their squalor—that he has nothing at all in common with them and can exist in isolation. Yet this theme becomes blurred in the very opening lines of the story, and is replaced by a sense of the isolation inherent from birth in Winik's nature. True, he had "won himself a place of calm security in his home town as an energetic doctor and intellectual, welcomed in the houses of the wealthy." But the very fact that a wealthy old man who meets him one morning in the street "eagerly returns his salutation with a beaming smile" awakes in him a searing memory that had, apparently, been long hidden within him and now only at that moment come to light.

> Previously, when he was a poor youngster at the Bet-ha-Midrash, this same wealthy man had once sent him home to see whether the samovar was hot, and had told him to ask his wife to give him an apple for his trouble. The apple was small, red, and shiny. It had a special smell about it, as if from another world, the smell of the rich woman's pantry, and to this very day he loved to recall that sweet, strange smell. He kept thinking about that apple with regret. Why had he taken it from the woman? Had he not done so, his standing would be different in the rich man's eyes; he could stand more erect, more proud. . . .[44]

The feeling of regret pulsating through this passage is a psychological seed that gradually develops until it overcomes the expressed sense of isolation in Dr. Winik's personality. The social aspects symbolized by the small red apple and the patronizing tone of the rich lady form an outward facet of the Jewish scene in these villages, the mutual relationship of the various classes within the society. Berkovitz preserves this level throughout the story, especially the relationship between Dr. Winik and his brothers. The superiority that gives him an entrée into the houses of the wealthy cuts him off from their irremediable poverty and squalor. In his soul, however, Winik is gnawed by regret, for he has torn himself away from ugly roots in the hope of finding salvation in another and better world, only to discover that he is suspended in an abyss devoid of all the meaning he had hoped to find.

In fact, Berkovitz in this story is searching for a style suited to reveal the abyss of despair Winik has experienced, the remorse fermenting the personality of this young man. The regret he feels in recalling the incident of the apple arises from a deep realization that he will never escape a feeling of inferiority in the presence of the wealthy, even if they welcome him into their homes with open arms. Yet even this remorse is not as great as that which he feels at having been cut off from his true roots in the poverty-stricken world of his brothers. The former sorrow is symbolized effectively by the apple, which shows that all his success and superiority in his home town is superficial, a mere veneer. On the other hand, his regret at being parted from his brothers is infinitely more complex, and demands a totally different form of expression both in the social setting and in the depiction of the individual.

Because of the realistic quality of his writing Berkovitz did not lapse into Brenner's angry expressionism (previously discussed in connection with *Around the Point*), that dreadful guilt Brenner felt on seeing the poverty, failure, and disillusionment in the home of Davidowsky's parents. The fact that Berkovitz does not allow the narrative to adopt the style of the characters, that he will not permit it to "live" the poverty of the town and convey in its own self the suffering of Winik's brothers, is his salvation. The narrative always reflects the author's view of what is going on in Winik's heart as, through the force of circumstance, he returns to his brothers' world and becomes reintegrated into their way of life. Hence the extraordinary perceptiveness of Berkovitz's writing. Unlike Berdichevsky and his circle, Berkovitz saw no need to identify himself personally with the problems of his characters; their suffering makes no claims upon him. As a result, he achieves an epic vividness of objective perception that permeates all his stories.

The climax of "The Uprooted," which occurs in the fourth chapter, functions on a number of different levels, each interpreting in a different way the return of Dr. Winik to his brothers' world. Together they testify to the epic force of Berkovitz's writings. One of Winik's brothers falls sick and the young doctor comes to examine him. This visit underscores the gulf between him and his sick brother Shelomo. "One bright morning, after a week of wavering between hope and despair, Shelomo died." That is the way the fourth chapter begins, introducing us to the first stage of Winik's return "home."

The opening paragraph is marked by a sense of wonder as the young doctor approaches his brother's house. There he found "the neighbors who lived on the street, both men and women, already crowding sadly into the small courtyard." The neighbors themselves either sit by the house talking quietly among themselves or gaze at the beautiful garden the dead man had always tended with such loving care. Without a trace of irony or satire, Berkovitz remarks: "Their sorrow did not prevent them from talking about mundane matters; they wandered out into the street and glanced at the contents of the farm carts trundling by to see if there was anything worth buying." Winik, however, begins to see with new eyes the neighborhood and house from which he had uprooted himself years before to enter a more elevated world, free from soul-destroying poverty and suffering. Through the closed windows rise from time to time the muffled sobs of the women, and he feels a sense of wonder that on such a lovely summer's day, with the sun beating down gloriously from the pure blue heavens, "this little house should be singled out for wailing and grief by the Creator of this beautiful universe."[45]

It is worth noting that the contrast afforded by this paragraph is shared by Berkovitz with other writers. In Bialik's "City of Slaughter" the poet conveys in a similar fashion the despair that lies beyond grief, placing the reader on the brink of an abyss in the world of the Jew.[46] The uniqueness of Berkovitz lies in the fact that the contrast between the beauty of the world and "the little house singled out for wailing and grief" does not arouse in Winik a fatalistic despair and grief leading to emptiness. The wonder that Berkovitz suggests here is original insofar as it produces in Winik a deep feeling of belonging, as well as grief, even though the author never states this explicitly. Winik's wonder is thus the first step in his return to the place from which he has been uprooted. The paragraph we have quoted is the most subtle and perceptive part of the entire story.

As soon as Winik sets foot in the house where his brother lies dead, the style of the story adopts a naturalistic tone mingled with expressionism, of the type we noted in our discussion of Brenner's *Around the Point.*

> In the middle of the room a cheap straw mattress lay on the mud-trodden floor, and upon it was stretched the dead man, covered with a black overcoat. At his head burnt two candles, in a pair of rusty candlesticks. On the empty bed two old women sat sewing the shrouds, their faces fixed in an expression of annoyance at everything that was going on in the room. Around the table crowded the women, some sitting, some standing, whispering and nodding piously to each other as if such was fate and it must be accepted; the older women wiped their noses on their aprons while the younger ones used handkerchiefs. The widow of the deceased, who was pregnant, stood in a dark corner between the stove and the saucepans wailing aloud, her swollen belly shaking up and down just as if she were laughing.[47]

Nevertheless, even this description does not arise from the author's desire to reconstruct the squalor and tawdriness of the room into which the young doctor had walked as though from another world. Consequently, it is free from the constriction that affects Brenner's writing. Indeed, this description is particularly powerful in conveying the young doctor's experience, for Berkovitz introduces an ambivalence that presents the doctor as disgusted by the filth and squalor, while at the same time forced to acknowledge that he belongs within these poverty-stricken surroundings. This very ambivalence demands that the style be free of restriction and responsive in both directions. In this, then, the story differs from those of Brenner, both long and short, which aim at identifying the author with the suffering of man and fascinate him with the artistic expression of suffering and failure. Berkovitz retains his objectivity even when he finds it necessary to reveal to the young doctor, who eventually comes to examine his sick brother, a scene such as this:

In a dark corner he could discern a pregnant woman, her face puffed and pale, clutching a filthy two-year-old child in her arms. The child was sucking its thumb, its nose running profusely, and it gave the impression that instead of being held in its mother's arms it was resting securely on her swollen belly as an integral part of her body.[48]

Hidden in the folds of the story, however, are sparks of humor and irony arising not only from the situation of the characters but also from the author's response to Winik's ambivalent position. There is a fine example in the speech the author puts into the mouth of the doctor's aunt; in fact, it serves as an echo of Winik's inner monologue when he visits the houses of the wealthy.

"There's nothing to it, I tell you. That doctor of yours could give two minutes of his valuable time to his sick brother. A bagful of gold wouldn't fall out of his pocket if he was to come once, especially since he has a fine carriage of his own with bells on it and wouldn't have to tire his feet. . . . On the contrary, he'd enjoy meeting him. . . . I just don't understand him—must he only treat nobility? Are they closer relatives of his than his brother, his own flesh and blood? Why are you so scared of him? He's his brother, isn't he?. . . . That's something he can't deny, even if he wants to. He's his brother whether he likes it or not. . . ."[49]

There is clearly an echo here of Shalom Aleikhem's mingling of humor and irony, which without our noticing affects the oppressiveness building up in the atmosphere when Winik enters. Somehow he feels a pang of regret, without knowing clearly who is guilty or of what. He stands there for a long time among the people who had gathered in the house, his head swimming and heart aching, weary after many sleepless nights spent by the bedside of his dying brother. Then suddenly:

From among the younger women gazing fondly at him, as the common people are wont to do, peeped the lovely face of his cousin Malka. She looked at him gently, her eyes filled with tears; it was a caressing look that seemed to draw him to her as she smiled sadly at him, sharing in his sorrow. As he caught sight of her, his heart felt soothed and he found himself smiling back.[50]

Here the story opens a new level of realism in its description of the bereavement in the house. The language of the story seems to achieve this effect on its own, by means of the all-inclusive objective perceptiveness, responsive to the outer and inner world, recording all the levels of Winik's experience. The lonely doctor suddenly has a wonderful feeling of belonging, of striking roots. From this point on, everything becomes integrated by this feeling of belonging. The beadle of the synagogue, who has grown very old since Winik left his home environment, unconsciously relieves the intensity of grief in the house by speaking in a tone of kind sympathy and of resignation to the decision of heaven and opens the gateway to Winik's return home with the question, "Do you happen to have a cigarette, doctor? I seem to remember from long ago that you smoke. . . ."

Here is the turning point of the story. Whether deliberately or not, Berkovitz introduces into the mournful atmosphere of this chapter something of the communal bond among Jews, and this element in their poverty-stricken lives relieves Winik's loneliness as he stands in the house of his dead brother. Without all the stylistic efforts of Gnessin, Shoffman, and Berdichevsky, and with an utter simplicity of language, the story rises to artistic heights rare in the literature of isolation that I have been discussing in these chapters. As a natural part of the plot, the beadle, Yosef Shmuel, enters. It is he who takes charge of the funeral, and he who perceives that the young doctor still feels an outsider, separated from his fellow Jews. The doctor has not yet made the ritual tear in his clothes for the death of his brother. The beadle, "an awkward, stooping Jew who limped along swinging his gray beard from side to side, ambling like a heavily laden ox," helps him make the tear, and Berkovitz describes the incident with a profoundly epic simplicity.

> In Reb Yosef Shmuel's words and tone of voice could be felt a gentle fatherliness, and he made the rent in the doctor's clothing in the way that some kind person would treat a small, helpless orphan. Indeed, at that moment Winik's face wore the look of a little lost orphan—an expression of mingled gratitude and trust.[51]

Once again Berkovitz leads the story back to childhood, but the movement is a natural continuation of Winik's meeting with the wealthy man, who recalls to him the incident of the apple. Between that earlier experience and his visit to the house of mourning, however, he had to experience a number of psychological struggles, until he recognized himself as an integral part of the environment to which fate had led him back. "His university days, and the period when he had worked as a doctor far away from his home and his poor brethren from whom he had become estranged so senselessly and pointlessly" now seemed to him as merely "a strange dream" proving that he "had committed a grave and unforgivable sin." From this point on, Winik can weep with the mourners, can share in the communal grief typified by his Cousin Malka, and eventually his own weeping becomes

> a kind of confession and secret lament for a solitary, lost soul, for a confused wanderer who, uprooting himself from his birthplace, from a world that belonged to him, and going in search of foreign fields in which to strike roots, had simply lost his way in a wasteland. Now he had shamefacedly returned to his poor brethren. He looked on their poverty and lowliness and they aroused in him now as in the past a feeling of emptiness and revulsion. Yet he had to admit to himself that he too was one of them, even though he had fled from the battle when his strength failed and, like them, had lacked the vigor to fight on. . . .

There is in this passage a tone of resignation to fate that seems indirectly close in upon the town and its future. It is historical in quality and I shall examine the effect of this quality on Hebrew literature in the next chapter. At the moment I only stress that, despite the tone of despair running through the plot of the story, stylistically Berkovitz maintains an epic level. Berkovitz's voice can be heard above the story as he scrutinizes his characters, and with wise artistry he never succumbs to their feeling of isolation. On the contrary, his literary work, which takes as its pivot the theme of isolation in all its various forms, always testifies to his deep roots in literary realism. In this epic quality within his short stories Berkovitz has stood alone in Hebrew literature up to the present day.

4

The Rise of the Prose Epic

By the first decade of this century the decline of the Russian shtetl had become imminent. Its economic, social, and religious strength dwindled away, and after the collapse of liberalism in 1905 the massive Jewish emigration to America began, together with a smaller emigration to Palestine, the Second Aliyah. Only in 1917, during the first months of the Revolution and the overthrow of the czarist regime, did the Jewish settlement appear to recover its strength. Following the October Revolution and the subsequent civil war, however, the Jewish shtetl in Russia came to the end of its existence. With its disappearance, the dynamic literature motivated primarily by a sense of isolation began to decline.

Nevertheless, the downfall of the shtetl gave rise to a new form of Hebrew literature—nostalgic reminiscence, wherein the picture of the Jewish shtetl was tinged by the longings of the author for what was past and gone. This nostalgia blurred the sharpness of the vision; vague childhood memories toned down the realism, and the town was seen, as it were, through a veil from the large cities in which almost all the authors were now living. The towns were emptied of their best inhabitants, who left for a strange, alien world overseas. There is a hushed tone about these stories, a sense of subdued voices and bated breath as if one is listening to the silence of a past whose roots strike deep in the soil. In the story by Mosheh Ben-Eliezer,[1] the beadle's com-

166

ment on Rebbe Mordekhai, who is leaving for abroad, reflects the changes taking place in the Bet ha-Midrash, now deserted by its scholars and leading members. Similarly, the story by Simhah Ben-Zion is permeated by a longing for the light and shade of childhood: a little girl watches her grandparents' mingling of grief and happiness as, on the first day of Pentecost, they take the "bride" of dead Uncle Meir, the Scroll of the Law that has been written in his memory, under a wedding canopy to the synagogue.[2]

The delicate impressionism of these and similar stories introduced a pleasant lyricism into Hebrew literature; the harsh reality of the shtetl disappears as these writers gaze at the distant horizon of their origins. Yet this literature, motivated primarily by a longing for Jewish roots, was not restricted to insubstantial memories expressed in impressionistic stories, for many of the works had a realistic bent and conveyed the vivid actuality of the Jewish town. They did not shy away from detailed description of Jewish family life or class distinctions in the shtetl, but examined perceptively the traditions created by generations of Jews living within it. It is worth noting that this vein of realism is particularly strong in the writings of those who joined the Second Aliyah, leaving the shtetl forever and emigrating to Palestine because they could see no hope for a revival of Jewish creativity anywhere in the Diaspora. Perhaps it was the fact that they intended to strike new roots in the Holy Land which led them to write about the past as well as about the new Jewish scene devoted primarily to agricultural pioneering in Galilee and Ein-Ganim. Whether the authors were conscious of it or not, these new interests diverted their attention from the isolation that, in all its different forms, was the main motif of modern Hebrew literature.

There are many outstanding names in this school of writers from the Second Aliyah.[3] Some were searching for "salvation" for themselves and for the Jewish community abroad—salvation from the disappointment and despair experienced by Russian liberals and socialists after the failure of the 1905 revolution. This group included Devorah Baron, Shelomo Tzemach, Mosheh Stavsky,

Aaron Reuveni, M. Siko, Aaron Kabak, Dov Kimhi, and Asher Barash.[4] They had in common a wish to express in literary form their deeprootedness in Judaism. Some of them, like Devorah Baron, succeeded in giving their memories of family life an epic quality. These stories contain numerous levels of inner experience and present the Jew of the old Russian shtetl created anew in the settlements of Palestine. Nevertheless, the Jewish town itself dwindled in importance as a literary theme among the writers in Israel: they were, after all, dedicated to the task of ending the Jewish exile and hence the Diaspora.

For this reason, Kabak, for example, made an unsuccessful attempt to leave Jewish reminiscence behind him and create a historical novel on the theme of the Messiah, whereby the longings for the redemption of Jewry throughout the generations could find literary expression in a novel of epic dimensions.[5] Similarly, Kabak's second attempt, in which the ambitions both of the author and of Hebrew literature as a whole were largely fulfilled, provided an epic account of the life of Jesus, set against the period of the Second Temple.[6] He also planned a complete Hebrew saga, *One Family's History*, but he died before he could produce more than the first volume in the series, *In a Vacuum*.[7] Thus, the shtetl as a literary theme began to disappear a few years before World War I both in Eastern Europe itself and in the reminiscences of the pioneering Aliyah, whose whole aim was to end the Diaspora as represented by the Jewish town. The abandonment of the shtetl theme left a sort of vacuum in Hebrew writing, causing considerable concern in cultural circles; only at the outbreak of the war and the revolutions that followed was the theme replaced.

The second decade of the present century saw the complete disintegration of what had once provided the inspiration of modern Hebrew literature: the Jewish settlement in Russia was totally destroyed by the Revolution and civil war. The previously Jewish towns in Russia, Poland, and Lithuania were almost emptied of their Jewish inhabitants due to emigration to America during the first few years of the century, the trek to the larger cities in the same countries, and the illegal immigration to Palestine. Although a surge of activity in Hebrew poetry occurred in the nineteen twenties, a deep silence fell upon Hebrew prose in Eastern Europe, as if it had nothing more to say. The younger Hebrew poets attempted to express their world in apocalyptic terms, employing myth to symbolize the destiny of the Jewish people. For this reason, their verse had a modernistic quality during the twenties and thirties.

Prose, however, in its continual search for a literary form suited to express the sense of isolation within the shtetl, did not achieve its full epic power before the outbreak of World War I, nor did it have great artistic standing at the time of European Jewry's final collapse. The original home of Hebrew prose in Russia, Poland, and Lithuania was no more, and there was now a danger that this prose would itself die out completely; but there arose two redeemers who provided it with a new impetus infinitely superior in psychological insight and epic dimensions to that which Hebrew prose had previously possessed. The two redeemers were Haiyim Hazaz and Shmuel Yosef Agnon. Whether consciously or not, they provided a remedy for the modern Hebrew epic. Hazaz came from the Ukraine and Agnon was from Galicia, but both emigrated to Palestine. Together they opened new vistas into the past and the future, and each in his own way began weaving an epic work that took as its central pivot the survival of the Jewish people.

The Fiction of Haiyim Hazaz

The stories of Hazaz are not laid out on the broad canvas of plots and narration that had become familiar in the realistic literature of Europe. At a first and superficial glance, most of them more or less resemble those short stories published in Hebrew at the end of the nineteenth century, when the novels of the Enlightenment began to disappear before the "New Trend" of Feierberg, Gnessin, Shoffman, Brenner, and Berdichevsky. A more careful examination, however, reveals an important fact: Hazaz's stories are all unified by the author's grasp of history, whether they deal with the Jewish town in the Ukraine during the Revolution and civil war, with the Yemenite communities in Palestine, or with the ingathering of the exiles from all corners of the world and their inner and outer struggles to become adjusted and achieve mutual understanding. By means of this historical grasp, the fictional writings of Hazaz succeed in weaving an epic tapestry.

His themes are many and varied, from the almost pastoral idyll of *In a Forest Settlement,* through *The Concealed Puddle,* a comic depiction in the style of Mendelé of the economic, social, and spiritual life of the Jews, to his study of the Yemenite Jews in their quarters in Tel Aviv and in their native Sanaa itself in *She Who Dwelleth in Gardens* and *Ya'ish.* Eventually he found his fullest achievement in *The Belt of Stars* and *Chained Together.* The former is a magnificently illuminating study of the ingathering of the Jews from all parts of the world (and of the spiritual strength of the individual Jew wherever he may be), while *Chained Together,* a story devoted to the terrorists fighting in Palestine against the British mandatory government, tells of two people sentenced to death, a Polish and a Yemenite Jew. These two stories, *The Belt of Stars* and *Chained Together,* illustrate, each in its own way, the epic quality of Hazaz's writing.

There is a certain problem, however, in Hazaz's work that sometimes confuses the reader. Unless one possesses a certain key to his writings, it is easy to make a serious error and to imagine that one has entered the realm of Mendelé Mokher Sefarim's "fine creatures." Hazaz never isolates his stories from economic, social, and spiritual problems, and when he comes to discuss them in the setting of the Ukrainian shtetl—the topic of his revolutionary stories—a certain irony creeps into his narrative which occasionally lends it a touch of the comic grotesque. In *The Concealed Puddle* the author not only writes of the depressing conditions in the town, with all their appeal to our sentiments, but also provides a naturalistic description of the characters' gesticulations and grimaces which is unsuited to the revolutionary theme that serves as the basis of the story.[8] The characters are remnants of another world, a world that ended with the cruelty of the Revolution. The descriptions of their gestures and grimaces make them seem disembodied and rob them and their environment of all meaning.

Haiyim Hazaz

Hence arises the comic element in all his stories, despite the sympathy that both author and reader feel for the characters themselves. Nor is this true only of the stories dealing with Ukrainian Jewry during the Revolution, for it applies also to his great work *Ya'ish,* which deals with Yemenite Jewry and the individuals within it (although it is true that in this work the effect of the grotesque is somewhat weakened by the more exotic atmosphere). The reader who is unaware of the very serious artistic purpose that permeates the work of Hazaz may erroneously imagine that he is once again in the Jewish world of Mendelé.

Nevertheless, this reaction is soon nullified by a wonderful sensation aroused with growing effect as one reads through the stories. The author's purpose becomes increasingly clear: even though each story is set in its own era, and the plot and characters are dependent upon that particular era, the characters are all (at least to the eye of an experienced reader) profoundly aware of their place in Jewish history. This awareness seems to well up over the banks of that era and join the stream of Israel's historic destiny throughout the ages, and the reader catches a glimpse of a much broader landscape. The disembodied Jewish atmosphere within the stories of the Revolution or in *Ya'ish* becomes filled with a vision of the future, a vision that unites all of Hazaz's stories as part of a Jewish epic despite their differences in plot. The grotesque element borrowed from Mendelé disappears in the face of this epic vision, which lends to the writings of Hazaz a quality Hebrew literature had not known for many generations.

The first aspect of this innovation is that the theme of isolation, which had motivated Hebrew literature from the end of the nineteenth century up to the time of the Russian Revolution, no longer serves Hazaz as the cornerstone of his writings. Only at rare intervals do his stories deal with the Jewish intelligentsia, whether in the shtetl or the big city, as had those of Gnessin, Brenner, and the other writers concerned with the psychological isolation of their characters in search of some lost reality. For the most part Hazaz is concerned with the common people of the Ukrainian Jewish town, and in them he finds the material for his literary work. Above all, he sees the Jews as devoid of all eco-

171

nomic, social, and cultural standing, dominated by the commissar —a petty ruler generally originating from the poverty-stricken back streets of town. It is he who acts in the name of the Revolution without understanding its aims and nature, and who is directed by a single thought: now is the time for the people at the top to descend to the bottom and those at the bottom to rise to the top. However, beyond the new poverty into which the Revolution had plunged the Jews by destroying the sources of their livelihood and imposing upon them new masters drawn from the lowest levels of the town together with the need to crawl abjectly and grotesquely before them—beyond all this there pulsates among the Jews a wonderful comradeship arising from their faith in the true redemption that would soon come to them from somewhere. Hazaz creates his characters from this comradeship, which serves as the motivating force in his stories, whether they deal with the Jewish village in the Ukraine, the Jewish quarter in the Yemenite city of Sanaa, or the city of Tel Aviv.

The poor Jews in all of Hazaz's stories form the main substance of the tapestry and are united in their inner beings. In *The Belt of Stars* and *Chained Together* there is an epic, tragic quality in their struggles for communal and individual survival as Jews. There the irony that runs through the narrative strikes the reader entirely differently from that of Mendelé's stories about the Jewish poor. It is not the result of any negative attitude on the part of the author toward his poor characters, but is rather the result of an ambivalence that grasps two levels. One is the comic element in the wretched condition of the Jews from the towns of the Ukraine who come to the immigration centers in Eretz Israel, where the problems of integration are almost insurmountable. On the other level Hazaz grasps the tragic nobility of those characters in their dreams and struggles for survival as individuals and communities. The irony eventually disappears in the epic quality of the work as a whole. The different levels in Hazaz's writing often seem to be separate, at times even contradictory, but at the end they come together by means of that comradeship in the real world which only an epic could succeed in relating. This basis overcomes all the contradictions and contrasts

172

existing between the stories, transforming them, despite their many differences, into variations upon the theme of awaiting the redemption.

A striking instance of this ambivalence, and one that arouses strong reactions because of its strangeness and unconventionality in relation to the world of the hero, is the story "The Sermon," which is almost a monologue. Yudké the pioneer has been a member of a kibbutz for many years, and is one of the silent types occasionally found among the members of the Second Aliyah, who immigrated in the first decade of this century, or of the Third Aliyah, who came in the twenties. He never expressed an opinion at kibbutz meetings, either on factual matters concerning the kibbutz or on matters of ideology. He seemed to keep everything closed up within himself, vague thoughts that could never find verbal expression. Once, however, Yudké is suddenly impelled to release a stream of words, not on a matter under discussion at a kibbutz meeting but because of some inner ferment that drives him to deliver a sermon on a most peculiar and ominous topic—the negative aspects of Jewish history throughout the generations. His words fall like fire and brimstone upon the astonished heads of his listeners. It appeared that day by day, hour by hour, words had been closed up within him until, in his silent loneliness, they had fused into one burning thought that his self-control could no longer contain and that now made an irreparable breach in his silence. In this soliloquy Hazaz finds it unnecessary to offer any description at all of the speaker's outward appearance. Yet on first reading he emerges as a comic, grotesque figure unlike any in all the literature of isolation discussed in the previous chapters.

Nevertheless, one Israeli critic, who is known for his religious outlook (inherited from C. G. Jung, T. S. Eliot, and many others in German and American literature), finds in "The Sermon" evidence of a remorse gnawing at the author because of the "secular" nature of his stories. In other words, this critic argues, the story, without the author realizing it, suddenly slaps Hazaz in the face and says, "The national history of Jewry lacks all ultimate meaning unless it bears the stamp of religious rites and of a religious outlook." This critic uses the same approach in dealing with Bialik's poetry, as well as the rest of modern literature, and it derives less from his own religious outlook than from the religious element that crept into literary criticism in the West as a result of the modernism of the twenties and thirties.

A sensitive reader, however, will respond to what really happens in "The Sermon." The sudden outburst of Yudké the pioneer, an outburst combining violent denial of faith with a cry for mercy, a groan of despair, and a plea of profound and irremediable loneliness, serves as the author's commentary on his own ambivalent tendencies. It is as if Hazaz were saying: "Here we have a Jew whose sense of belonging to Jewish history weighs upon him unbearably, eventually driving him to despair." Yet all this only shows how loyal Yudké was to Jewish history, both for its intrinsic quality and through his personal sense of destiny. At the very moment he seems to be rejecting history, he is walking toward it as the only meaningful part of his individual existence. Therefore, it is clear that for all the psychological turmoil of "The Sermon," the author's epic view of history pervades the whole story, as it does the rest of his works. There is just a touch of irony, suggesting that the author is writing not only about Yudké the pioneer but also about himself. The irony lends a tragic note to the entire story: at the very moment when Yudké's outburst tears Jewish history apart, the meaningfulness of that history invades the narrative itself. This stylistic element casts considerable light on Hazaz's literary techniques.

From this epic viewpoint, Hazaz's play *At the End of Days* parallels "The Sermon."[9] At the play's climax Joseppa demands that the last Jewish house in the Diaspora be burned down as the first and last condition for the coming of the Messiah. Like Yudké in "The Sermon," he too yearns for the "ending" of Jewish history in the grief-stricken Diaspora, and the play as a whole, like the story, pulsates with the fatefulness of that history, with a meaningfulness that was to raise to epic heights a story he wrote some years later, *Chained Together.*

All this accounts for Hazaz's unique style, which reflects this literary ambivalence. True, his language grew out of the rich soil of the Mishnah, but it never becomes a standardized vehicle for his writings. Like the language of the Mishnah it opens new perspectives of sight and sound, adapting itself to whatever it describes. It never, however, adopts the Mishnah's authoritative tone. In fact, the author frequently deviates from it in spirit, sharpening his own style like a keen instrument to describe in modern terms the world of the Jew in all its varied forms. He seems to strip off the ephemeral, more comic aspects of his Jews, penetrating into their deep, inner world, and his language assumes the task of expressing their united trust in the future redemption. By means of his language, Hazaz succeeds in drawing man to man, community to community, and story to story until they form a single "belt of stars." Only the period of the ingathering of the exiles, with all its struggles and suffering, with all its grotesqueness and yet its historic sense of destiny, could transform that "belt" into a powerful epic.

As the nineteen-sixties approached, Hazaz's writing began to lose its ambivalent viewpoint and gain in epic quality. His collection of stories, *The Belt of Stars,* published by Am Oved ten years after the state of Israel came into being, did, it is true, deal with a number of themes examined in his earlier stories, such as "A Flowing River" with its study of the Jewish shtetl at the time of the Revolution.[10] The more recent stories are, however, more epic in scope, no longer requiring the ambivalence of his previous writing or the touch of irony that had been noticeable in his narrative. The comic vein has disappeared completely from the characterization and is replaced by a profound sense of history concentrated on the sequence of events and on the realistic depiction of characters moving within the Jewish town at the time of the Revolution. The grotesque is nowhere to be seen in the individual characters, who respond either consciously or intuitively to a destiny of which they themselves form a part.

Henekh, the son of Reb Nathan Neta, has returned from Siberia, where he was exiled by the czarist regime in punishment for his socialist activities. He is bruised in body and soul, struggling with doubts that rob him of the last shreds of inner peace.

Hanka, the daughter of Reb Yehiel-Mikhel Mashbetz, listens on the one hand to her father, who draws his moral strength from the discipline of Jewish tradition and who for that very reason cannot fathom the deeper meaning of the Revolution, and on the other hand to her husband Mottel Pikelni, a tailor's apprentice whom the Revolution has raised from the backstreets and appointed as strict governor of the Jews who had once occupied the seats of honor in the synagogue. These characters do not exist in the kind of vacuum we find in Mendelé. Each is vividly drawn by the author as an individual with his own inner world. The town that provides the setting for the story is, it is true, small compared to the dimensions of the Revolution as a whole, but the events occurring there as a consequence of the Revolution provide a tragic picture of the general Jewish situation at the time.

In fact, something of each character remains with the reader after he has finished the story. Henekh the revolutionary, with his powerfully mystic thoughts brought back from Siberia, finds a place in the reader's heart, leaving, as it were, echoes of far places beyond the realms of silence. Similarly Pikelni the commissar remains in our memory. Suddenly faced by a crazy world in which the Revolution places upon him the heavy burden of changing the order of the universe, Mottel cannot grasp what has happened —why he, of all people, should be in charge of the new world. His revolutionary ideas cannot keep pace with it all, nor can he find words to cope with his new situation; and yet he is aware of the responsibility placed upon his shoulders. The same is true of Hanka, who picks her way quietly through the various paths of the Revolution, responsive to her father's religious world, her husband's search for self-expression, and, most of all to the secret beauty of her sorrow for Henekh's suffering. Each character, like the town itself, is integrated organically into the whole story, which is pervaded by the author's deep understanding of the historical and hence epic element.

The other stories in the collection reveal the same understanding. That alone endows them with the breadth of vision necessary for great art and transforms them from mere journalistic reporting of the strange customs of the oriental immigrants. Hazaz's epic sense of Jewish history places the immigrants like stars in the belt

Shmuel Yosef Agnon

that embraces the varied eras and communities of Jewry. If this is true of *The Belt of Stars*,[11] it applies even more to *Chained Together*.[12]

Chained Together deals with Menahem Halperin from Poland, a member of the Palestinian Etsel organization, and with Eliyahu Mizrahi from the Yemen, a member of the Herut, both of whom have been condemned to death by the British mandatory authorities for their terrorist activities. They are in the same cell, discussing the establishment of the state of Israel. Menahem Halperin speaks fluently, for he has spent his life in political circles where ideologies are debated, even though such language is too abstract to express the deeper emotions of the individual. Eliyahu Mizrahi, however, speaks with difficulty, as if his language comes from the mysterious distances where man may one day find expression for his inner being and its longing for a wonderful redemption for itself and for all the Diaspora in the coming of the Messiah. For this reason the words never form easily on Eliyahu's lips, but seem to hang in the air of the cell, waiting to be redeemed. However, the moment the two of them decide to blow themselves up, together with the entire prison, British guards and all, their language soars on the wings of their messianic longings. Within the cell all the generations of Jewry seem to parade before them, unified, despite their diversity of custom and habit, by their hope of messianic redemption.

The story itself glows with the splendor of these two Jews walking toward their death as if toward some glorious fate, and it is a splendor all the more remarkable since Hazaz refuses to pay any attention to the party differences that divide the state of Israel even today. The two men, so diverse and previously unacquainted, are drawn together by the part they are destined to play in Jewish history and by their act of holy martyrdom. The story is presented with the majesty and dignity that Hazaz imparts to all his pictures drawn from Jewish history.

Shmuel Yosef Agnon's Techniques of Characterization

The prose writings of Shmuel Yosef Agnon, whether they deal with past or contemporary Jewry, are always faithful to reality. His stories invariably begin with the phenomenal, everyday world and remain in it. Nevertheless, in both his short stories, such as "The Kerchief,"[13] and his broader canvases, such as *The Bridal Canopy, A Wayfarer Tarries the Night,* and *The Day Before Yesterday,*[14] there is a long stretch between the opening and the conclusion and there one finds all sorts of imaginative digressions, archetypal struggles, and internal as well as external adventures. Each story, however, remains firmly anchored in the real world and returns to it for its concluding scenes.

Indeed, at first the story seems often to be telling itself, moving of its own accord without external direction, chancing upon some incidental story that also tells itself, mingling with the main story and flowing into it, as if in the hope that something more will happen in the not-too-distant future. The reader is carried along by this stream, a little surprised but gradually becoming accustomed to this unique style. Not only does the reader begin to recognize the technique of the story within the story but he also begins to sense a unifying force that emanates from the inner traits of the hero. At the same time, he discerns the way the author really controls everything from beginning to end within the powerful movement of his stories. This technique forms the subject of this chapter, with particular reference to *The Bridal Canopy, A Wayfarer Tarries the Night,* and *The Day Before Yesterday,* Agnon's three longer novels, which together constitute, for the first time in modern Hebrew fiction, a great epic work.

The artist's eye, as I have already suggested, gazes throughout at the eternal quality of his hero's experiences, a hero who emerges in different forms in each generation, donning various guises but remaining essentially the same. In *The Bridal Canopy,* Reb Yudel Hasid wanders through the Jewish towns of Galicia, collecting charity for his daughter's dowry, and leaving her waiting with her mother and sisters in dire poverty. From town to town, and even from house to house, he meets with miracle after miracle. His ear is ever open to tales of wonders and prodigies, and, in the course of relating them, they become transformed for him from legend to reality. Instinctively he blends dream with reality and reality with dream like one window framed within another, so that both are always real to him. Chronology collapses,

178

past and present cannot cancel each other out. Everything reflects the "ultimate aim," which is itself a reality within reality, so that when Reb Yudel is collecting donations for his daughter's dowry he is also walking toward distant echoes of a coming Messiah. For the most part this "ultimate aim" takes place beyond the level of consciousness. He does not even worry about a thought that strikes him—often he intends to travel in one direction but is carried by someone or something in the very opposite direction —for in fact all his paths are aimed in the direction of the coming of the Messiah.

At this point we may sense the dialectic element in Agnon's writing, which is a mingling of midrashic discourse on the one hand and everyday actuality in a Jewish Galician town on the other, sayings of the rabbis, folktales, Jewish minstrelsy, and wonderful descriptions of the Jewish weddings of Galicia. Agnon needs them all to create the character of a hero responsive at all times to the overlapping of vision and reality in which his collection of donations for his daughter is at the same moment at movement toward the Messiah, who always is waiting "just around the corner." It is only through a character like Yudel that Agnon can write the first part of his epic trilogy, which draws upon the Jewish world of Galicia in the eighteenth century just as Mendelé Mokher Sefarim's *The Beggars' Book* relies upon the eighteenth-century Jewish world of Lithuania.

The story of *The Bridal Canopy* is set in the Galician ghetto many years before the Emancipation, and vividly evokes its atmosphere. With the joy of a true artist, the author sets about the task of describing it in detail, of grasping it almost physically. At times Agnon tends to loquacity, heaping detail upon detail until the story sounds less like a written narrative than a spoken monologue in the style of the primitive folktale, which would not at first sight seem suitable in a fully developed work of art. The reader's impression is that the flow of words has no purpose except to satisfy the author's need to talk, that his curiosity links ideas solely by spontaneous association, and that it is an endless sequence of comic and serious events connected only by the author's unconscious and unpremeditated impulse. Such was the tradition of the ancient storytellers and jesters before the authors and poets learned to master their material and create individualistic works of art. In Agnon's writing, too, one always feels the presence of a troubadour or storyteller gazing at the life of the Jews and jotting everything down on paper. For the most part he remains hidden, not showing his face openly, although his individualistic presence is felt throughout: in the questions and answers in the talmudic style, in the numerous characters that people the stories, in the tales from legend and history, in the maxims of the sages, in the realistic setting of the fictional events, and in the detailed picture of Jewish life, which reaches its climax in the description of the wedding and jesters' songs at the home of Yudel Hasid in Brod. Stylistically, *The Bridal Canopy* is intended to convey a universalistic picture of Jewry.

Moreover, Galician Jewry in the eighteenth century—generally cut off from the world at large and spiritually torn between messianism and reality, fact and dream—finds expression in the character of Reb Yudel Hasid. The community comes alive because of him. He is a character created from the world of his day, hewn out of its substance, and yet it is he who elevates that world by his partly mystical universality. The ostensible theme of the story—Yudel's journeying in search of a dowry for his daughter—takes on a deeper meaning at the various levels of Yudel's own being and becomes part of the mingling of past and future, of visions of Jewish redemption which permeated the atmosphere of the Jewish town in Galicia. Deep within him, Yudel holds fast to something that gives a profound meaningfulness to his life, something rooted in religious tradition, in halakhic and aggadic tales, in Hasidism and the popular Kabbalah, in national dreams and minstrelsy—a potpourri containing the ancient past and the distant future and in which the Galician shtetl occupies a central position. Yudel is longing, perhaps unconsciously, to embody within himself the messianic, apocalyptic visions of his people. It is this longing that creates the epic quality of Agnon's writings, as yet unparalleled in modern Hebrew literature.

In this way, the joyfulness of *The Bridal Canopy* responds to the Jewish vision implicit in it. Everything, whether on the realistic level of the Galician community or on the psychological level of inner longings and impulses, glows with an inner light, illuminating everything around it. The farther the reader proceeds in the story, the more brightly does this light shine, endowing everything with an ultimate significance. As a result, the story becomes simultaneously realistic and fantastic, reaching its climax in the gently sympathetic description of the wedding in Yudel's home, in the love of Israel that pervades the simple joy of the wedding, and in the jesters' songs in the famous Jewish city of Brod. All this endows Yudel Hasid's character with a symbolic sense whose source is the messianic vision.

Moreover, this story of Agnon's functions at two separate levels that do not seem to harmonize, a technique of characterization which links Agnon to the modernistic trends in world literature. The various levels of externality and internality intermingle with a powerful immediacy that rejects the chronological sequence of cause and effect of the nineteenth-century novel and confirms the impression of Agnon's modernistic tendencies. On the other hand, Reb Yudel Hasid is a character profoundly responsive to the sense of unity that wells up within him—a deep conviction that the Holy One alone is responsible for everything that happens to him and everything that will happen to him in the future. As a result, he emerges as the kind of character to which European literature had devoted its finest efforts for so many years. These two aspects—traditional characterization and modernistic techniques—are interlaced in *The Bridal Canopy* by Agnon's literary sensitivity. For while he portrays the unconscious drives of man that give purpose to his life, he creates at the same time a character who will eventually find his fulfillment in the real world of the society from which he was created and in which he lives.

In creating his characters Agnon never departs from the Jewish scene. In *The Bridal Canopy,* as in his other works, there is no figure that remains completely isolated from Jewish society. In fact, the individual does not occupy an all-important place in Agnon's work, and not one character in the entire trilogy is cut off from the Jewish community either consciously or subconsciously. The moment he ceases to draw nourishment from his

Jewish sources, he ceases to exist. All this is stated clearly in Agnon's more important works. Agnon has reservations about modernistic art—its belief that literature should rely on its own strength and be able to manage without such external sources as history, sociology, psychology, or any other abstract discipline divorced from the particular—yet he insists on the uniqueness, the particular significance and quality that give his characters their individual force.[15] Each step that the character takes is part of his personality; it has its own echo and it forms part of its own destiny.

Thus, Reb Yudel Hasid's character never becomes blurred because of his humble status as a beggar, nor is it warped by his success as a marriage broker. He never loses his sense of individuality, of personal destiny, despite the many physical and spiritual vicissitudes that befall him. Yet at the same time he reflects the life of Jewry as a whole, of Jewish society and the spiritual forces that impel it. It is this mingling of individual and community in Yudel which opens the door into the wonderland he finds in every object along his way; for the fantasy remains linked to a firm, enduring realism that constitutes the everyday life of the community. Through his personality the Jewish environment itself reflects the magic of the present, where past and future blend, and man can hear the footsteps of the Messiah from beyond the wall. The hardships of that everyday existence and the poverty and mendicancy of the Galician Jews are elevated again and again in the fantasies of Reb Yudel. This transformation gives *The Bridal Canopy* its importance in the epic writings of Shmuel Yosef Agnon.

As the story of *The Bridal Canopy* unfolds the reader becomes aware of one aspect dominating all of Agnon's literary work: the various levels by which the author elevates his story in accordance with a prearranged plan. On the surface the story may seem, as I have noted, to respond to numerous aspects that do not normally mingle with ease; yet Agnon leads us through the maze with sure artistry that draws upon numerous sources produced by Judaism throughout its long history.

The first stage is the everyday world of Reb Yudel Hasid—his house in one of the Galician Jewish towns. Agnon opens his story with a description of the dreadful poverty of this family and the begging to which their poverty forces them, and yet from time to time there is a gleam of the satirical irony of Mendelé Mokher Sefarim and the humorous irony of Shalom Aleikhem. Nevertheless, even on this level the author's tone carries us in a different direction from Mendelé's naturalistic satire and Shalom Aleikhem's humorous realism, by turning to the ancient folktale, in which he can reflect a number of different levels of life at one moment. In other words, Agnon employs a style generally regarded as outmoded among Hebrew writers in order to achieve a modernistic style more complex than any that naturalism could offer. Here are two extracts that illustrate the function of Agnon's prose in describing the real world of Reb Yudel Hasid:

> Now this Hasid was burdened with many daughters, each a few years older than the next; that is, Gittele the youngest was around seventeen, the next in age, her sister Blumme, was about nineteen, and the oldest, Pessele, was twenty, and they used to wander about naked and barefoot, without clothes or shoes, shut up in the house and unable to show their faces outside. They were all pious and witty and pretty, "their breasts were fashioned and their hair grown," but in their hearts sorrow flourished, for they had grown into maidenhood and there was none to redeem them from the shame of their virginity. When the youngest reached maturity, Frumit, the hasid's wife, made a stand and upbraided her husband. Frumit said to her husband, "How long will you harden your heart like a vulture toward your children and not pity your poor daughters, who sit here forsaken, sighing over their lot, their eyes worn out with weeping, their hair turning gray while you sit there like a dummy, not lifting a finger to marry them off. Just look at their friends, how many babies snuggle up to them while all my three sweet daughters are forsaken, with no husband to relieve them of their shame." These words touched the heart of the hasid and he was filled with paternal compassion. He heaved a bitter sigh and turned back to the Gemara, placing his trust in God, who created everything according to His will.[16]

The opening sentence in this quotation reads like the naturalistic descriptions of Mendelé, but soon the sarcasm comes to the fore as open satire. The punctuation of this sentence aims at catching the tone of Mendelé's writing; as the first part realistically describes in one long breath the hasid burdened with his "many daughters," the middle section lists the names and ages of those who had reached maturity, while the final section has a staccato quality as though of annoyance, which will soon be more clearly audible. But as he proceeds, the author transforms it all into a sort of rhymed nursery tale in which the lighter vein goes rippling along the surface while the more serious vein responds to a secret joy in which derision triumphs, rather like the medieval maqama, whose power in popular literature has never waned.[17] The rhyme in the Hebrew original of "they were all pious and witty and pretty . . . ," together with the punctuation that emphasizes the rhyme, creates an effect of light comedy, offsetting the naturalism and leaving a sort of vacuum the author must fill with some other effect that he has had ready all the time.

The technique is repeated after the rhymed passage. Indeed, when Frumit harshly upbraids her husband for hardening his heart like a vulture and not pitying his poor daughters, she reminds one of Tuvia's wife, Golda, and Shalom Aleikhem's stories. Frumit's rebuke, however, loses its realism as a result of the mocking rhymes which might be rendered more freely in English as "the girls are full grown, all three are alone, with no one to wed, they'd be better off dead." At the end of the passage the author found it necessary to fill the vacuum he had created with one puff of his banter. He continues the rhymes to the end of the introductory passage but then injects a more serious note—a hint of something wonderful appearing on the distant horizon which is soon to enter the reader's world: "He heaved a bitter sigh and turned back to the Gemara, placing his trust in God, who created everything according to His will."

From this it is abundantly clear that the author has no intention of employing pure realism in *The Bridal Canopy*. Not only does he remove some of the seriousness by making the bride of the story the daughter of Reb Yudel Hasid, but at the very opening of the story he introduces his main character, Reb Yudel, as a passive receptacle for all that goes on in the world. The entire story thus becomes a sort of play that continues entirely on its own, as if it had no text and the producer simply tells all the actors to carry on just as they please. Nevertheless, all this is merely an optical illusion. The reader who chooses to see (and the literary form of *The Bridal Canopy* lends itself to visual effects) the various levels of the story as a whole and at the same time as separate, will soon realize that in fact the story never leaves the realm of realism. Yudel goes from door to door to collect contributions for the dowry of his daughter, who does, at the end, actually get married. This realism, however, takes on different layers of meaning with every step, with every turn of the hero's, in a way normally provided only at the conscious level.

Therefore, the element of passivity we sense in the final sentence of the above quotation—is really intended to provide a psychological insight into the various adventures and experiences that follow. For those experiences contain a mighty impulse that unifies all the realistic levels of the entire story—Reb Yudel Hasid's deep longing for the Redemption. The story thus works both at outer and inner levels and indicates the literary innovation of Agnon in uniting the two elements realistically.

The author's ambivalence comes full circle in the story. It employs the immediately visible realism of Reb Yudel Hasid's home, where Agnon inserts into the dialogue sly touches of realistic satire; there is also the irony, to which the rhymed, folkloristic maqama is so well suited; there is the humor, which rises to the surface as soon as Reb Yudel Hasid leaves his home to go from door to door, and his two horses, Moshkheni and Narutza,[18] begin chatting to each other; there is the folklore beckoning from wonderland as if scales have fallen from Reb Yudel Hasid's eyes and he can now see it clearly for the first time; there is the dream element, in which the balance between reality and folklore is nullified and Reb Yudel Hasid moves into another reality that bids him cut off all connection with the material world and the very purpose of his journey, and then we return to the realism of that material world in the wedding of his daughter, which is free of all satire and irony, and illumined solely by the legendary folklore of the distant past.

The following passage also comes from the opening pages of

the story and illustrates the motive force of *The Bridal Canopy*. Reb Yudel has climbed up into the wagon, bidden his family and friends a fond farewell, and offered up a brief prayer.

> As soon as he had finished his prayer, he began singing Adir Gadol ve-Nora—"Mighty, great, and revered is the Lord."[19] Nota cracked his whip above the horses' heads, and they at once pranced forward eagerly, kicking up the dust with their hooves and covering the wagon with it, and beautiful houses flew by in a flash, and mud huts loomed through the dust, and people stood by them shading their eyes with their hands as they gazed after the wagon. Within a few minutes, they left the city and dust behind them, and the open heavens became visible as the canopy of the earth, just as if sky and earth were kissing each other. When Reb Yudel saw that they had travelled beyond the point to which citizens were permitted to walk on the Sabbath, he recited with great devotion and piety the prayer for setting out on a journey. He recited it in the plural, since a communal prayer is answered more speedily than that of an individual. When he had finished his prayer, he crossed his legs and looked at the world around him, singing Adon Olam—"Lord of the Universe"— and nodding at those he passed, whether circumcised or uncircumcised, impressed by the bright light that God in His goodness had shed with such beauty over the earth. Reb Yudel began perfuming the air with holy words, and did so with great devotion, for there are souls who did not manage to repent in time and therefore could not find rest, so that they wander about the universe, sometimes hanging from trees, and when a man of Israel utters a holy phrase, they come and clothe themselves in that phrase and ascend heavenward, where the angels of anger and law have no power over them. . . .
> Nota cracked his whip at the horses and thought to himself that it was a stupid world if Moshkheni and Narutza had to be troubled for such a fool. But Reb Yudel was above such thoughts and said, "The wise author of *Hovot Halevavot* wrote that man is composed of a body and a soul, both given him by the goodness of his Creator, and now that his soul was feeling good it surely would look after his limbs, for it could never desert them in time of trouble." It did not take long before they reached the village of Pinkewitz.[20]

The more clearly one perceives the pattern of satire, irony, humor, legend, dream, and reality in Agnon's writing, the more obvious is the presence of the author within his story. At first he seems merely to be accompanying Reb Yudel on his travels, concealing his presence in the series of adventures and experiences. Before long, however, we begin to notice the powerful individuality of the hero, an individuality that permeates every corner of the tale. Moreover, Agnon deliberately emphasizes the folkloristic basis of his writing in all its forms, as well as the midrashic and aggadic basis, which is also folkloristic, in order to be sure that his tools are reliable in fashioning the modernistic element in his writing. Whenever the element of fantasy is dominant, as in the scene of Reb Yudel's meal at the house of the mendicant Heschel, or in Nota the wagoner's dreams, or in the visions of "the man who feared the nights," and so forth, Agnon makes sure that adequate expression is given to the inner world of Reb Yudel Hasid. All this he does by placing one narrative within another and linking them solely by the associations of his thought, like wheels within wheels connected by links invisible to the naked eye. Eventually, however, we realize that the whole sequence had been premeditated by the author before he set pen to paper.

It is for this reason that the less perceptive reader becomes confused by the different levels as he reads the story. At first, he imagines that the story functions at the level of popular fantasy alone. In his view the author has touched up a number of ancient stories, amusing himself by stringing them together and placing them in the mouth of Reb Yudel Hasid, who relates them in the language of the sages while meditating to himself or meeting his fellow creatures. For Yudel is a simple soul, believing all sorts of nonsense—kabbalistic sayings, moral teachings, and hasidic axioms from the common people he meets as well as phrases containing empty ideals, visions, legends, and dreams. Even the dialectic style of Agnon's stories, both the short ones and novelettes, seem suited to this technique. Before he can finish telling one story, he already raises a question about it, answers the query, and asks another question, so that the story seems to be telling itself, only allowing the reader to pause for a breath when he reaches the end of a chapter.

This personal dialogue, however, contains the explanation of Agnon's technique, for all the aspects listed above are merely the means by which he achieves a clearly modernistic effect. Reb Yudel Hasid journeys along, together with Nota the driver, through the Jewish towns of Galicia; by providing the contrasting character of Nota Agnon offers his hero the opportunity of free association in his response to the outer and inner worlds of Galicia, thus freeing the plot from any conscious, logical progression and breaking the architectonic line of the story, which lends it an ambivalence that can record the various levels of reality, despite the apparent contradictions between them. It is not chronological order or any sense of continuity such as realism requires which brings to life the imaginings of Nota the driver, or the visions of Reb Yudel Hasid at night as he lies on the straw in Nehemiah's house, gazing at the light filtering down to him from the seven heavens and their stars.

It is as though at one stroke Agnon has opened the door to all sorts of secret thoughts that until now had been suppressed by the conscious mind. In "the man who feared the night," those secret feelings begin to find expression and burst out of their hiding places, causing all sorts of results in which the fear that was always closed up and hidden within Reb Yudel Hasid breaks forth. Agnon's tendency to make those inner thoughts respond immediately to his touch is reminiscent of the surrealist school of painters, who based all their work on spontaneous association completely free from conscious artistry. In Agnon's case, however, his purpose is quite different from that of the surrealists, for he wishes to express the unified character of Reb Yudel Hasid journeying through the towns of Galicia to collect alms, while deep within he listens at all times for the footsteps of the Messiah already standing "on the other side of our wall." He seems to carry the echo of the Messiah's footsteps in his heart, in both the inner and outer aspects of his character, and it is his listening for the Messiah that unites these two aspects. In fact, the various literary devices we noted earlier—the grotesque comedy introduced into the atmosphere of poverty and idleness, the touches of satire and irony, the elevation of the story by means of the author's humorous identification with Reb Yudel and the dreams they share, the folklore intermingling with realism whereby Reb Yudel leaps from realism into his dream world—all these form part of the spectrum Agnon pepares for Reb Yudel in his search for the Messiah on one level and his search for his daughter's dowry on another. All the adventures, trials, strata, and substrata, on both the realistic and the psychological planes, eventually become united in the magnificent conviction that there is a plan and a purpose, that there is order in the world intended for man, and that they endow him with the splendor of spiritual unity.

In fact, the entire story of *The Bridal Canopy* achieves its apotheosis in the chapter devoted to the wedding of Reb Yudel's daughter. Everything he had experienced and dreamed during his travels finds its fulfillment in that chapter, and the very motive force of the story reaches its climax there, in what might be called "the love of Israel." It is almost as if the author can no longer restrain his affection for all the delightful creatures of his story. The deep bond uniting Agnon and his characters eventually finds expression in the popular Jewish songs of the Galician town of Brod. The sublime music of those songs awakens and brings to life the real world of Galician Jewry and permeates the wonderful trilogy of Agnon, consisting of *The Bridal Canopy, A Wayfarer Tarries the Night,* and *The Day Before Yesterday.*

The term "trilogy" applied to these three stories requires some further explanation. From the point of view of actual plot, *A Wayfarer Tarries the Night* is not an immediate continuation of *The Bridal Canopy,* nor is *The Day Before Yesterday* a continuation of the former, even though the leading character, Itzhak Komer, is the grandson of Reb Yudel Hasid. From the viewpoint of their motivation force, however, they constitute a continuous series, each arising from its predecessor and becoming progressively clearer in artistic purpose. In creating the character of an individual Jew, born out of the longings for redemption thoughout the various epochs and changing conditions of Jewish history, Agnon provided an epic concept new to Hebrew fiction. This concept also constituted an abrupt change from the traditions established during the period from Mendelé in the seventies and eighties to the experimental twenties, with Feierberg, Gnessin, Brenner, Shoffman, and Berdichevsky. The change can be seen in Agnon's concept of the Jew as well as in the means by which he brings that concept to fruition.

In *The Bridal Canopy* Agnon begins to settle accounts with Mendelé's world of Kabtziel. The vacuum into which Mendelé threw his characters is replaced by the deep meaningfulness of Reb Yudel Hasid. Externally, he is in many ways similar to the men of Kislon, Batalon, and Kabtziel, but while Mendelé's characters are devoid of any creative vision (in his desire for naturalism, he makes all their dreams, stories, and visions into mere pastiche), Agnon fills the squalid surroundings of Reb Yudel Hasid with messianic visions that elevate and ennoble the Galician beggar. Obviously, in introducing this change Agnon had to create a language that offered the possibility of inner dimensions in a way excluded by Mendelé's unambiguous naturalism, and the realism of his followers in the "New Trend."

Agnon, however, was not the first to tamper with the realism of modern Hebrew literature. We have already seen how Mikha Yosef Berdichevsky and his younger contemporary, Uri Nissan Gnessin, strove to penetrate the inner psychological world of their characters. Berdichevsky even used folklore as a means of expressing his artistic struggles, and also devoted his finest resources to creating a Jewish character bearing within him the visionary longings hidden in myth and legend. Yet, as I noted above, the effort involved made such heavy demands on the author, particularly in the richness and immediacy of language, that the realism vanished. The epic power evaporated when his realistic depiction of the actual world, which was to form the framework of the psychological development, was swept aside by the inner struggles of his characters. That is what happens in *The Hidden Thunder* and *Miriam,* which Berdichevsky regarded as the finest of his literary achievements. The same is true of Gnessin's work, where the author, by transferring to the story his own sense of isolation, destroys the structural, epic unity of the work, its plot continuity, and ultimate purpose.

Agnon, however, is the most purposeful of Hebrew writers, creating his characters with complete objectivity. Of course, he allows Reb Yudel to digress into all sorts of visions, dreams, legends and hair-splitting casuistry, but all this functions according to a prearranged plan. These digressions contribute to the creation of a Jewish character credible at the level of his inner being as well as in his everyday life. Agnon's sureness of touch and his overall plan are the marks of epic greatness. Hebrew literature up to our own day contains no such detailed description of an eighteenth-century Jewish wedding in Galicia as we find at the end of *The Bridal Canopy*. On the one hand it is vividly realistic, with all its jesters' poems and the songs of the "singers of Brod," while on the other hand it conveys a feeling of great fulfillment, transcending the realistic setting and redolent of gladness and joy. The popular tradition and the movement toward a happy ending become so strong in the final pages from one sentence to the next that it suddenly breaks out into a folkloristic song in honor of Reb Yudel's emigration to the Land of Israel. Agnon recounts blessing after blessing that the Holy One bestows on the house of Reb Yudel Hasid after the wedding, relating how Reb Yudel found good husbands for all his daughters, and saw grandsons born who were destined "to study the Torah and observe the commandments and do good deeds that bring honor to those who perform them," and how the Holy One "heaps blessings at every step on those who perform His will in love, and in that way Reb Yudel's daughters enjoyed every happiness in this world." As for Reb Yudel himself:

> . . . his happiness was even greater than theirs, for he and his wife were rewarded by the privilege of emigrating to the Holy Land and seeing it in this life. If we were to relate all the adventures of Reb Yudel and Frumit his wife while traveling by wagon from Brod to the River Tuna and once they were aboard the ship, we would never reach the end of our story. But to give Reb Yudel the credit due to him, we ought to record that he accepted every trouble and pain with joy, and used to say that it was worth suffering all the troubles in the world in order to reach the Holy Land. Even Frumit his wife agreed with him eventually. For some years before he left for the Land of Israel he used to wear a kerchief over his eyes so that they should have no pleasure outside the Holy Land. My learned friends, you can

imagine for yourselves Reb Yudel's joy when he reached the
Land of Israel and was privileged to dwell before the Lord
in this world. He soared beyond the heights of wisdom and made
himself rules that a man may live by in this world as well as
in the world to come, and wrote letters in the holy spirit.

> The author's words are ended
> And a poet's lines appended:

So ends the story of Yudel Hasid
May heaven protect us and save us from need.
Let our hearts always burn with religious desire
And the Holy One send us the promised Messiah.[21]

Despite the varied levels of meaning, the Jewish aspects of Reb
Yudel's personality achieve solidity, credibility, and concreteness
of form. An almost primitive realism exists in the story side by
side with the world of illusion, and reaches its fruition in the
individualized character of Reb Yudel Hasid. By exploiting the
popular element in his character, Agnon was able to move back
and forth from the world of reality to that of the imagination,
and by this means the story could flow smoothly along, eventually
achieving stability within his character. In *A Wayfarer Tarries
the Night*,[22] however, the realism of the Jewish town is already
more blurred, heavy with the pain and suffering that accompanies
despair. The town of Shibush, which the wayfarer visits, is no
longer a bustling place from which the author can produce a
firmly individualized character. Indeed, the whole town (which
was, in fact, Agnon's birthplace) is dominated by the personality
of the outsider, of the traveler who is merely coming to spend the
night. His is a personality that existed prior to the story, beyond
the bounds of the dying town, and bestows its own freshness and
its own significance on the atmosphere of desolation. The traveler
is a mixture of past and present, and by virtue of that blending
is able to revive the town.

Thus it is that the entire story is related in the first person; for
this character recognizes his own duality, the mingling of inner
and outer reality, the fusions of past and present expressed in the
I of the omniscient narrator. On further reading, however, it
becomes clear that we are encountering the first of Agnon's
"crises," which are to recur in his later writings.

The crisis is basically this: the realism of the story shies away, as it were, at the approach of the traveler, who has come merely to spend the night in the town but who, struck by its desolation, decides to remain and await the time of its salvation. The dying life of the town slips from his grasp and is never tangibly conveyed. Indeed, throughout his comings and goings in the town, the traveler is almost always alone. Shibush has lost the framework of its Jewish way of life. All the vitality of *The Bridal Canopy* has seeped away, and the setting, as well as the characters within its walls, has become blurred as the desolation descends. An indefinable mood invisibly affects the atmosphere, filling it with a longing for final cessation. The traveler reaches the town on the eve of the Day of Atonement, the very night when he used to feel the security of belonging within the Jewish community and the significance of being a Jew. But where that night used to be filled with hope and reverence, now the synagogue, with all its worshippers, candles and prayers, the river with the bridge over it, the heavens and the tahanun prayers,[23] the people coming and going, both believers and scoffers, the hotel and its "candle of life," and the traveler himself, who has chanced upon this town— all of them have ceased to speak for themselves and their lives, but rather turn their attention to something burgeoning beyond the horizon. The traveler himself is only a spectator, waiting for the destined end.

Once again, all these objects serve only as symbols of something beyond reality that cannot be named precisely—something that has no reality of its own, forms no part of logical cause and effect, and produces the longing for death. At the very beginning of the story Agnon introduces a note of mystery that lends to the entire work a second level of reality. Nevertheless, the story does remain realistic in its setting and characters, with all their physical and spiritual problems. Agnon's prose, which leans heavily on midrashic Hebrew, soars aloft in the second half of the chapter, "The Eve of the Day of Atonement," which relates the narrator's experience as his thoughts wander.

> The central synagogue, which in my childhood I had believed was the largest building in the entire world, seemed to have shrunk in height and breadth; to eyes that had gazed on castles

and palaces, the synagogue seemed even smaller than it really was.

In the synagogue there was not one person I recognized. Most of the worshippers walked to the front, seized the best seats on the eastern side and ignored the other places. Some walked back and forth, either to display their importance or because their seats were uncomfortable. The light that used to glow upon the heads of worshippers on the eve of the Day of Atonement did not shine upon them, and their prayer shawls lacked the old radiance. In the past, when everyone who came to the synagogue would bring a candle with him, adding it to those already burning in the candelabra, the synagogue used to glow with light, but now that the candelabra had been neglected during the war and few came to pray, there were few candles and little light. In the past, the prayer shawls used to be ornamented with silver collars reflecting the light onto the heads of the worshippers, but now there was no silver ornamentation and hence no light.

The cantor did not spend long on the service; or perhaps he did, but, as it was my first visit there in the synagogue of my childhood and that night was the Day of Atonement when people stay long in prayer, I wanted to stay longer, and thus it only seemed to me that he was cutting the service short. When he had finished, all the worshippers gathered around the Ark and recited kaddish, the memorial prayer for the dead. There was not one who did not recite it.[24]

Such is the mood of nostalgia and decay in the Jewish town whose foundations were collapsing socially, economically, religiously, and culturally, as well as from the viewpoint of the inner world of the individual who could no longer find his way either in the community or in his own life. And it is a mood already familiar to us from significant literary sources other than the writings of Agnon. It occupies an important place in the works of Gnessin, as we saw in an earlier chapter, and in the Yiddish writings of Bergelson, who, although he inherited much from Gnessin, by his own efforts elevated the theme of nostalgia and decay to its artistic peak in such stories as *Around the Railroad Station* and *The End of Everything*[25] before he became caught up in the October Revolution. Nevertheless, *A Wayfarer Tarries the Night* is unique in that Agnon's central character speaks in the first person, so that in effect the narrator is the hero, a descendant of Reb Yudel Hasid, who has turned aside to this Jewish village in order to restore its visionary reality, to make it, as had Reb Yudel Hasid, part of the ancient past and the messianic future of Jewry.

Therefore, the motive force of *A Wayfarer Tarries the Night* is a dialogue between two opposite poles. On the one hand, the story itself is vividly real, the reality being created by the language of the story, and the narrator elevates the tone at will. Yet all the actuality of the story seems to dissolve in the silent blending of action and mood. The traveler gazes right through the physical setting of his birthplace, seemingly peeling off the external. In this way, Agnon employs a literary technique in this story which is the exact reverse of his *Bridal Canopy*. There the dreams and imaginings of Reb Yudel Hasid flow into the chain of real events that reach their climax in the wedding at Reb Yudel Hasid's house. His devotion to the messianic ideal and his mingling of past and present are the primary cause. But in *A Wayfarer Tarries the Night* this devotion has reached its nadir and the real world disintegrates progressively. That is why the wayfarer wanders about the town seeking the key to the gates of reality, which have been broken down and ruined beyond repair.

On the other hand, the wayfarer is struggling to rectify the atmosphere of disintegration, to restore some stability in its real world, to endow it with some of the vision that has disappeared from the thinning community and its oppressed individuals. In this story too Agnon makes full use of his language, but unlike *The Bridal Canopy*, he does not employ it in this story to evoke a popular tradition overflowing with literary creativity in its primitive desire to connect ideas spontaneously in a magical flow of words and endowing everything in the phenomenal world with a responsiveness to the inner, subjective world. In *A Wayfarer Tarries the Night* the flow of language provides a complex dialogue responsive at one and the same time to a number of contradictory elements that the narrator brings together under the aegis of the prearranged plan. This plan elevates everything to the plane of a higher reality in which may be found the solution to the existence of all the characters in the dying town.

Agnon's midrashic style of narration reflects the way everything withdraws into itself, whether in the individual's world or in that of the community as a whole. The flow of language increases in proportion to the sense of silence and mystery. The collapse of society and the degeneration of the individual both complement and reflect each other, spreading over the whole story a decadent beauty reminiscent of the European Decadent movement at the beginning of this century. Yet, at the same time the author's style counterbalances the impression of degeneracy he has been at such pains to create, for Agnon is determined to soften the harsh realism of the atmosphere by imbuing it with the hope of rebirth in the Holy Land. These two currents join force in Agnon's work, transforming *A Wayfarer Tarries the Night* into a fantasy in which the mingling of dream and reality creates the effect of a nightmare, offsetting the vivid, everyday realism. It would seem that Agnon hesitated to describe the disintegration of his birthplace in terms of mystery and symbolism, and felt that something was wrong in the very quality of his description that a deep longing had prompted him to create. This affects the story from its very beginning up to the climax, when the key to the synagogue is handed over to the traveler and mislaid, a new one fashioned superior to the original, and the latter brought to the Holy Land.

The dialectic pattern in the narration of *A Wayfarer Tarries the Night* makes it very hard for the critic to illustrate the story from the text. To quote from the stream of narrative is to spoil the passage by removing it from its ambivalent context, from its different levels of inner and outer meaning in the actual town. The passage becomes petrified and loses its force when the critic suddenly tears it from its literary setting, a setting that so subtly reflects its various facets. In fact, at the very opening of the story, Agnon rejects any realistic grasp of time or place. He removes any trace of the logical development usual in a realistic novel, both in his description of the environment and in his individualization of character within that environment. First Agnon concentrates on such characters as the tailor, the shopkeeper, the hotel keeper, and the carter—figures who form part of the folklore as long as the realistic narration leaves no room for examining the inner world of their human experience.

Shmuel Yosef Agnon

The tailor's head is always bent over his needle and thread, his eye fixed on his cloth; the shopkeeper seems to focus on some distant point in the empty air; the hotel keeper is constantly noticing something mysterious in the faces of his guests; and the carter's mind is always far away in the snows where he will eventually become lost. All of them respond to the death wish permeating the atmosphere of the town; all are closed in themselves and at the same time are longing for someone to come and free them from the mysterious weight pressing on their hearts. No style could be more ideally suited to such characterization than the meandering style of the midrash that Agnon employs, for it conceals and reveals at the same moment, it asks and replies, combines speech and silence, and, in concerning itself with the minutest detail, penetrates to the heart of the universal. Agnon says of the hotel keeper:

> Perhaps I was wrong to say that he used to close his eyes in order to preserve what he had just seen. He closed his eyes in order to stop seeing what he had just seen. It is easy to be mistaken about men like that; you think something about them, but it's not so.[26]

The same is true of the tailor, the shopkeeper, and certainly of the carter. The narrator softens the harsh realism of their characters by means of the dialectic descriptions that the midrashic style makes possible. This technique frees the narrative from the normal logical sequence of events, transferring the reader to some strange world in which everything is isolated and actions act themselves out independently without forming part of an overall plot. The wayfarer who tarries the night is required to listen with equal interest to the tailor, who forces him to look at the beautiful cloth from which Prince Halaf had bought a length for his beautiful wife, and to the shopkeeper, who says that the tailor never sells that cloth, not because he does not need the money, but because it is so very beautiful that he likes to place it under his sick wife's head.

In the course of conversation, the shopkeeper mentions the heat of the Holy Land, from where the traveler has just come, and compares it with the heat of the town. For a moment, therefore, he mingles the Land of Israel, where the Zionists live "who cannot stand the young communists," with his town, in which there lived a young man who was previously a communist and who was the brother of Daniel Bakh, "a cripple, lame in one leg" and an atheist. He speaks of another character, Yeruham the Freethinker, who went out to the Land of Israel as a pioneer; the Zionists wanted to expel him from the country but an Arab anticipated them: "An Arab felt like firing a bullet, so he fired one at him and killed him." All sorts of stormy winds, which used to blow through the town long ago, seem to blow once again in every breath of the shopkeeper's speech, and then become silent. A moment later, the shopkeeper enters into casual conversation with his wife about some topic that lost all its significance long ago—and the wayfarer finds his head spinning with matters of which nothing but echoes are left in the real world. At that point, Agnon's style becomes modernistic and surrealist, almost as it was later to become in his *Book of Deeds.*

> The sun remained fixed in the sky, rooted there and inseparable from it, and a mild warmth suffused the air. This air, together with the light of the sun, changed the expressions on the faces of people passing back and forth and they became more friendly to each other. People I did not know nodded at me and bade me good day. Ignatz came and attached himself to me, asking whether he could carry my parcel. The shopkeepers looked at it and at the one I was holding. There were many shops and few customers, and whoever purchased something from one shop roused the anger of all the other shopkeepers.[27]

The modernistic element in *A Wayfarer Tarries the Night* gradually increases, covering all the narrator's wanderings through the town. Its primary purpose is to reconstruct the world of the town by renewing the visionary reality of that world, which has been spoiled by a quality foreign to it. Here the narrator deals with the weakening of religion in the town. Daniel Bakh pours a stream of complaint heavenward at the way the Almighty treats His creatures. Daniel Bakh no longer dons his phylacteries, and, what is worse, he discourages his elderly father, Shelomo Bakh, from emigrating to the Holy Land in order to be "buried in its dust." The whole affair is permeated with a feeling of the grotesque that transcends the satire and the anger it contains. Daniel has served in the czarist army, gone to war, and stood with his fellow Jews in the trenches of the battlefield. One day his trench was hit by a shell and he alone was left alive, searching the trench to see whether he could be of assistance to anyone. His hand became caught in the strap of a phylactery and he tells the traveler, "As I pulled at the strap and fumbled with the phylactery, a horrible smell arose and I realized that the phylactery was wound around the arm of a dead man." This grotesque incident eventually lends a nightmare quality to the whole of Bakh's depressing world, endowing everything with a feeling of rank decay. The tailor and shopkeeper are in the same situation, as is even Yeruham, the atheist, of whom Agnon says:

> All day long, from sunrise to sunset, he sits in the streets of the town banging with his hammer, chipping stones or creating dust as he fills in holes and repairs the streets of the town that had been damaged during the war. The expression on his face makes it clear that he does not enjoy his work, but he devotes himself to it like one who has no other before him, and because he has no other before him, devotes himself to it. I have heard that the town councilors are pleased with his work and pay no attention to the ideas for which he was driven out of the Land of Israel. I am telling no tales and revealing no secrets, since the matter is widely known, but this young man was involved in some wrongdoing, and before being expelled from the Land of Israel was imprisoned for the crime of having distributed pamphlets to Jews and Arabs. At any rate, since he returned here he has not been involved in any wrongdoings. He has nothing to do with the other communists in the town, and has nothing to do with anything, even with himself. How can a man have anything or nothing to do with himself? If he sings and talks to himself, he has something to do with himself; if he does not sing or talk to himself, he has nothing to do with himself. From sunrise to sunset he does his work and is silent.[28]

The same is true of most characters in the story. At times it seems as though the traveler came back to his town merely to find a vehicle for the nightmarish desires pressing ceaselessly upon him, and that all the characters are really ghosts arising from the narrator's own subconscious. It would appear that Agnon deliberately removes all meaningfulness from their lives so that he may finally be able to say of himself: "In my childhood I saw everything I wished to see. When I grew older my vision became limited and I saw only what was shown to me. Now I see neither what I wish to see nor what is shown to me." Nevertheless, this brief statement, although it seems to close the door on the future of the town as well as on the "vision" of the wayfarer, at the same time opens a new door for the story's dialectic power. The atheist Yeruham, the "other Yeruham," who was shot by the Arab in the Land of Israel, Daniel Bakh, whose faith has deserted him, the tailor, the shopkeeper, and the carter, whose lives all seem to have lost their purpose—all these, as they move toward the final point of despair, become charged with the narrator's renewed longing for his childhood. It is a longing for the vision that penetrated the surface of the characters in the town to the truth that lay beneath —in other words, a longing "to see everything he wished to see."

Therefore, although Agnon's dialectic style plunges him into ever deeper gloom and the characterization grows increasingly surrealistic, at the same time the story offsets this gloom by the dream visions of the children, who gradually become the real heroes of the story, compensating for everything else. As Agnon delves deeper into the inner world of Daniel Bakh, he finds that faith has deserted Daniel at every level of his being. He cannot believe in a God who could behave so cruelly to his creatures during the war, in the same way that he cannot keep faith with a Zionism that drove Yeruham the atheist out of the Land of Israel or allowed the "other Yeruham" to be killed by an Arab bullet. He can not even believe that his pious, and sincerely orthodox, father, Shelomo, ought to travel to the Land of Israel to die and be buried in its soil, and he scoffs at the significance of such a burial.

Agnon's modernistic outlook perceives a certain perversity in the town that neither heaven nor earth can cure. The townspeople have closed their Bet ha-Midrash and handed over the key to the wayfarer, and even the key becomes lost; on the surface of things, there are no believers left. All this is forcefully conveyed by Agnon's powerful style, with its piercing, penetrating vision always at the level of a dialogue that never seems to deal with

actual objects, people, or events in a really stable world. Some
thing, however, escapes from this closed world of modernistic
dialogue and finds refuge in the half-starved, half-ailing children,
all of whom possess an intense dreamlike vision.[29] However hopeless Daniel Bakh's despair and disillusionment may be, he is redeemed by his sick child. The child's vision is, indeed, a mingling
of dream and reality, but in place of the harsh realism with which
Daniel Bakh is described, Agnon weaves into the sick child's fantasies a new realism that blends past and future, and that imbues
with palpable truth his faith in God, his vision of the redemption,
and even his grandfather Shelomo, who embodies this past and
future. It is in the fantasies of this sick child that many of the lost
characters of the story find their fulfillment, on the level of the
actual setting of the town as well as on the level of the mystic symbolism that finds its own realism within this childish fantasy.

There are many similarities between the sick child and Rachel,
the hotel keeper's daughter, who "has a habit of shrugging her
shoulders as if someone had just laid a hand on them, and of half-
closing her eyes . . . not like her father, who wants to preserve
what he has just seen, but as if she wants to see what is coming."
This child too is endowed by Agnon with a sensitivity of vision, so
that from the hidden realms of man's inner world she imbues the
hotel with a truer realism. The same is true of Henikh, with his
horse Hartom, and Hanokh, who is frozen to death on his journey-
ings: both possess a childlike vision, and by their intuitive dreams
they achieve true insight into the future of the town.

The narrator betrays a secret sympathy and affection for these
characters, since it is they who testify to the overall plan that con-
ducts all the confused aspects of the town to the bright light of
meaningfulness. Each of these child-figures has been injured—has
been made the victim of some accident that has left his body tense
—but this physical tension, which leaves the soul on the border
between dream and reality, allows the various gulfs to be bridged,
the different levels to mingle, and every dip to become the prelude
to an ascent into a new way of life. The entire disintegrating town
and its dwindling population seem to revive under the impetus
of the new note in Agnon's style whenever he begins talking about

the child-figures. The further we move through *A Wayfarer Tarries the Night* and the more the wayfarer himself seems cut off from his roots in Jerusalem, wandering through the desolate world of the "naked souls" of Shibush, the town of his birth, the more do these child-figures seem to lead us toward some realistic solution. The wayfarer is sitting in the old, empty marketplace of Shibush when suddenly everything becomes clear to him: "I hadn't clarified things sufficiently. Now that everything is clear, I shall try to put it all in writing, and if my words have no relevance here, they will have relevance elsewhere." This wonderful change throws light on Agnon's purpose in the incident of the key.

An entrance, a door, a threshold, a key—the standard tools of symbolist writing from its earliest beginnings. They always represent the transition from the logical, conscious world of the senses, with their appearance of solidity, to the dim world of the subconscious. Agnon resorts frequently to these symbolist techniques in *A Wayfarer Tarries the Night.* Once the reader has grown accustomed to the apparently traditionalist style of Agnon's story, with its echoes of aggadah, midrash, and even talmudic dialectic, he readily accepts the narrator's venturing into the realm between dream and reality. There is no other story by Agnon so permeated with dialogue as *A Wayfarer Tarries the Night,* whether it be between the wayfarer and one of the other characters in the story or between the wayfarer and himself—a dialogue that questions one thing and answers yet another, beyond the scope of the first. Nevertheless, anyone familiar with Agnon's writings will recognize this fundamental point: he never, even in *A Wayfarer Tarries the Night,* allows himself to desert the real Jewish world as had so much of modernistic Hebrew fiction. True, Agnon descends in all his writing into the inner, psychological world of his characters, but he always returns to strengthen the actual world he seemed at first to have left. That is what he does in *The Crooked Shall Be Made Straight,* the first story in which Agnon revealed his unique, epic insight in which myth and everyday realism in the world of the Jew work hand in hand. This is the technique he employs in *The Bridal Canopy* as well as in *A Wayfarer Tarries the Night*. None of his "apparatus" illustrates this technique better than the Bet ha-Midrash in the town to which the wayfarer comes—the Bet ha-Midrash itself, its door, and, above all, its key. In the adventures of that key are explained Agnon's creative struggle and his literary approach.

As we have seen, the townspeople of Shibush hand over the key of the Bet ha-Midrash to the wayfarer, and this incident constitutes the crux of the story. Elimelekh Kaiser represents the town's entire Jewish community. All its bitterness, disillusionment, and despair find their full expression in the suppressed mockery in the ceremony of handing over the keys.

> Elimelekh said, "It is clear that you, my dear sir, are waiting solely for the coming of the Messiah. Perhaps you would stay with us until the Messiah comes to witness your joy." I silently nodded my consent.
>
> He then looked at me and said, "You nodded in silence; your head moved, but your lips kept their peace." Placing my hand on my heart, I said, "My head and heart are one, but I have not managed to utter any speech from my mouth."
>
> Elimelekh Kaiser replied with a sneer, "Perhaps you are waiting for permission. If so, it is granted. If you like, my dear sir, we will give you the key to the Bet ha-Midrash and you can be lord and master there." Someone else nodded and added: "We are leaving here and have no need of the key. Better to give him the key than throw it in the garbage." The beadle saw that I had stretched out my hand to receive it. He stood up and climbed up the steps. . . . Then he held out the key to me, the same key I used to open the old Bet ha-Midrash with when I was a boy, studying Torah there from morning to night. It was many years since I had last seen it—even in a dream—and suddenly I was being publicly presented with it forever, inside the Bet ha-Midrash on the Day of Atonement. I took the key, closing my hand over it. Members of the congregation who had not joined in the discussion came and peered at me. I wanted to say something to them but the words stuck in my throat.[30]

From this point on it is this difficulty in uttering speech that becomes the central problem of the story. I have already discussed one aspect of the problem in connection with Agnon's longing for childhood and for the visionary fantasies of childhood, which shed a softening realism over the harsh atmosphere of death and decay. A second aspect, perhaps more important from the artistic point of view in *A Wayfarer Tarries the Night*, is the incident of the key, which affects the entire story. With that, in the passage quoted above, the narrator begins his story, and with that he concludes it. In the same way as the key serves as a symbol of the disintegration of the town, it serves also to mark Agnon's artistic struggle for a means of literary "speech" that will by its epic quality reconstruct the disintegration and reawake the Jews in the town. By means of this key the outer and inner worlds become fused within the "speech" of the narrator.

In popular folklore, the Bet ha-Midrash has a literary tradition all its own. From the moment it is left deserted, emptied of men and their problems, of their experiences and prayers, there awaken within it all sorts of hidden powers that can arise only in the dim atmosphere of man's inner, psychological world. Not only do the dead gather there at night, drawn by its gloomy emptiness, but so do living people who have been torn apart by the primitive struggles within them. Their disintegrating selves wander there, stripped of the rags of reality, having lost their grasp on the real world and their sense of individuality.[31] The ascetic and the kabbalist, whose souls have suffered deeply and are struggling toward some grotesque abyss, the beggars, the scoffers, the crazy, and the idle—all of them gather in this nightmarish atmosphere of the very Bet ha-Midrash that, in the light of day, becomes filled with the realistic activity of man's daily life. This nightmarish realism, which the popular aggadah inherited from the strange messianism of the Lurianic Kabbalah, took hold of Hebrew fiction, which never returned to the didacticism of the Enlightenment era.

Hebrew fiction, as I explained in the previous chapters, was searching for symbols of the unique, inner world of the Jew, and the aggadah served this purpose admirably—particularly that part of the aggadah that concentrated on the atmosphere of the Bet ha-Midrash at night. Feierberg, Berdichevsky, Peretz, Anski, and many others had exploited the demonology of the Bet ha-Midrash, each in his own way. Agnon too was drawn to the Bet ha-Midrash, not only to its nighttime aspect, when it was filled with ghosts that disappeared at the crack of dawn, but also in the strong light of day, including the Day of Atonement, when it was shrouded in desolation and filled with a feeling of decay. Nevertheless, in contrast to the earlier authors, Agnon did not turn to the Bet ha-Midrash to identify himself with its shadowy nighttime atmosphere, but in order to rectify it, to create a handhold strong enough to dispel the feelings of dissolution within the town by means of the vision of a new revival in the Land of Israel. All the symbolic elements in the incident of the key are aimed at reconstructing the vivid vision whereby the Jewish town of Galicia may obtain its spiritual reawakening.

When the first key is handed to the wayfarer, the narrator himself is enveloped in a feeling of despair. The atmosphere of decay in everything around him, in the thoughts of the people and the events outside him, has had its effect upon him. As he pores over his books in the Bet ha-Midrash, he is aware of the inner dissolution of the town in the hotel, the homes, and in the marketplace—the nightmare desolation that flows into the Bet ha-Midrash even in broad daylight. At times it seems almost as though Shmuel Yosef Agnon himself has succumbed to that atmosphere, and his dialectic style, the midrashic basis of which allows him to move back and forth between the inner and outer reality of the town, here finds its full flowering, answering the author's deepest yearning for a full artistic expression.

Agnon, however, had to struggle against the sense of isolation that had so long dominated Hebrew fiction of the twentieth century. We have already seen how the theme of isolation in all its varied forms caused on the one hand a literary revival among the young Hebrew writers of Eastern Europe, and on the other discouraged great subjectivity in writing, since the authors transferred their personal sufferings into the framework of the literary work itself. As a result, the epic potentiality of the theme was nullified in the works of such writers as Feierberg, Gnessin, Brenner, and Berdichevsky, and its effects were felt in the first stages of Hebrew modernistic writings by the fact that the shtetl could never achieve epic status. If, in his shorter stories, Berkovitz succeeded in bestowing on the town a certain epic quality, it is only on the realistic level and is confined solely to the short story.

Agnon, whose artistic grasp was by no means restricted to the level of realistic description, and whose style was never suited to mere actuality, did, it is true, concern himself with the borderline between everyday reality and the dim inner world. But by the dynamic power of his writing he struggled with the nightmarish fantasy he created in *A Wayfarer Tarries the Night* in order to rectify it and make it a positive part of Jewish history. He takes the theme of isolation in the Jewish town to its fullest extreme—the souls of his characters are emptied of all meaning, as is the Bet ha-Midrash, which seems here to have been handed over to the ghosts wandering naked through the night. But from this point on, he concentrates on filling this vacuum with the traditionally Jewish visions of another reality displayed by Rachel, the sick child, and the other marginal characters. By the force of this visionary power, the wayfarer enters the Bet ha-Midrash alone, as though he had been appointed its night watchman. True, the first key given to him by the members of the Bet ha-Midrash is lost, and every faint sign of reality in the village leaks away like an ebbing tide, toward a dim nothingness; but once a new key has been made and the wayfarer has taken up his abode in the Bet ha-Midrash, the great and powerful link with the past is renewed, the link hewn out of the lives of previous generations and tempered on the anvil of Jewish philosophy and religion. Once again the breath of life returns to the books, the volumes of halakhah and aggadah that had never surrendered to the dusty silence. And on his return to Jerusalem, the wayfarer finds in his hand once again the old, heavy key.

The wayfarer who makes his abode in the empty Bet ha-Midrash regards himself as its guardian, responsible for its upkeep, and even the nights he spends there gradually become filled with the light of day, with the realism of the town's community, which is so much in need of strengthening and encouragement. This everyday realism serves the same function in this story as it did in *The Bridal Canopy;* it creates a handhold for some solution in the midst of the emptiness that Agnon's psychological explorations have cast over his work. Here, Agnon obviously employs ancient Jewish traditions that gave to the generations of Jewry their philosophy, whether kabbalistic or hasidic. For writers and artists, even if they were involved in an extremely individualistic art, nonetheless turned to the Jewish community and its concrete world to elevate its thought by imparting a social vision by which the individual too would be strengthened. Something of the same effect is produced by Agnon on the wayfarer after he had lost the first key and felt himself to be wandering in an abandoned, desolate, and pointless world—like Franz Kafka's empty universe where God is hidden and his voice no longer heard. Hence it is that Agnon puts into his narrator's mouth the following "utterance":

> These eyes of mine can not see by themselves. In my childhood I could see everything I wanted to see. When I grew a little older, my vision was reduced and I saw only what I was shown. Now I recognize neither what I wish to see nor what I am shown. How do I know? A voice sometimes reaches me, coming forth from God's creatures.[32]

It is only when he is entirely cut off from human voices that he feels he "can see nothing," and begins to think of the "merits of Jerusalem." These thoughts serve merely as harbingers of what he will soon hear from Rachel and from the sick child.

> There are places in the Land of Israel which seem like a dream even when you are awake. And most of all Jerusalem, which God selected from the entire country to be surpassingly fair. Therefore, there is no cause to wonder at a man who lies on his bed in Shibush and dreams of Jerusalem.[33]

Obviously, this dreaming of Jerusalem within the town of Shibush is a natural offspring of Reb Yudel Hasid's dreaming in *The Bridal Canopy*. Not only does it fail to spoil the realistic setting, but it endows it with a new vitality and continuity. The mystic symbolism that originally gave expression to individualistic longings and to the dim, inner world of the individual eventually becomes illumined by the light of the Jewish past. The first key to the Bet ha-Midrash the wayfarer has, indeed, lost and with it he has, as it were, lost the Jewish town, whether of Galicia, Poland, or the Ukraine. But the wayfarer has a new key made in the same pattern as the first, which opens wide the Bet ha-Midrash to the light of day and to the spirit of Jerusalem. From this point onward, everything becomes illuminated by the light and spaciousness of Jerusalem. The new key opens new doors to the visions of past and future, and the vacuum of Shibush is gradually filled by these visions. The dream of Jerusalem heals the blemishes in the souls of all the characters in the long story, and their longing for death vanishes before this new dawn. All the silence of the story seems to tremble in anticipation of the great solution.

The final chapters of *A Wayfarer Tarries the Night* are filled with a wonderful clarity in which everyday realism blends with a profound symbolism. The "finding of the key" pulsates with a dynamic force derived from the halakhah and the aggadah, in which the two complement each other within the realistic Jewish setting of this changing era. Indeed, the town has almost collapsed into decay, but just then a new Jewish child is born. It is a symbol of the survival both of the Jewish community and of the individual Jew; a hopeful sign of the renewal of life in the town in the spirit of Jerusalem. This revival Agnon presents with all the beauty and meaningfulness with which his art has been endowed. They reach their high-point when the wayfarer discovers the old key on his return to Jerusalem. He sees that his wife, who had opened his rucksack,

> was holding in her hand a large key. "I found it in the folds of the bag," she said. I stood there utterly amazed. It was the old key of our Bet ha-Midrash, which I had given to the atheist Yeruham's son on the day of the circumcision. How had it found its way here? Clearly, Yeruham, the atheist, who had rejected all the commandments, was annoyed that I had appointed his son guardian of the old Bet ha-Midrash and returned the key by hiding it in my bag. . . . That was the key the elders of the Bet ha-Midrash had handed to me before the concluding service on the Day of Atonement.[34]

In this way, Agnon transforms the key into a symbol of the continuity of Shibush-Jerusalem and at the same time brings his story back to the level of epic realism. The author, Shmuel Yosef Agnon of Shibush and Jerusalem, knew very well that every generation has its own forces, its own heart searchings, and that no generation resembles any other in its weaknesses and strengths. For this is the confession he makes:

> I stood up and placed the key in its container and held the key in the container over my heart. Why did I not hold the key to our old Bet ha-Midrash over my heart? Because my heart could not bear its weight. The old craftsmen used to make their keys very large and heavy; they do not suit the size of our hearts today.[35]

Indeed, as the author says, they are too large for the "size of our hearts today." The motive force of his story is derived from the cosmic vision of the passing generations. Whether the vision struggles up from the hidden recesses of silences, or rages at times of momentous transition, it is always ready to nourish the creative writing of the new Hebrew author.

The writings of Agnon as a whole display an overall structure of remarkable psychological insight. The gradual development of the central figure—at the first stage, Reb Yudel Hasid, at the second, the wayfarer who tarries the night, and at the final stage, Itzhak Komer, in the Land of Israel during the time of the Second Aliyah in *The Day Before Yesterday*[36]—is achieved by means of this structure. With this in mind, one must trace the long "history" that provides these three characters with an epic unity that underscores the uniqueness of Agnon's contribution to the history of Hebrew fiction.

Obviously, the modernistic tendency in Agnon's stories is liable at times to surprise the reader by its contradictory elements. While the author is busy creating his main character and following his various adventures against a realistic Jewish background, suddenly, as if in the course of conversation, he introduces a section about ghosts. Often the reader is snatched away from the everyday world of the Jewish hero into a maelstrom of digressions, dreams, visions, and nightmares interwoven one with the other, inverting the "order of the universe," overthrowing chronology, and, it would seem, threatening the epic quality of the main character with disintegration and collapse. The story seems to desert the framework Agnon has built for it to take matters into its own hands, shaking off all control in favor of a grotesque comedy having no bearing on the development of the central figure.

This aspect of Agnon's writing is clearly influenced by the modernistic trend usually called "stream of consciousness," which reached its peak in the work of James Joyce. This stream releases conscious thought from the control of logic, and leads the story into the realm of spontaneous association prompted by the subconscious impulses of the character's personality. The stream of consciousness frees the story from its architectonic realism and looses the psyche from restraint. The flow of narration seems no longer to be subservient to any prearranged plan within which the author intended his hero to develop, and the latter has no particular purpose to achieve. No such concepts as beginning and end apply to this type of writing, except in a physical sense—that is, we begin reading at one page and end at another. But the narrative itself merely serves as a channel for an endless flow of inner thoughts picked up by the narrator instinctively and spontaneously. In this modernistic school of writing, the narration offers what may be termed "islands of memory" in the ocean of the hero's subconscious—islands which appear and disappear without the purposeful causality essential for creating an architectonic structure in which a character can develop.

This modernistic technique is clearly visible in *The Bridal Canopy* and increases in force in *A Wayfarer Tarries the Night,* since in the latter Agnon does not employ the primitive folkloristic element of *The Bridal Canopy*. This folklore is, by its very primitive nature, concerned with the demonology of legend and myth and with magical incantation, which also tends to move from item to item by means of spontaneous association. While in *A Wayfarer Tarries the Night* Agnon does infuse his midrashic style with this popular folklore, the result frequently is a mysterious symbolism entirely different from the simple "tale after tale" or "tale within a tale" of *The Bridal Canopy*. The narrative flow in this story at times has a hidden silence within it that compensates, as it were, for the town's disintegration, and the narrator's voice seems to be coming from beyond the veil of the town and going out into a nothingness that swallows the sounds in eternal silence. This thread in the tapestry of *A Wayfarer Tarries the Night* supports our theory that these three stories, *The Bridal Canopy, A Wayfarer Tarries the Night,* and *The Day Before Yesterday,* constitute a single epic unit in which for the first time the figure of the Jew is presented as embodying both past and present. This needs further investigation: for if Agnon's primary artistic purpose was indeed the creation of a Jew firmly implanted in his own era and generation but at the same time responsive to the dynamic vision of Jewish history in which past and future intertwine, then this purpose is intrinsically self-contradictory.

At this point we reach an essential criterion in Agnon's writing, and one typical of all creative Jewish writing throughout history. It is here that Agnon's work becomes an organic part of Jewish literature throughout the generations. Most readers, as they grow accustomed to Agnon's unique style, move back and forth across the dialectic lines of narration, not only identifying themselves with the central character in the external, realistic setting of the town, but also with the narrator himself, who stands over and above the story, looking down at its rich content. The author's insight in allowing himself to become detached from his story and to look at it from a different perspective is quite remarkable, since in effect it introduces a second hero into the story. This additional hero is the narrator, who knows omnisciently from the very first how the story and the individual character will end, and constructs the story in advance in order to suit these purposes. And yet en route the story somehow finds its own way in its complex levels of psychological realism. Only when he recognizes this does the reader begin to be aware of the thin veneer of irony spread over all Agnon's writing.

The irony never disappears—it is found on the folkloristic level and the realistic, on the illusory level in *The Bridal Canopy* and in the mystic symbolism of *A Wayfarer Tarries the Night.* It is even present in the incident of Balak the dog in *The Day Before*

Yesterday, with which I shall deal in the next section. The irony accompanies the story throughout its wanderings as a sort of "personal supervisor" over the development of plot and the psychological experiences of the characters. The irony is not, in fact, embedded in any particular situation of this or that story, or in any particular experience—there are many situations suited to ironic treatment throughout the stories, but they do not provide the basis for the irony under discussion. It is dependent upon Agnon's fundamental style rather than any situation. The discerning reader will find in this irony the mark of the narrator's presence in the story and will identify it with the author's reflections on his own creative writing.

The irony is, then, Agnon's "stocktaking" as the plot of the story develops. The epic quality of his writing, his depiction of characters spanning the eighteenth and nineteenth centuries and closing with the Second Aliyah in the first decade of the twentieth century, the return of the hero from the "wide world" and from Palestine to his birthplace after World War I, and his eventual return to Palestine in the wave of immigration in the twenties—all this is more than a superficial account on a realistic level of the changes taking place in Jewry during these various periods. It is rather a study of the deeper psychological changes undergone by Jewry during this era of transition. Agnon's ear was sensitive to all these changes, and in the wide sweep of his epic the main characters seem almost to be coming one by one to demand their portrayal—Reb Yudel Hasid, the wayfarer who tarries the night, and Itzhak Komer, together with the minor characters dependent upon them. Therefore, the author's examination of the outer, realistic world of Jewry invariably leads him to a study of the characters' inner world as both individuals and members of a community. If Agnon has a premeditated plan whereby the story will develop according to his wishes, in fact the story seems always to be wandering off of its own accord into numerous digressions the author had not planned. Here we stumble upon a certain ambivalence in Agnon's artistry which is the source of the irony apparent throughout his work.

On the one hand, no main character in his work ever sets out on his journeys without a settled "view of the world." This view of life, this visionary purpose, forms an organic part of all Jewish writing and especially of Agnon's epic works. They are the direct descendants of that view of life inherent in scriptural narrative, in prophetic writings, in the wisdom literature, and in the halakhah, the aggadah, the Enlightenment, and Hasidism. Agnon's heroes too could not exist without a firm view of life and a vision of the world. Reb Yudel Hasid is always listening for the steps of the Messiah as he goes from door to door in search of a dowry for his daughter; Hanania of *In the Heart of the Seas* spreads his kerchief on the surface of the water and the way to the Holy Land leaps open before him; and the wayfarer who tarries the night accepts the key to the Bet ha-Midrash from those who have no further use for it and finds that same "old" key in the Land of Israel, even though he continues to use the new one because it is "not so heavy." Itzhak Komer of *The Day Before Yesterday* is actually working for the upbuilding of the Land of Israel and the establishment of the state. All these are clear instances of an overall plan and vision in Agnon's mind before he even thought out his characters. This is the source of his characters' solidity and credibility, and also of the epic quality of the trilogy.

On the other hand, whenever Agnon touches his characters even with the tip of his pen, the story, as we hinted above, seems to leap out of the boundaries established by the scheme, the purpose, and the vision of the work. The language begins to respond to demonic impulses and the narrator, far from subjecting this psychological world to the discipline of consciousness and condemning it to silence, on the contrary releases these complexes with the sheer delight apparent in his treatment of them. At this stage Agnon sems to be nullifying all that he has achieved in the epic characterization that gives the trilogy its unity. The reader too eventually responds to this delight in the mingling of the outer and inner worlds within the stream of consciousness in *The Bridal Canopy* and *A Wayfarer Tarries the Night*.

Agnon is aware of the ambivalence inherent in his writing, and as a result there arises the irony present throughout the trilogy, born of his knowledge that the narrator is, indeed, continuing with his epic purpose but the "speech he utters" is somewhere breaking through the bounds of his original plan. It is then that the reader begins to wonder at this technique and to be puzzled by the question, whether it is not the narrator himself who is giving vent to those powerful expressionistic forces that have for so long been driving him toward the whirlpool of surrealism to which the text keeps veering, and, therefore, whether it is he himself who is endangering the epic quality of the story. But the ironic eye of the author catches the eye of the reader and the reader too begins playing hide-and-seek in the belief that it "will all turn out for the best." In *The Bridal Canopy* and *A Wayfarer Tarries the Night* the reader never loses his faith in the positive aspect of the story and the epic fulfillment at which the author aims. The text itself seems to announce the epic conclusion that we expect. There is only one book by Agnon in which this does not hold true, and this is *The Book of Deeds,* which was written before *The Day Before Yesterday* and immediately after *A Wayfarer Tarries the Night.*

The entire literary purpose of *The Book of Deeds* is summarized in its title. From the very beginning it disclaims any premeditated plan such as we expect from an architectonically designed story. Each of the tales in the book seems to be devoid of any conscious purpose. They are self-contained, living out their "lives" in a vacuum of time and place. Neither Berdichevsky nor Gnessin adopted this technique in their yearning for the infinite depths of the human soul, wherein their works departed from the traditions of the "new trend" in Hebrew literature at the beginning of the twentieth century. For, in fact, Berdichevsky and Gnessin devoted their main strength to struggling against the established conventions of Hebrew fiction, in order to endow their surface realism with a deeper significance drawn from man's inner world —whether it was the "religious" significance of "Shadows" by Feierberg, or the archetypal eroticism of Berdichevsky's short novels, or the despairing search for lost reality in the writings of Gnessin.

In his *The Book of Deeds,* Agnon seems to accept both the external world and the inner world, but each of them floats in a vacuum. They collide and merge without any result, creating a purposeless fantasy lacking the messianic awareness of Reb Yudel Hasid and the visionary hope of the wayfarer who tarried the night. No other work by Agnon is so filled with people, events, and images, and no other work raises such problems of modernistic expression; but its motive force comes from beyond the limits of logical planning. Indeed, all the tales in this book resemble the imagist technique of the surrealists: they hang in an artistic vacuum, each independent, ignoring the instructions of the author, who is supposed to know more or less in which direction he wishes to travel. The deeds in *The Book of Deeds* seem to be attacking their creator, demanding expression, each insisting upon the right to "utter speech" within the words of the narrator. The same "uttering of speech" that Agnon had dwelt upon in *A Wayfarer Tarries the Night* has become lord and master by virtue of a primitive force that compels the narrator to deal with each in turn, driven as he is by an irresistible, primeval desire. As the stories take command of the author, so he longs for the light touch that in *The Book of Deeds* replaces the epic vision of the trilogy. All sorts of boundaries and fences collapse before these deeds, which struggle along without any concept of an "ordered world" derived either from ancient heritage or from visions of the future. Agnon's epic dialogue falls completely apart; it is no longer subordinated to any Jewish ideal, whether of the community or of the individual.

> I was looking for someone who could tell me where the house was. My eyes closed again. I struggled with all my strength to open them. They opened to admit only a slit of light. The moon came out and shone its dusty-gray light upon them. I saw a little child. She beckoned me with her finger and said, "Here it is!" I wanted to ask her how she knew what I wanted. My eyes opened and I saw my father holding a glass of wine in his hand and about to recite kiddush, but pausing, waiting.
>
> I was afraid I might disturb the quiet of the house, and tried by a look to convey to my father the reason for my long delay. My eyes closed again. I struggled to open them. There was the sound of a sheet being torn. In fact, no sheet had been torn, but a cloud in the sky had parted. And as it parted, the moon came

out through the clouds, shedding a sweet light on the house and on my father.[37]

The language here is deeply sensitive. On the one hand it tends to formlessness, to a whirl of events devoid of all order and meaning, free from the control of the narrator. Some distant experience has swept away the artist's consciousness, and his language has become responsive to aimless, purposeless incidents occurring without any sequence. His pen seems to be moving of its own accord, without beginning or end, with no ear or eye to impose any order, discipline, or meaning on the confusion. The spontaneous movement has a nightmarish effect on the reader, echoing sacred myths lost in the antiquity of man.

On the other hand, this formlessness gradually merges with a dreamy musicality in which every action and object loses its solidity and realism. Every action and every object is both itself and something else too. Time and space seem to coalesce and the language of the stories weaves the pattern of a strange phantasmagoria in which the narrator has lost all self-awareness and his existence all meaning, sense, beginning, and end. The style of *The Book of Deeds* brings Agnon into the world of Franz Kafka, created by the gulf between man and God in a universe devoid of all significance and purpose, and in which objects and events float in a vacuum. The narrator, in his world of fantasy, continues:

> After this, I told myself that I ought to find my wife. My thoughts troubled me and I lost my way, suddenly finding myself in a street I had never seen before. It was no different from any other street in the city, even though I knew that I had wandered into a place I did not recognize. At that hour, all the shops were closed and small lamps burned in the windows among all sorts of merchandise. I saw that I had wandered far from home and knew that I would have to take another route, but did not know which. I gazed at a staircase flanked on both sides by iron railings. I ascended it, arriving at a small flowershop. There I found a small group of people standing with their backs to the flowers, and Doctor Rishel was standing among them, telling them of his new suggestions concerning grammar and style.
>
> I greeted him and asked him the way to . . . but before I could name the street, I began to stammer. I had not forgotten

216

the name of the street, but my tongue refused to pronounce it.
You can understand how a man feels when he wants to ask
the way somewhere and, as he is about to ask, he cannot pronounce
the name of the place. But I pulled myself together and pretended
I was only joking. I suddenly broke out in a cold sweat. I was
forced to admit what I was trying to conceal. When I tried once
again to ask where the street was, the same thing happened as
before.[38]

Every story becomes increasingly involved. The experience
builds up, but it fails to reach any conclusion—it has no desire to
reach a conclusion. It makes no effort to free itself from its dark
oppressiveness. For this reason, neither *The Book of Deeds,* nor
many other stories that Agnon wrote after *The Day Before Yesterday,* partake of real tragedy, and of the struggle that marks
such tragedy. For inherent in all real tragedy is the struggle between a formless, aesthetic impulse, whose sole purpose is directed
toward expressing itself with complete freedom from any "outside" influences (such as social or national, which do not arise
from man's inner world), and the intellectual consciousness that
restrains and subdues this impulse in the name of creative art.
Tragedy always enters the work of art by means of a recognition
of the selfhood of man, of his mastery over the abysses, whether
external or internal, which open before him on his path. But in
The Book of Deeds, man's self is weak and his actions whirl him
about as if caught up in uncontrollable gusts of wind.

At times, however, these undisciplined actions and emotions
are suddenly illumined by a flash of insight from the author. It is
then that we sense the author's sorrow that he has released upon
his central character this unconscious inner world. "This is the
dark sorrow," the author writes both of himself and his hero, "of
creatures of the universe whom God has raised, but not sufficiently, so that they are still far from the heavens." Or, "I placed my
hand on my heart and, feeling it, saw that between each pulse my
time was slipping away. Only in a dream can we see this. As yet,
our imagination does not suffice." Or in the story about his friend
who becomes blind, "Eventually, he opened his eyes. . . . His two
proud eyes filled with light and I saw myself standing by my

217

house." But flashes of this kind disappear as quickly as they come and are lost again "as time slips away between each pulse of the heart."

In this respect *The Book of Deeds* stands in direct contrast to *The Bridal Canopy* and *A Wayfarer Tarries the Night*. The latter, for all their modernistic and expressionist tendencies, are permeated by a vision of universal stability, of redemptive purposefulness, which grows throughout all the demonological digressions of the hero and reaches the level of consciousness for both the individual and the Jewish community. In *The Book of Deeds*, however, Agnon succumbs to a feeling of isolation that is far superior in his characters to the isolation I examined in the earlier chapters. Feierberg, Gnessin, and Brenner were authors who attempted to transfer their personal sense of isolation to the objective world of their writings. Gnessin served as a powerful stimulus to modern Hebrew literature, and Berdichevsky and Berkovitz originally attempted to create an individualized character torn between his inner and outer worlds. Yet none of these negated in their writings their hero's self-awareness. On the contrary, this awareness is an essential ingredient of their literary purpose. But Agnon, by his profound concern with modern expressionism, seems to make the principle of isolation part of himself, denying the reality of human self-awareness controlling action in the comings and goings of the individual. Nevertheless, before he completed his trilogy, Agnon drew back from the total vacuum of *The Book of Deeds* and from its extreme form of expressionism derived from European literature.

He had still to write *The Day Before Yesterday,* which was included in the ninth volume of his writings—that is to say, it was written after *The Book of Deeds*. There he escapes from the nightmare world in which deeds "wander about lost" in the empty void of life, uncontrolled by any vision on the part of him who performs the deed, and lacking all significance for the Jewish community at large. The dark Kafkaesque world and the surrealist nightmare are dispelled by the redemptive vision of *The Bridal Canopy* and *A Wayfarer Tarries the Night,* to which was now added *The Day Before Yesterday*. We shall now examine this final volume in Agnon's epic trilogy.

Shmuel Yosef Agnon

Agnon passed from the surrealism of his *The Book of Deeds* to this final volume of the trilogy like someone emerging from nightmarish darkness to the broad light of day. But it was not only the phantasmagoria of *The Book of Deeds* that disappeared as he began *The Day Before Yesterday;* even the element of fantasy dominating *The Bridal Canopy* and *A Wayfarer Tarries the Night* evaporated. The mingling of inner and outer worlds gradually lifts here and the author brings his vision of redemption to realistic fulfillment. The somewhat grotesque void of *The Book of Deeds,* in which man, stripped of vision and purpose, wanders with vague half-desires, vanishes before a new meaningfulness that the hero of *The Day Before Yesterday* discovers in the pioneering world of the Second Aliyah, during the first decade of the present century in the Land of Israel. Even the folkloristic demonology of Reb Yudel Hasid in *The Bridal Canopy,* and the silent atmosphere of a longing for death in *A Wayfarer Tarries the Night,* eventually undergo a change in the pattern of literary realism that directs the narrator to the "recidivists of the nineteenth-century school," as they were called by the younger Hebrew critics as yet unable to free themselves from the shock of European and American modernism in the forties and fifties. This realism, however, elevates *The Day Before Yesterday* to the level of great art and transforms the story into an epic in the fullest sense of the term.

It is the story of a young man from Galicia named Itzhak Komer, the grandson of Reb Yudel Hasid, who left his small town for the European city, and, after much suffering, eventually reached the Land of Israel at the time of the Second Aliyah, with the goal of becoming a Zionist pioneer. In the course of time, however, as he works as a housepainter in the city of Tel Aviv, he responds to certain "inner changes" as a result of his immigration. Agnon places him in the turbulent social setting of Palestine, providing profoundly perceptive insights not only into the character of Itzhak Komer himself, but also into the historic figures of that era, among them Yosef Haiyim Brenner, Aaron David Gordon, and their comrades in the settlements of Kinneret and Deganiah,[39] as well as those in the young city of Tel Aviv—all of whom molded the character of the Second Aliyah and had so deep an effect on the future destiny of the country. Outwardly, they were men dedicated in their daily activities to the national and social struggle for "the conquest of labor," for "the conquest of defense," and for the adoption of modern Hebrew as the national tongue. Inwardly, however, each of them as an individual was "forlorn of God," seeking deep down for some meaning in life and in his own individual existence. Their inner lack was due to the profound despair that had gripped them on reaching the spiritual crossroads in Europe after World War I. From the point of view of the story as a whole and of the subtle differentiation between the various characters, Agnon achieved in *The Day Before Yesterday* the peak of epic writing in modern Hebrew literature.

One of the sure signs of this new process is the absence of the dialogue technique, which he had needed to blend realism and fantasy in his earlier stories. There are, indeed, numerous midrashic echoes in the style itself, but these serve solely to create the atmosphere of an overlapping of past and present. This is the most striking change in Agnon's style as his interest in surrealistic techniques waned and he concentrated exclusively on the epic. The stylistic mannerism of talmudic question and answer, by which Agnon had previously moved from intense realism to messianic vision to grotesque existentialism, begins to disappear from *The Day Before Yesterday*. In *The Bridal Canopy* the narrator himself keeps emerging, disappearing and then reemerging from the stream of narration. In the wealth of changes and transformations that occur at the numerous levels of Reb Yudel Hasid's strange journey, the narrator is always present, ready to come to his hero's assistance, to protect his spiritual integrity from his dreams and illusions. Similarly, in *A Wayfarer Tarries the Night,* the author is on his guard against his own hidden aesthetic impulses, the secret individual desires that demand artistic expression in his literary work. In contrast, the narrator of *The Day Before Yesterday* frequently uses the term "we." In other words, he acknowledges that he is relying upon his own memories of the people of the Second Aliyah, which he feels he must "immortalize" in epic form. And yet, the element of identification suggested by this word "we" really testifies to the motive force of the entire trilogy, beginning with the wanderings and adventures, continuing through wonderful dreams and silent decay, and concluding with the portrayal of a character molded by both the halakhah and the aggadah.

It is now easy to deduce why Agnon felt it necessary on a number of occasions to allude to the fact that Itzhak Komer was the grandson of Reb Yudel Hasid. What seems strange to Yudel Hasid and hidden to the wayfarer who tarried the night in the town of his birth becomes clear in *The Day Before Yesterday*, in the realistic portrayal of the Jewish pioneer by means of a combination of halakhah and aggadah. This is the way Agnon describes the beginnings of Ein Ganim:

> Itzhak made a move one day, left the confines of Petah Tikvah and went to Ein Ganim. The reddish-black soil that used to grow weeds, thorns, lizards, and scorpions now produced trees and vegetables, poultry and cattle, houses and sheds, men, women, and children. During the day, the men worked in Petah Tikvah as day laborers or on a monthly wage, but returned from work in the evening to expend their energy on the village in which they had settled.
>
> How had it happened that this desolate, uninhabited place had become a settled village? Well, just at that period when it seemed we had no future in Palestine, there arose a small band of pioneers devoted to the Land of Israel who said: "We will not move from here." They met and formed an association to establish a village settlement—that is, to purchase a certain number of dunams of land and till the soil. On the days when they found work elsewhere, they would do their own work when they were finished, and on the days when they found no work elsewhere, they would spend the entire day on their own land. They had no money on which to live and certainly none to purchase any land, for they were day laborers and work was not available every day. But their will and determination drove them to overcome all obstacles. This is not the place to relate all the details, for they are well known.
>
> At any rate, they purchased a piece of land and every day, when they returned from work in Petah Tikvah, they would go out with their wives and children cutting down weeds, turning over the soil, and making bricks. They had no water, for the well was a long way from the settlement through sands, weeds, and thistles, and they went barefoot in order to spare their shoes.

But they would not spare themselves, and they used to fetch water from far away in order to make bricks and build themselves homes. Near the houses you would find good soil, which welcomed those who worked it. They ploughed, sowed, and planted. They had no water, for the well was a long way from their settlement. But they would not spare themselves any effort and used to fetch water from far away in order to water their gardens. The gardens grew well and produced fine saplings, whose praise was in everyone's mouth, and many people came to buy them. However, they would not sell their saplings, but let them grow into fine trees. These men labored hard, suffered hunger and disease, and with the money could have purchased a little quinine to ease their fever, but they exercised self-control through hope in the future. The women were just the same. Even the most delicate of them took from their own mouths in order to feed the poultry. Like mother, like daughter; like father, like son. Such was Ein Ganim, the first Hebrew workers' settlement in the Land of Israel, purchased by the workers' own toil.[40]

The remarkable simplicity of style in this passage contrasts vividly with the sophisticated dialogue of the previous stories. And yet it is rich in the insight into life that has always been the first requirement of the epic throughout world literature. It becomes elevated here by a vision of humanity inherited from the Bible, the Mishnah, the aggadah, and the Midrash organically interwoven and combining the past and future. This stylistic simplicity conceals a powerful undercurrent that endows the working community of Ein Ganim with greatness and beauty, and at the same time highlights Itzhak Komer as one of the pioneers.

The overt theme of *The Day Before Yesterday* is the social, economic, and religious world in which the men of the Second Aliyah live, with their national and individual aspirations. Each of them has his own private dreams and fears. The plot of the story, which is centered on Itzhak Komer's sojourn in Jaffa and Jerusalem, develops by means of a progressive accumulation of incidents, characters, landscapes and experiences. It is a broadly sweeping novel taking in the whole of the day-to-day scene by means of the narrative flow with its undercurrent of the meeting of past and present. There are Komer's friends before he leaves for the Land of Israel; his childhood home in Galicia, forgotten yet ever present; Komer's gradual awakening from his romantic, provincial illusions; the harsh conditions in Palestine at the beginning of the century; Jaffa and Jerusalem in all their beauty and squalor; the historic blending of old and new; the backbreaking toil dignified by the idealism of the pioneers; the teeming variety of characters—workers, writers, teachers, orthodox, atheists, and searchers after God, aesthetes and anarchists; lives for the most part outwardly drab but inwardly illumined by the anticipation of something great and wonderful that was in the air, bursting forth with tidings of a mighty reawakening due at any moment. All this provides the story with its content and with its clear, forward movement that never digresses into any side issues, with the sole exception of the Balak incident, which I shall deal with later.

At times *The Day Before Yesterday* becomes filled with a deep love for the landscape of the Holy Land—not by means of vague hints, as in the previous stories, but clearly and openly. The author's eye examines the plants and living creatures in much the same way as it examines the people in Ein Ganim, in Jaffa, and in Tel Aviv. They have a special beauty, a particular significance, and they are treated with an affection arising out of a sense of their profound meaningfulness. Aaron David Gordon speaks of them in this way to his friends in Kinneret and Deganiah, as does Yosef Haiyim Brenner, when among his friends.[41] The "ordinary" workingman suddenly loses his mood of depression and becomes fired with a sense of meaning and purpose. The language in which all this is conveyed seems to burgeon naturally from the new atmosphere created by the Jewish workers, from the author's conviction that Itzhak Komer had not been wrong in his dream, in the same way as his friends in Deganiah and Kinneret had not been wrong. This is the inspiration of the story, even though the author never hesitates to deal with the less attractive features of the Land of Israel, or with the mood of depression that so frequently descends upon the characters.

Such, then, is the overt theme of the first part of the story—what Agnon called "the first volume." There is an inner theme deep within Itzhak Komer himself, which gradually becomes interwoven in this first volume with the spiritual problems of the entire community of the Second Aliyah. All his impulses and desires are given meaning and purpose, content and vitality, ideal and outlet. The folkloristic digressions in *The Bridal Canopy,* the powerful longings for mystic symbolism in *A Wayfarer Tarries the Night,* and, above all, the surrealistic tendencies of *The Book of Deeds,* are all "pacified" in the realistic atmosphere of this first section. The actions, speech, meditations, characters, and events no longer take place in a vacuum, but form an integral part of the new world created by the Jew. In this first volume, there is also a remote, mighty source of humor that sometimes smiles at the romantic illusions of Zionism—the messianic illusions—which permeate the souls of these youngsters and at times tinge the realism of the scene with a visionary quality.

This is not true of the other portions of *The Day Before Yesterday.* From the beginning of the second volume until the end of the book, the story concentrates all its attention on Itzhak Komer's love for Sonia, his settling in Jerusalem, his work as a house painter, and his relationships with the residents of the orthodox Meah Shearim quarter of Jerusalem. There is a different tone in this part—a new, almost primitive, breeze has begun to blow. The squalid atmosphere of certain quarters of Jerusalem at the beginning of this century seems to have ensnared the author's style with a disillusioned naturalism completely devoid of the epic tonality that animated the first volume. This naturalism has none of the confidence and perception of the earlier part, but breaks through into the demonological world within the realistic setting of the Meah Shearim quarter, at both the individual level and the level of the squalid community, but most of all in relation to Itzhak Komer himself, who is drawn there by his love for Sonia. The peculiar intensity of language introduces satiric undertones, often more biting than the familiar satire of Mendelé Mokher Sefarim a few generations before. For Mendelé's satire, whether intentionally or not, was aimed at correcting the faults of Jewish society, while the satiric undertone in Agnon, however concealed, is there for its own sake through the whim of the author. One passage, describing the illness of Faish, an inhabitant of Meah Shearim who had been bitten one night by a mad dog called Balak, will illustrate this growing tendency in Agnon's writing.

> Slowly Reb Faish's thoughts ceased. His limbs relaxed and his thoughts left him. Sleep descended upon him and he dozed off. The Torah and its commandments, good and bad deeds, Gehinom and the Garden of Eden, this world and the world to come, disappeared and nothing was left but his body, stretched out between cushions and eiderdowns, and heavily perspiring. His lips parted and became wet with saliva. At times they appeared blue, at times purple. At first Rivka kept drying them, but when she saw that there was no end to it, her arms grew tired and she left his lips alone. But Shifra would not leave them alone. Like a butterfly on a rainy day fluttering its wings to keep them dry, so Shifra fluttered the colored rag with which she dried his lips. He would stir, gaze at her as though through a thick cloud, and slip back into a doze.[42]

The staccato rhythm of this passage is typical of the style in the section following the first volume. The language is weighed down not so much by the fact that Faish is lying ill in bed as by the strange devotion mingled with a grotesque undercurrent by which the author describes Reb Faish's illness in the development of the plot. This is the new quality that Agnon introduces into the account of Komer's move to Jerusalem, and particularly into the descriptions of him in Meah Shearim. The central pivot of this new tone is to be found in the dog Balak.

In Jerusalem, Itzhak Komer leaves the pioneering world of his earlier days and becomes a house painter. By chance he meets in the course of his work a starving, stray dog that clearly wants a little affection from a human being. In a moment of flippancy, he paints on the back of the dog the word "klb"—"dog" spelled backward with the alteration of one letter, to read "Balak." This act, a purely chance incident arising from a moment's good humor, dominates the rest of the story and serves as the foundation without which the section beginning with the second volume and ending with the final chapter would collapse.

The second volume lacks any visionary impulse; it begins in a vacuum and ends without any real conclusion. Even before the appearance of the dog, with all the grotesquely evil consequences concealed within its entry into the story, the irony in Agnon's style begins to rise to the surface, introducing a sardonic note into the narrative. Jerusalem, with its orthodox and its atheists, its intelligentsia and its laborers, lacks the vitality that animated his earlier descriptions of Ein Ganim, Jaffa, and young Tel Aviv. The humor with which Agnon describes Itzhak Komer in Jerusalem even before he meets the dog seems to be searching for some literary "adhesive" whereby the author could cement the story into an organic unit. The incident of Komer and the dog provides this adhesive, and the resultant story surpasses in its expressionistic force everything Agnon had previously written. Whenever Komer achieves some personal distinction, the story "returns to Balak"— to use the phrase that Agnon affixed to many chapters in the story. Balak becomes, in effect, Komer's alter ego. The flippancy Komer displayed in painting of the dog reveals the grotesque aspects of Jerusalem. It brings Balak to despair and madness because of his evil thoughts about mankind, and he eventually bites Komer, destroying the latter's life too.

The story of Balak, therefore, runs parallel to the story of Itzhak Komer, contrasting the adventures of Komer in Jerusalem with those of the dog. In the sections devoted to Balak, there is a new intensity of language that testifies to the author's delight in achieving his demonological, comic purpose. This delight is sometimes restrained by an assumed seriousness, when the author pretends to sympathize with the dog, whom an ironic fate is driving toward catastrophe; at times he acknowledges his amusement at the sport a mocking fate is having in the quarters of Jerusalem. This is the source of the intensity even in the descriptions of scenery, which are more frequent here than in any of Agnon's previous stories. In the following passages, in which these descriptions of scenery are intertwined with the adventures of Balak, the reader will discern at once the difference between the descriptions of Ein Ganim and Jerusalem.

> While Balak's thoughts were roaming about, dawn rose and the time arrived for the creatures of heaven and earth to sing their morning hymn. But where were those waters of which it is

written: "When He uttereth His Voice, there is a multitude of waters?" Where were the rivers of which it is said: "The rivers clap their hands?" Where were the springs that sing their hymns? Jerusalem was as dry as a desert. Were it not for two or three score trees and shrubs, there would be no hymns at all heard in Jerusalem. At that moment, the sun could be heard saying: "At the light of Thy arrows they went, at the shining of Thy glittering spear." Jerusalem awoke from its sleep and from every house, hut, and shack people began throwing out all sorts of slops into the street. But before Balak could slake his thirst, the burning sun had dried them completely, leaving nothing but a heap of filth.[43]

The ironic humor of this passage is typical of all the descriptions of nature occurring in the book in association with Balak's adventures. The author juxtaposes the two characters; whatever Itzhak Komer achieves and transforms into positive qualities in the course of his labor, for his pioneering vision never deserts him completely, is reflected with a horrifying surrealism in the Balak theme. This is how Agnon descibes Komer and his friends bathing at Jaffa beach one Sabbath eve.

Gradually the sun sank and disappeared into the sea. The gateway to the west reddened and the waves rose higher. The ocean roared, but there was silence within the roaring. The sea foamed, the foam covering the crests of the waves that changed their hue as they rose into the space between heaven and earth, between sea and sky. The heavens and the earth changed their quality too, and hidden longings began to throb in the air, longings that could not be felt by the five senses but only by the heart, which shared in those longings. Those in the sea now left the waves, came up, dried themselves, and dressed. They were all cleanshaven, their moustaches trimmed, for they had been to the barber before coming.[44]

The sensitive reader will detect at once the difference in tone between this descriptive passage and the one before it. This one has a far greater dramatic force than the description of a Jerusalem dawn. Moreover, it has an epic confidence and musicality in which the staccato rhythm compensates for any failings in the author's aesthetic perceptiveness. The changing hues of the sunset, the changing sounds of the sea, and the changes taking place in the heavens and on the earth all occur because of the invisible Sabbath atmosphere, which suggests that man's inner depths are led by that Sabbath beauty toward complete spiritual integration. This is the exact opposite of the description of Jerusalem at dawn, which conveys the emptiness of Balak's world. The difference is not between the mighty waters of Jaffa beach and the infinite desolation of Jerusalem; it is rather between the pioneering atmosphere of Itzhak Komer's sojourn in Ein Ganim and Jaffa and that of his stay in Jerusalem, which is struggling for its pioneering quality and at the same time is caught up in the devilish fate symbolized by the adventures of the dog Balak. Indeed, the identification of Itzhak Komer with Balak is expressed openly in a number of passages as the reader approaches the scene of Balak's biting Itzhak's leg and of Itzhak's death in the terrible agonies of madness. One such passage will suffice to illustrate the point.

> Once Itzhak dreamed that he was standing in a place that was hot and without shade. He was assailed by thirst, and thought he would faint. He saw a girl passing with a pitcher of water but he could not reach her. Worse than his thirst was the fact that he did not recognize where he was and had no idea why and how he had got there or why his shoulders felt so heavy. He saw Pnina standing there, ploughing, and Itzhak asked her, "Where are we?" Pnina replied, "Can't you see we are in Um Juni?" Now he no longer felt surprised at why he was there, but was surprised that her voice was that of Shifra. He took the hoe from his shoulder and began hoeing. Askanowitz came along with a photographer while he was standing behind the people who were ploughing. Suddenly Itzhak was wakened by the sound of a dog barking under his window.[45]

Here begins the note of flippancy in Komer the house painter, a flippant mockery that at first seems innocent and devoid of any evil intent but that later becomes "a chain of reactions" containing some grotesque blemish that will lead only to destruction. Now the author removes the story from the category of the epic, the mingling of realism and vision in Itzhak Komer, and turns to the naturalistic expressionism of the Balak incident, which is empty of all vision and which directs all the artistic impulses to achieving its satanic intent. The dog unintentionally terrifies

Jerusalem, transferring to all its areas the same demonic horror
that has been placed upon the dog itself. The language is now
devoted to an existentialist nightmare of which Balak is only the
symbol. Within the world of the dog everything has lost its meaning, everything is without significance; the universe moves without supervision and in the direction of madness. Everything is
suspended in a savage abyss consuming all the messianic longing
that Agnon frequently invokes in his passages on Jerusalem and
that at times even touches Balak himself. The dog never understands why his past friends have suddenly begun throwing stones
at him and running away from him. The inhabitants of Jerusalem, who have always been good to him, never realize that someone has been "playing a joke" on *them*—that a pioneering house
painter felt like playing a joke one quiet afternoon and therefore
implanted madness in their hearts. Only the author himself
knows. He looks down upon all this craziness and laughs loudly,
ironically, even expressing the madness in a popular ballad of the
type he used so frequently in *The Bridal Canopy* to adorn the
messianic longings of Reb Yudel Hasid.

> The moon disappeared behind its clouds, light breezes began
> to blow, rustling the olive trees; dew descended upon them and
> the air was filled with their scent. Balak awoke and peered
> through the sweet darkness, listening to the bells of the camels
> that, in caravan after caravan, were bringing food and supplies
> to us in Jerusalem. The sound of the bells and the night dew
> soothed Balak's spirit and calmed the anger that had been throb-
> bing through his body like poison. Balak gazed at the scene be-
> fore him, feasting his eyes, and was glad that his Creator had
> given him such understanding. . . . Then some evil spirit mur-
> mured to him that perhaps all the peacefulness was only tem-
> porary, that no one had seen him enter and in the morning, when
> the Holy One shed light on His universe, people would see him
> and attack him with sticks and stones. . . .
> So Balak lay down as if the whole night belonged to him. He
> began nodding his head as he sang, as if he were alone in the uni-
> verse with no other creature to hear him:
>
> > I gaze at the earth,
> > No candle is nigh;
> > I alone am awake
> > With the stars in God's sky.

No traveler here
Disturbs my domain,
Why then should my soul
Be grieving in vain?

The night is still long,
Still distant the day.
Close thine eyes, then, in sleep,
And slumber away.

Throughout the whole earth,
No human stirs now.
Be silent, all creatures.
Bow-wow, bow-wow-wow![46]

In fact, the story of Balak is not an allegory in the way that "my horse" is in Mendelé Mokher Sefarim, nor is it symbolic in the sense that some Hebrew critics in Israel think. The entire theme of madness is introduced here for its own sake, for the aesthetic pleasure in expressionistic writing it offered to the author. Nor was he satisfied till he had brought Itzhak Komer himself, the grandson of Reb Yudel Hasid, to the end fated for him at the moment he flippantly painted the name Balak on the dog's back. He is bitten by the dog, and, of course, goes mad himself, losing all the brilliant clarity and meaningfulness he had achieved through his pioneering ideology and his deep longing for salvation for himself and for his people. He becomes infected with the existentialism of the mad dog, who is totally lost. Through his pioneering work, Komer had, unknown to himself, become free of his sense of purposelessness. Now, however, Agnon devotes all his powers to the naturalistic description of the madness and death of the hero he had created and developed with such care.

What is the point of his putting an end to the life of Reb Yudel Hasid's grandson, the heir of the wayfarer who tarried the night in the town of his birth in order to revive the lost vision of redemption? What inner logic can be found in this episode, which marks the continuation of all the humanistic and messianic struggles of the trilogy? Agnon realized that his story needed some "correction,"[47] some apology, for he turns to his "good friends" and says:

> Now, my good friends, as we gaze at what has happened to Itzhak, we are amazed and dumbfounded. Why should Itzhak,

who was no worse than any other creature, have been punished
so? Because he teased a dog? But he only did it for a joke. What
is more, Itzhak Komer's end is not suggested by his beginning.
According to his nature and his abilities, he ought to have settled
on the land, to have made his home there, to have brought to
Palestine his father and his brothers and his sisters—those poor
creatures who had seen no pleasure in their lives because they
so longed for the Holy Land. . . .[48]

In these unanswered questions is contained the author's surprise
at the extraordinary deviation in his story. Agnon's self-perception
always serves as a charming conclusion to round off the last chapters of his works, and this is perhaps the most simple and direct
of them all. Actually, it complements the chapter in which Itzhak
throws in his lot with those settling at Ein Ganim.[49] It occupies
a page and a half at the end of *The Day Before Yesterday,* all of
it devoted to the rain that fell, stopped, and fell again after the
death of Itzhak Komer. But between the lines of this chapter, as
though between the drops of rain described in those lines, can
be felt the comfort, the vision, and the hope. The play is ended,
the nightmare is finished—only a deep and broad gravity is left in
the world. This seriousness has a hint of Komer's beginnings in it,
and serves as a fine epilogue to his travels in his ancient and
now revived motherland. In this epilogue all the satanic comedy
of the Balak episode is completely purged. The air of Jerusalem
is cleansed by the rains, and a pastoral charm descends upon the
universe. By means of the epic musicality of language that can be
heard once more in Agnon's writing, the ironic, expressionist
squalor is replaced by something Agnon had yearned for in all his
earlier stories, and it is fitting that this final chapter should conclude an examination of Agnon's art and of the struggles of
modern Hebrew fiction.

> On the day that Itzhak Komer was laid to rest, the sky clouded
> over. The sun was overcast, and a wind sprang up, accompanied
> by thunder and lightning. The sky trembled with the force of the
> thunder and began to shed large, warm drops of rain. The next
> day the clouds dispersed and the sun shone, and we knew that
> all our hopes had been in vain. Even the winds that we thought
> would refresh us brought no relaxation with them, for they were
> hot, and bit like leeches.

But at night the winds cooled down and the world became cooler too. By morning the sun was squeezed between the clouds, and, before it could complete its orbit, was driven from the sky. The sun had been a burning fire that with its intense heat had scorched all the grass of the field, parched the trees and dried up the springs of water. The dark clouds chased it until there was not one small corner of the heavens in which it could rest. And as we lifted our eyes heavenward to see whether the clouds were deceiving us, the blessed rain began to fall. Only the day before yesterday we had been standing in prayer, offering up selihot, sounding the shofar, and reciting the hoshanot, and now we were singing songs of praise and thanksgiving.

Once the rain began to fall, it did not cease day or night. The water cascaded down onto the roofs of our houses and under our houses, sweeping away utensils and causing houses to collapse. But the cisterns filled up with water. We now had water to drink, to cook with and to wash our hands. For six or seven days the rain fell, and when it stopped, it began all over again. At last the rain stopped, the clouds disappeared, and the sun shone. When we went outside, we saw that the earth was smiling with flowers and blossoms. From one end of the country to the other shepherds came with their flocks, and the bleating of sheep was answered by the chirping of birds in the sky. There was joy and happiness everywhere. There had been no happiness like it. All the villages in Judah and Galilee, in the plains and the mountains, were filled with fruit and produce, and the whole country was like the garden of the Lord. Every bush and blade of grass poured forth its perfume, as, of course, did the oranges. The country was like a lovely dwelling whose inhabitants had been blessed by God. And you, my brethren, you chosen ones of Kinneret and its environs, of Ein Ganim and Um Juni, which is Deganiah, you went out to your work in the fields and gardens, to the work that our friend Itzhak was not privileged to perform. Our friend Itzhak was not privileged to stand on the soil, to plow and to sow; but he was privileged, like Reb Yudel Hasid and many other righteous sages, to be buried in the soil of the Holy Land. Let those who will mourn for his sad death. But we will relate the deeds of our brothers and sisters, children of the living God, who work the land to their everlasting praise and glory.

The story of Itzhak is ended. The story of the rest of his friends, of the men and women, will be told in the book *A Plot of Land*.[50]

Appendix

Literary Ingathering/*Ha-Tekufah*

Concern over the future of Hebrew literature was expressed very forcefully at the Congress of Hebrew Literature and Culture held in Vienna in 1913, the year before the outbreak of World War I. It was here that Haiyim Nahman Bialik made his great plea for a "gathering together" of all Hebrew literature throughout the generations and throughout the various countries of the world, as well as of all literature in foreign tongues that had been produced by Hebrew writers. Bialik deliberately stressed the practical aspects in his talk, which even contained a detailed plan for making this literary collection.[1] Yet, in reading his lecture today, one is struck by the deep concern it betrays for the future of Jewry itself. He believed that the Jew must, as it were, retrace his footsteps through the ages, the wanderings of his destiny; he must recapture his hopes, longings, and sufferings together with his literary impulses and achievements from the beginnings of his history until our own era. He must reenact the pageant of the Jewish people as well as his own private dreams until the vision of Jewish identity is revealed to him, stretching from antiquity into the future. Such indeed is the poetry of Bialik (a subject I shall deal with in a separate volume), and it was this vision that prompted his plea for the collected works of Judaism, which he launched by producing with his friend Yosef Haiyim Ravnitski *The Book of Aggadah,* as well as other works.

Bialik, however, was not alone in his recognition of the dire necessity for such a collection. Berdichevsky earnestly supported him in his own particular way. By descending from the lofty, barren peaks of Schopenhauer and Nietzsche to the hasidic and folkloristic stories of Judaism, he showed how desperate in his eyes was the plight of Hebrew literature during the period of European crisis. The writers seemed to feel that some dreadful calamity was threatening Jewry, and they wanted to set up a wall

of defense against the spiritual disintegration that at the beginning of the century was becoming apparent in all branches of
European art. Bialik's literary collection was to serve as a divider,
blocking off Jewry from the inner destruction that had begun to
ravage the "enlightened" world. If Bialik never openly acknowl-
edged the reasons offered here for his project, whoever reads today
the speech he delivered at the Congress of Hebrew Literature and
Culture is at once impressed by the feeling of deep concern that
lay behind his plea, the longing for stability, for the preserva-
tion and continuity of Jewish philosophy and literature in the
future. For his plan included everything, from biblical and apocryphal writings to contemporary Hebrew literature. He seemed
to be saying that Jewish liteature had traveled a long road, from
pre-biblical pagan mythology to monotheism, with its spiritual
unification of man in the Bible itself; from apocalyptic concern
with demons to early mystical folklore and the Kabbalah to the
humanistic brilliance of Hasidism; from medieval writings to
modern literature. This long journey testified to the Jewish
people's power of survival throughout history, and it was the task
of Hebrew literature to gather these writings together at a time
when numerous troubles threatened a Europe that was suffering
from a growing sense of destruction.

At the same conference where Bialik delivered his plea for the
collection, there was another speaker—the critic David Frishman.
Frishman had made a most important contribution to Hebrew
literature, for he had, with painstaking care, weeded out the high-
flown phrases from Hebrew literature and concentrated on mod-
ernizing the language. He himself kept clear of all nationalist or
socialist ideologies—he could not bear the conformity and discipline imposed by such movements—and instead concerned himself with European art forms, tending frequently to an individualized romanticism in his translations and often demanding a simple
beauty in his critical works. He came to the congress with a plea
for "good literature," not in the form of any precise plan, and
certainly not with any practical suggestions. In an article entitled
"Youth or Childhood,"[2] Bialik poured his scorn upon Frishman

for having demanded from the congress "novels . . . and creative writers with new ideas," for seeing no solution for Hebrew literature except in "beautiful writing, namely, vision and poetry," when, in fact, Frishman and others like him had nothing to offer except negative criticism leveled against the Hebrew tradition.

Bialik was perhaps justified in his annoyance at Frishman's negative response to the idea of a "collection" of Jewish literature. Nevertheless, the poet failed to understand Frishman's fears for the humanistic literature of Europe, whose modernistic trends before World War I already showed signs of that spiritual barrenness spreading over the Western world. It is clear that Frishman himself had not yet formulated his ideas in the manner expressed here. At the 1913 Congress of Vienna, nobody foresaw that the "lights would be going out all over the world" for the long period of two world wars, and that in the wake of the various revolutions human values would be destroyed. Yet Frishman's realization of the need for "withdrawal" grew among Hebrew writers until it found expression in the establishment of the important publishing house of Stiebel and its collections *Ha-Tekufah* ("The Era"), of which Frishman was the first editor.[3]

The project was founded in 1918, and the Stiebel publishing house chose *Ha-Tekufah* ("The Era") as the name for its periodical. Did they mean to suggest by that name that the periodical would deal with the problems and achievements of Hebrew and world literature in that generation? For the era in which it began publication was one ravaged by crises in human history, by the destruction of the ideals, moral values, and aspirations that had accumulated during the centuries of the European Enlightenment. The literary sphere of *Ha-Tekufah* included creative writing of the great humanistic tradition, which even at that time was threatened by the spiritual fragmentation of the modernistic movement. Under these conditions, Hebrew literature, in its struggle for survival, introduced literary techniques from that very humanistic school, because that was what it needed. What future could it hope for in the barrenness infecting European writing from the symbolist poetry of Baudelaire through the modernism of the red, brown, and black revolutions, to the nihilism of T. E.

Hulme, T. S. Eliot, and their many disciples?[4] Thus we should not regard *Ha-Tekufah* as a literary anachronism any more than we should regard Bialik's plea for the "collection" as a literary anachronism. Both of them were pleas loyal to the faith and vision of Hebrew literature, whose vital strand snapped in Russia just a few years after 1918.

In those years, the last flickerings of democratic liberalism and socialism were visible in Europe. World War I had just ended, the first chapter in the apocalypse of western civilization whose destructive impulse reached its fullest force in the rise of German Nazism and World War II. The lull between the two wars was empty of all meaning for mankind. Somewhere in the ruins of World War I still glowed the embers of a faith in a better world for man, in the victory of political and economic democracy as the cultural heritage of humanity. In France, England, and the United States, people still spoke prophetically of the rule of reason, of the brotherhood of nations, of equality and justice for creative man. At the beginning of this inter-war period it still seemed that the terror gripping the heart of Europe and threatening its destruction was dying down. Even there the feeling of ruination began to be replaced by a new faith.

There were still some eminent figures on the European political stage, as well as in the realm of literature and humanistic philosophy. Cecil and Briand were still alive, fanning on the altar of humanism the flames that had been subsiding since the last decades of the nineteenth century. Even European socialism, which had, at the outbreak of World War I, been swept along by the ugly current of chauvinism to lend its blessing to murder and slaughter, now seemed to be reviving, prophesying a great future for western democracy. But it did not last long. Throughout Europe signs became visible of its decline in the twentieth century.

First of all, European literature gave way to a feeling of utter despair at its irrevocable fate. This literature, which in France, Russia, and other countries had previously fought for man's existence and for the meaning of that existence grew silent. An instance of this darkening can be seen in the French novelist Romain Rolland. His writings had previously been charged throughout with faith in the future and the nobility of man. He was dedicated to his great literary work and to his vision of man's advancement as an individual within a progressive society. He caught the spirit of life with a wonderfully varied musicality and harmonized it by means of his creativity, touching all his characters with his own visionary powers. Yet even Romain Rolland turned at this period to the lonely paths in which man grows silent as before some great oncoming evil.

In fact, this melancholy oppressiveness had infected European prose even before the outbreak of World War II. The bright rays that had shone upon the reader, emanating from the tragic figure of Tolstoy, the harshness of Ibsen, and the fierce anger of Zola, vanished, leaving in Europe and America only the faint glow of spiritual defeat, of the grotesque psychological distortions typical of Russian and Italian expressionism, of the neo-romantic chauvinism apparent in Nazi Pan-Germanism.

An incredibly strange sort of "nightmare complex" swept across Europe. Humanistic realism was pushed aside by the nightmare symbolism of chauvinistic neo-romanticism. The German Movement, which turned its back on urban civilization in favor of the soil and race and bloodshed, and royalist movement in France, which turned its back on democracy in favor of the nobility of the ancient past, opened literature to the demonic impulses that nineteenth-century realism had suppressed. The proof is to be seen in Gerhart Hauptmann and Knut Hamsun, who became so admired by the German intelligentsia that they eventually took on the coloring of Naziism. Only a few, like Thomas Mann, remained faithful to the vision of mankind conquering its destructive impulses by means of its intellectual powers. It was within this latter tradition that the idea of the "ingathering" arose, whether in Bialik's sense of finding in the treasures of the Jewish past a guarantee for the future, or in Frishman's sense of looking in the humanistic treasures outside, as well as in the young and fresh writings of Hebrew literature itself.

A glance through the thirty-five volumes of *Ha-Tekufah* shows that its contents were not selected on literary criteria alone. They contain many types of writing, often connected only indirectly with literature, but they are unified by a central idea that runs through the whole collection. In time, it may be that these volumes of *Ha-Tekufah* will become recognized as unique documents in the history of the Jewish battle for survival, marking a chapter in the series of collections produced at transition periods in Jewish history, such as the Mishnah, the Gemara, the Hebrew writings of the Middle Ages, the Kabbalah and Hasidism, which ensured the future of the Jewish people. There is a tradition that each of these collections possesses its own central idea while at the same time forming part of the general struggle for Jewish survival. What, then, is the special characteristic of *Ha-Tekufah?* What national or individual purpose did the first editor have in mind when, with his great breadth of knowledge, he went in search of material both in its original language and in translation, in both Jewish and world literature?

It would be wrong to assign this far-reaching work to the personal interests of any one man, yet as we read through the varied material contained in these volumes of *Ha-Tekufah,* the unique humanism of Frishman himself comes across clearly. To anyone looking back at this material after World War I, it must appear something of an anachronism, for what organic connection had Hebrew literature with the "world at large"? Yet in the same way that Zionism itself could never have succeeded without emphasizing its affinity to humanistic ideals, so Hebrew literature could not have survived had it followed in the wake of the fatalistic pessimism that was devouring world literature.

They were fateful times. We who lived through them know what lay hidden beneath the veneer of European culture and aestheticism. Frishman published in his *Ha-Tekufah* the writings of Rabindranath Tagore, with their dreams of unity between East and West, with their songs of universal love, simple, sacred, and purifying. Mikha Yosef Berdichevsky found in *Ha-Tekufah* an anodyne for the spiritual struggles of his hasidic stories and his short novel *Miriam,* while Shaul Tchernikhovsky created there a Hebrew idiom for the Jewish joie de vivre in his idyll, "The Marriage of Elkah,"[5] set in the steppes of the Ukraine and charged with a tragic significance drawn from his Jewish characters and from the ancient Russian and Scandinavian epics. Homeric poetry from Greece and the Latin elegiacs of Rome came to live in a revitalized Hebrew side by side with young Jewish writers whose works throb with creativity. Dr. Simhoni, aflame with love for ancient Hebrew writing, and Matityahu Shoham, the visionary gazing into the tragic depths of the human soul, found in *Ha-Tekufah* a sanctuary for themselves beside Goethe and Heine, with their universal concepts set within Western culture.

Bialik the realist, who had taken such care that his *Halakhah ve-Aggadah* should avoid any romantic associations, won a place for himself in *Ha-Tekufah* by means of his brilliant Hebrew translations of Anski's *The Dibbuk* and Schiller's *Wilhelm Tell*. Hillel Zeitlin, with his burning messianic faith and desperate search for divine redemption, entered the collection in the mystic garb of the holy Zohar, together with Lev Shestov, who also was crying out for salvation from within the depths of his despair and his apocalyptic visions of East-West struggles. Shmuel Yosef Agnon began his long journey into the epic in the pages of *Ha-Tekufah,* an epic beautiful in its traditional folkloristic element and its profound affinity to modernistic literary trends, while Gershon Shoffman achieved there his stylistic compression, conveying the essentials of human experience. In *Ha-Tekufah,* Shmuel Abba Horodetsky drank deeply from the sources of Kabbalah and Hasidism, and Ya'akov Steinberg, in his spiritual isolation, became involved in modernistic poetry while his heart remained faithful to the brilliant tradition of Jewish writing. Ya'akov Cahan, fascinated by the beauty of the Swiss landscape and by Jewish and universal longings for redemption, began within *Ha-Tekufah* to relate his folktales and then matured into symphonic dramas filled with nobility of thought. Uri Zvi Greenberg, envisioning the messianic era coming to those places where his Jewish brethren lived under oppression, began in its pages his rebellious song of the ascent of David's scion to the throne of the Holy Land. The very wise Diezendruck, with the weighty burden of his message, began to strip philosophy of the harmony that man's heart could no longer bear, and Ya'akov Fichman wandered in a dappled landscape, hearkening to the murmuring of the trees in Jerusalem,

239

whose roots, in their struggle for existence, forced their way though the cruel rocks to the springs of fresh water beneath. And Ya'akov Klatzkin left his Gemara behind him to teach in the pages of *Ha-Tekufah* a new lesson, that of the "sunset of life." There too was the literary legacy of Brenner and Gnessin, ornamenting it by their inspiring struggles for literature and for life. Aaron Zeitlin, at that time never dreaming of Maidanek and Treblinka, revealed the splendor of Polish literature, and Hillel Bavli came from the far reaches of America to write of Negro poetry. Ze'ev Jabotinsky, armed with a wonderful command of the Hebrew language, entered *Ha-Tekufah* with his translation of Dante's *Inferno*, while David Shimonowitz, enveloped in the deep melancholy of the Russian autumn, appeared there on his way toward his writings of idylls on the summer harvest in the land of his fathers. And there were many more, old and young, veterans and newcomers. All came under one roof—the tabernacle of literary creativity that God has bestowed on man.

The first editor of *Ha-Tekufah*, like those who followed him, never guessed that the lights were about to be turned off throughout Europe. The periodical was filled with the optimism of its broad project and of the aims of its publishers, as well as of the creativity of Jewry and the world at large. Who at that time was able to recognize in *The Blessing of the Soil* and *Pan* by Knut Hamsun the blind gropings of Wagner toward the dark and his lament for the "twilight of the gods"? Who could then discern the myth of desolation welling up within modern European literature? Many young Jewish writers were thrilled by the wondrous beauty of Gerhart Hauptmann's *The Sunken Bell*. With the gradual collapse of the shtetl, they were left confused, not knowing what powerful forces of evil lay hidden within the dramatic works of Hauptmann, who was later to become an open supporter of German Hitlerism. These young Jewish writers were fired with enthusiasm for the innovations of Western literature, the problems raised by reading Tolstoy, Dostoevsky, and Ibsen. Perhaps they responded to some faint echo of the Kabbalah and Hasidism, in the midst of their spiritual struggles—a feeling that they were "descending in order to rise."

Literary Ingathering

Certainly, for the Hebrew reader there were clear signs of that struggle in a literature of inner confusion, concerned with a battle for the redemption of man's soul. Yet it was not only Dostoevsky, with his constant yearning to justify God's treatment of man, who captivated these younger Jews as he has captivated generations of other writers, but also Tolstoy, his contemporary, that genius in his understanding of the human lot, gazing at man's paths upon earth and knocking at the door of his heart. Hebrew literature prided itself on its translation of Dostoevsky's *Notes from the Underground* and others of his stories, as well as on translations of Tolstoy's *Anna Karenina* and *War and Peace,* for they proved the ability of the Hebrew language to cope with new experiences untried in the realm of Hebrew literature until then and gave writers the feeling that they were at last beginning to play a part in world literature. The same was true for the translation of *Jan Christoff* by Romain Rolland, whose epic harmony, rich, colorful movement, and dynamic force fascinated the reader.

The Hebrew language was beginning to achieve a tone of universality, deriving from a love of the world in all its details, whether in the marketplace or the holy temple; it was a harmony pervading all aspects of human experience, lending it a visionary force, a splendid faith that transformed the mundane into a paean of joy. Those muffled sounds from beyond the horizons of the Jewish world began to reach the reader of Hebrew, filling him with a vague fear and arousing strange emotions. Even the wordless mystery of Maeterlinck's plays and poems, with their involvement in death and depression, gave him a feeling of majesty that Hebrew literature had not offered throughout its history. The Hebrew writer was now attracted to such works by an indefinable artistic impulse, and *Ha-Tekufah* and the Stiebel publishing house gathered them all together, providing the "collection" of which Frishman had dreamed in his plea for the "beauty" that formed the basis of European literature.

The list of books produced by Stiebel marks the crossroads that Hebrew literature had reached after World War I, its desire to gather to itself the works of western Euopean literature in all the variety of its interests, experimentation, and dilettantism. The translations published by Stiebel include the melancholy de Maupassant, with his biting irony, the delicate Parisian urbanity of Anatole France, shrugging off all man's agony with his light banter as if to say that he knows very well there is no solution—man is wiser to be a little pensive, a little skeptical, not taking his tragic lot too much to heart. Peter Altenberg, who always sought the ultimate in both the content and style of his writing, contrasts with the English Galsworthy, whose middle-class wisdom led him to write a saga of a family's gradual decline through the generations. There was Jacob Wassermann, whose discerning eye formed part of the kabbalistic tradition of penetrating into the depths of the soul and who eventually himself suffered from the resultant confusion; against him stands Max Brod, with his pageants of the stormy messiahs of Israel who broke away from the authority of the law. In England, Charles Dickens presented the ugliness of human poverty as destructive of all that was good in man's lot, while in contrast the spoiled narcissistic aesthete Oscar Wilde of the Decadent movement, finding no explanation for his existence in this world, destroyed the beauty of his life. Zola, with all his naturalistic wrath at political, social, and economic corruption and his compassion for man's depressed condition, stands opposed to Emil Ludwig, with his gentle biographical style, devoid of genuine sympathy with the characters he describes, circulating around Napoleon and his comrades in their battles, heroism, victories, and defeat.

The Hebrew works produced by the Stiebel publishing house and by *Ha-Tekufah* thus contained much of European literature. Shakespeare, Schiller, Goethe, Pushkin, Chekhov—the Hebrew translator could select from all these, from all schools of art and thought in the great periods and even in the interim periods, unhampered by any predetermined plan or clear policy of selection. The sole criterion was the idea of making a collection, of bringing everything into the bosom of the Hebrew language before any catastrophe should occur to Hebrew literature in Europe. All the humanistic elements in European literature came to its support in the fight for survival, a survival threatened with imminent extinction. It may well be that even today, despite all that has happened in subsequent years, we are drawing upon the sense of human dignity and nobility that literary collection afforded, including the efforts of Bialik and Frishman.

On Frishman's death, the editors of *Ha-Tekufah* published a number of obituary notices. He was a man of gentle disposition, eagerly fanning every spark of Hebrew creativity in his generation. Every glimmer of beauty in modern Hebrew writing was for him a promise of its future. He was born in Warsaw, that melting pot of Jewry where different streams of thought and feeling, tradition and revolt, communal ferment and individual enthusiasm mingled to form a powerful love of life. Out of this maelstrom of ideas Frishman longed to create for Hebrew literature an artistic form of its own. He ignored the maelstrom, which at times seemed primitive to him, lacking in stability and continuity. For this reason he admired Mendelé Mokher Sefarim's powers of description and choice of flexible idiom,[6] while Peretz's sensitivity to subtle variations of tone, his impressionistic half-phrases, and his symbolist allusions did not appeal to him. Frishman found his fulfillment in translating world literature, where art had found its perfect harmonious expression. Whether he was translating Rabindranath Tagore or Nietzsche, Byron or Homer, he was fulfilling his literary dream within the Hebrew language.

In his attitude to European literature Frishman was perhaps alone in his generation—its sole emissary. It is interesting to speculate what Frishman would say today, what *Ha-Tekufah* would have selected from European literature, if he had known what was to happen to European Jewry and the humanistic dreams of Europe. Perhaps he would have remained completely silent.

Notes

NOTES TO THE PREFACE

1. On the Haskalah ("Enlightenment"); Jacob S. Raisin, *The Haskalah Movement in Russia* (Philadelphia: Jewish Publication Society, 1913); F. Lakhover, *Toledot ha-Sifrut ha-Ivrit ha-Hadashah*, 12th ed., 2 vols. (Tel Aviv: Devir, 1954), vol. 1, bks. 1 and 2; Israel Tzinberg, *Toledot Sifrut Israel*, 6 vols. (Tel Aviv and Merhaviah: Joseph Shrebek and Sifriyat Po'alim, 1956–60), vol. 5, bk. 9; Shalom Spiegel, *Hebrew Reborn* (Philadelphia: Jewish Publication Society, 1912); Mayer Waxman, *A History of Jewish Literature*, 5 vols. (New York: Bloch Publishing Co., 1941), vol. 4, *The Modern Period;* Simon Halkin, *Modern Hebrew Literature* (New York: Schocken Books, 1950), pp. 44–53.

2. On the Jewish national renaissance at the end of the nineteenth century: Simon Dubnow, *History of the Jews in Russia and in Poland,* trans. I. Friedlaender, 3 vols. (Philadelphia: Jewish Publication Society, 1916–20), vol. 3, the years 1818–1917; Nahum Sokolow, *History of Zionism (1600–1918),* 2 vols. (London: Langman & Co., 1918), 2:281–317; Richard Gottheil, *Zionism* (Philadelphia: Jewish Publication Society, 1914); Joseph Klausner, *Yotzerim u-Vonim,* 3 vols. (Tel Aviv: Devir, 1925), vol. 2; A. S. Waldstein, *The Evolution of Modern Hebrew Literature (1850–1912),* Columbia University Oriental Studies, vol. 9 (New York: Columbia University Press, 1916).

3. On Kabbalah and Hasidism: Gershom Scholem, *Major Trends in Jewish Mysticism,* 3d ed. (New York: Schocken Books, 1954); Gershom Scholem, *The Book of Splendor* ("Ha-Zohar"), (New York: Schocken Books, 1949); Isaiah Tishbi, *Torat ha-Ra Veha-Kelippah be-Kabbalat ha-Ari* (Jerusalem: Schocken Books, 1900); Isaiah Tishbi and F. Lakhover, *Mishnat ha-Zohar* ("The Teaching of the Zohar"), 2 vols. (Jerusalem: Mosad Bialik, 1946–60); Louis Newman, *The Hasidic Anthology* (New York: Charles Scribner's Sons, 1934); Martin Buber, *Die Chassidischen Bücher* (Helleran: Hegner, 1928); Martin Buber, *Die Geschichte des R. Nahman* (Frankfurt am Main, 1906); Martin Buber, *Ha-Or ha-Ganuz* (Jerusalem and Tel Aviv: Schocken Books, 1958); S. A. Horodetsky, *Ha-Hasidut veha-Hasidim,* 4 vols. (Tel Aviv: Devir, 1922): for English translations of some of these stories see Maria Horodetsky-Maidanik, *Leaders of Hasidism* (London, 1928); Simon Dubnow, *Ha-Hasidut* ("The History of Hasidism"), (Tel Aviv: Devir, 1929–30); I. Tzinberg, *Toledot Sifrut Israel,* vol. 5, bk. 10, "Hasidut

245

va-Haskalah" ("Hasidism and Haskalah"), pp. 163–257; Yehudah Steinberg, *Kol Ketavé* (Tel Aviv: Devir, 1959), "Sippuré Hasidim" ("Hasidic Stories"), pp. 285–308.

4. On New Criticism: René Wellek, *Concepts of Criticism* (New Haven, Conn.: Yale University Press, 1963), pp. 54–68, 256–81, 316–64; Murray Krieger, *The New Apologists for Poetry* (Bloomington, Ind.: Indiana University Press, 1963); I. A. Richards, *The Meaning of Meaning* (New York: Harcourt, Brace & Co., 1956); T. S. Eliot, *The Use of Poetry and the Use of Criticism* (London: Faber & Faber, 1933); Isaiah Rabinovich, "Ha-Bikkoret ha-Hadasha Biyridatah" ("New Criticism on the Decline"), *Moznaim,* January, 1965.

NOTES TO CHAPTER 1

1. An important source of the modern concept of poetry is S. T. Coleridge, *Biographia Literaria,* ed. J. Shawcross, 2 vols. (Oxford: Clarendon, 1907), 2:12.

2. Erich Auerbach, *Mimesis* (Berne: A. Franck, 1946), chap. 12 ff.

3. Mikha Yosef Bin Gorion (Berdichevsky), "Sippuré Ahavah" "(Love Stories"), *Tsefunot va-Aggadot* ("Mysteries and Legends"), (Tel Aviv: Am Oved, 1955), pp. 160–64; see also "Koveshé ha-Yetzer" ("Conquerors of Lust"), pp. 169–72, in the same collection.

4. On the Lurianic Kabbalah see Gershom Scholem, *Major Trends in Jewish Mysticism* (Jerusalem: Schocken Books, 1941), pp. 246–86.

5. M. Y. Bin Gorion (Berdichevsky), "Bi-Shené Olamot" ("In Two Worlds"), *Tsefunot va-Aggadot,* pp. 275–90.

6. See Rabbi Eliezer Baal-Shem-Tov in Biographical Notes, p. 261.

7. On Rabbi Nahman of Braslav, see Shmuel Abba Horodetsky, *Ha-Hasidut veha-Hasidim,* 4 vols. (Jerusalem and Berlin: Devir, 1922), 3:18–81; Hillel Zeitlin, *R. Nahman Braslaver* (New York: Farlag Matonés, 1952); R. Nathan (the most ardent follower, commentator, and biographer of Nahman), *Haiyé Moharan* (Lublin, 1922); S. A. Horodetsky, *Sippuré Rabbi Nahman mi-Braslav* (Berlin: Ein ha-Koré, 1923); Martin Buber, Preface to *Die Geschichten des Rabbi Nahman* (Frankfurt am Main, 1906); S. Z. Zetzer, Preface (Yiddish) to *Vunder Maases fun Reb Nahman Braslaver* (New York: Farlag Feierberg, 1929); Isaiah Rabinovich, *Shorashim u-Megamot, Darko shel Rabbi Nahman el Sippuré Maasiot Shelo* (Jerusalem: Mosad Bialik, 1967), pp. 163–219.

8. See, for example, Harry Sackler, *Sefer ha-Mahazot* ("The Book of Plays"), (New York: Ogen, 1944), *Yosi Min Yokrat,* pp. 9–62; *Nesi'at ha-Tsaddik,* pp. 199–268; *Ketoret be-Af ha-Satan,* pp. 331–36; *Ha-Hozeh roeh et Kallato,* pp. 338–44. See also the poem on Joseph

Notes to Pages 6–11

Dela Reina in *Shirim u-Poemot* ("Small Poems and Large"), by Aaron Zeitlin (Jerusalem: Mosad Bialik, 1949), pp. 165–211, as well as the notes on Hasidic motifs in the writings of I. L. Peretz, M. Y. Berdichevsky, and Yehudah Steinberg.

9. Joseph Perl, *Megalléh Temirin* (Vienna, 1819). On Megalléh Temirin see F. Lakhover, *Toledot ha-Sifrut ha-Ivrit ha-Hadasha*, 12th ed., 2 vols. (Tel Aviv: Devir, 1954), vol. 1, bk. 2, p. 14. On Joseph Perl see the article by N. Gordon in the *Hebrew University College Annual* (Cincinnati, 1904), pp. 136–67.

10. *Kol Ketavé Mendelé Mokher Sefarim*, ed. Joseph Klausner, 4 vols. (Jerusalem, Berlin, and Odessa: Moriah, 1921), vol. 4, bk. 7, "Shné ha-Mendelim" ("The Two Mendelés"), pp. 136–67. Among English translations from Mendelé's works there are: *The Nag*, trans. M. Spiegel (New York: Beechurst Press, 1955); and *The Travels and Adventures of Benjamin the Third*, trans. A. H. Friedland (Cleveland: Cleveland Bureau of Education, 1953).

11. David Frishman, Introduction to *Kol Ketavé Mendelé Mokher Sefarim*, vol. 1, bk. 1, pp. i–xxix.

12. Abraham Kariv, *Adabrah ve-Irvah Li* (Tel Aviv: Am Oved, 1951).

13. *Kol Ketavé Mendelé Mokher Sefarim*, "Reshimot le-Toledotai" ("Autobiographical Notes"), vol. 4, bk. 7, pp. 4–6; "Ba-Yamin ha-Hem" ("In Those Days"), vol. 2, bk. 4, pp. 33–36. See also S. Niger, *Vegen Yiddishe Shreiber* (Warsaw, 1912).

14. See F. Lakhover, *Toledot ha-Sifrut ha-Ivrit ha-Hadasha*, vol. 2, pp. 33–36. See also Charles A. Madison, "Mendelé, the Foremost of Ghetto Satirists," *Poet Lore* 33(1922): 255–67.

15. *Kol Ketavé Mendelé Mokher Sefarim*, vol. 1, bk. 2, "Be-Emek ha-Bakha," pp. 17–18.

16. *Kol Ketavé Mendelé Mokher Sefarim*, vol. 1, bk. 1, "Sefer ha-Kabtzanim," p. 49.

17. I. L. Peretz, *Di Goldené Keyt, Dramatishe Werk* (New York: Tzico Farlag, 1947). (This Yiddish version is both longer than and artistically superior to the Hebrew version, *Hurban Beth Tsaddik* [Tel Aviv: Devir, 1927].) See also I. L. Peretz, *Bei Nacht oifn altn Markt* (Vilna: Kletskin, 1922); and S. Anski, *The Dibbuk*, trans. Henry G. Alsberg and Winifred Katzin (New York: Boni and Liveright, 1926). (The latter play was originally published in Yiddish by Farlag Vilna, Warsaw and New York, 1928.) There is an excellent Hebrew translation of *The Dibbuk* by H. N. Bialik, *Bein Shené Olamot, Ha-Tekufah* 1 (Moscow: Stiebel, 1918). On S. J. Agnon's *Hakhnasat Kallah*, see pp. 178–92.

18. *Kol Ketavé Mendelé Mokher Sefarim*, vol. 1, bk. 2, "Be-Emek ha-Bakha," pp. 17–18.

19. *Ibid.*, pp. 7–76, and bk. 1, "Sefer ha-Kabtzanim," pp. 24–25.
20. *Ibid.*, "Sefer ha-Kabtzanim," pp. 1–3.
21. *Ibid.*, pp. 3–5.
22. On Mendelé's use of Hebrew see H. N. Bialik, *Divre Sifrut* (Tel Aviv: Devir, 1925), pp. 270–76, 277–80; on his style in Hebrew see I. H. Ravnitsky, *Kol Ketavé Mendelé Mokher Sefarim*, vol. 4, bk. 7, pp. 166–75.
23. *Kol Ketavé Mendelé Mokher Sefarim*, vol. 2, bk. 4, "Ba-Yamin ha-Hem," pp. 3–143.
24. *Ibid.*, pp. 20–21, and especially chap. 9, pp. 57–58.
25. Simon Dubnow, *History of the Jews in Russia and Poland*, trans. Israel Friedlander, 3 vols. (Philadelphia: Jewish Publication Society, 1916–20), 2:358–429; 3:7–65.
26. Shalom Aleikhem's works in Yiddish were published in 28 volumes by Folksfond (New York, 1917–23). English translations of his works include: *Tevye's Daughters*, trans. Frances Butwin (New York: Crown Publishers, 1949); *The Great Fair*, trans. Tamara Cahana (New York: Noonday Press, 1955); *The Adventures of Motel, the Cantor's Son*, trans. Tamara Cahana (New York: Shuman, 1953). Two very good books containing translations from Shalom Aleikhem's work and evaluations of his literary creativity are: M. Grafstein (ed.), *Shalom Aleikhem Panorama* (London, Ont.: Jewish Observer, 1948); Maurice Samuel, *The World of Shalom Aleikhem* (New York: Alfred Knopf, 1943). An excellent Hebrew translation of his works was made by his son-in-law, I. D. Berkovitz (8 vols.; Tel Aviv: Devir, 1956).
27. Haiyim Nahman Bialik, "Le-Ahad ha-Am" ("To Ahad ha-Am"), *Shirim* (Tel Aviv: Devir, 1926), pp. 156–58.
28. Shalom Aleikhem, *Tevye's Daughters*, "Modern Children," pp. 20–37.
29. *Ibid.*, "Competitors," pp. 38–52.
30. *Ibid.*, "Hodel," pp. 53–68.
31. *Ibid.*, "Hava," pp. 93–108.
32. David Bergelson, *Nokh Alemen* (Berlin: Vostok, 1921).
33. *Kol Ketavé I. L. Peretz*, 5 vols. (Tel Aviv: Devir, 1952), vol. 5.
34. On Symbolism in literature (especially French literature) see: *Columbia Dictionary of Modern European Literature*, ed. Horatio Smith (New York: Columbia Uniersity Press, 1947), pp. 291–94; Ernest Raymond, *La Melée Symboliste* (1918–36); Edmund Wilson, *Axel's Castle* (1931).
35. Shmuel Niger, *I. L. Peretz* (Buenos Aires: Yiddish Cultural Congress, 1952).
36. *Kol Ketavé I. L. Peretz*, 1: 1–6.
37. *Ibid.*, pp. 88–98.

38. *Ibid.,* p. 98.

39. See Stith Thompson, *Types of the Folktale,* 2d rev. ed. (Hatboro, Pa.: Folklore Associates, 1961).

40. For a concise article on Maurice Maeterlinck see the *Columbia Dictionary of Modern European Literature,* p. 501.

41. *Kol Ketavé I. L. Peretz,* vol. 2, "Ha-Illemet" ("The Dumb Girl") pp. 9–30; "Manginot ha-Zeman" ("The Melodies of the Day"), pp. 31–38; "Mi-Sippuré ha-Levanah" ("Tales of the Moon"), pp. 59–62; "Hazon Em" ("A Mother's Vision"), pp. 111–12.

42. *Ibid.,* vol. 3, Hasidut ("Hasidism").

43. *Ibid.,* vol. 4, "Niggun Hadash" ("A New Melody"), pp. 63–65; "Ha-Mekubbalim" ("The Kabbalists"), pp. 63–66. Among English translations of Peretz's works are: Solomon Liptzin, *Peretz* (New York: Yiddish Scientific Institute [Yivo], 1949), (gives both Yiddish original and English translation); *The Three Canopies,* trans. Tehilla Feierman (New York, 1948); *Stories and Pictures,* trans. Helena Frank (Philadelphia, 1906). See also Maurice Samuel, *Prince of the Ghetto* (New York: Alfred Knopf, 1948); Sylvia Rothschild, *I. L. Peretz: Key to a Magic Door* (New York: Farrar, Straus & Cudahy and Jewish Publication Society, 1959); *I. L. Peretz: Memorial Book* (London, Ont.: Max Grafstein and I. Goldstick, 1945), vol. 1, no. 1.

44. On the singing efforts of Rabbi Nahman of Braslav see Rabbi Nathan (his most ardent follower), *Haiyé Moharan* ("The Life of Our Teacher, Rabbi Nahman"), (Lublin, 1922), p. 6.

45. See Gershom Scholem, *Major Trends in Jewish Mysticism,* pp. 246–86.

46. H. N. Bialik, *Shirim,* "Hetzitz va-Met" ("He Looked In and Died"), pp. 243–45.

47. *Kol Ketavé I. L. Peretz,* vol. 8, "Petirat ha-Menaggen" ("The Death of the Musician"), pp. 81–84.

48. *Kol Ketavé I. L. Peretz,* vol. 2, *Hurban Beth Tsaddik* ("The Collapse of a Rabbi's House"), pp. 10–35. The Yiddish version, *Di Goldené Keyt* (New York: Tziko Farlag, 1947), is preferable and is used here.

49. On Stanislaw Wyspianski see: *Columbia Dictionary of Modern European Literature,* pp. 877–78; R. Dyboski, *Modern Polish Literature* (1924).

50. *Di Goldené Keyt,* pp. 26–27.

51. *Ibid.,* p. 34.

52. See note 34.

53. On Ibsen see: *Columbia Dictionary of Modern European Literature,* pp. 399–400; *Henrik Ibsen,* trans. H. Koht, 2 vols. (1931).

54. *Di Goldené Keyt,* p. 63.

55. *Ibid.,* p. 101.

NOTES TO CHAPTER 2

1. Shmuel Niger, *Itzhak Leibush Peretz* (Buenos Aires: Yiddish Cultural Congress, 1952), pp. 420–46.

2. Note, for example, the leading female character in his *Kiddush ha-Shem* ("The Sanctification of God's Name"), (New York: Matonés, 1947).

3. Joseph Opatoshu, *In Di Poylishe Welder* ("In the Polish Forests"), (Vilna: Kletskin, 1928), "A Nakht in Wald" ("A Night in the Woods"), pp. 57–62; "Reb Mendelé Kotzker" ("Rabbi Mendelé of Kotzk"), pp. 153–76; "Tif'eret" ("Beauty"), pp. 249–49.

4. S. Niger, *Der Nister, Di Yiddishe Shreiber in Soviet Rusland* ("Yiddish Writers in Soviet Russia"), (New York: Yivo, 1958), pp. 368–80.

5. *In-Zikh* ("In the Self") *Collection* (New York: Maizel, 1920). The important leaders of this literary school were the Yiddish poets Jacob Glatstein and Aaron Glantz of New York. On the In-Zikh movement see also Dov Sedan's Introduction to the Hebrew edition of Glantz's poems, *Shirim ve-Hezyonot* ("Poems and Visions"), (Jerusalem: Mosad Bialik, 1965).

6. On Hebrew fiction during the Haskalah period see: F. Lakhover, *Toledot ha-Sifrut ha-Ivrit ha-Hadashah*, 12th ed., 2 vols. (Tel Aviv: Devir, 1954), vol. 1; Joseph Klausner, *Historia shel ha-Sifrut ha-Ivrit ha-Hadashah*, 6 vols. (Jerusalem: Hebrew University Press, 1930–50), vol. 2, bk. 2. In English see: Simon Halkin, *Modern Hebrew Literature* (New York: Schocken Books, 1950), "The Dilemma of Haskalah Literature," pp. 34–53; Meyer Waxman, *A History of Hebrew Literature*, 5 vols. (New York: Bloch Publishing Co., 1941), vol. 4, chap. 1.

7. Haiyim Nahman Bialik, "Le-Ahad ha-Am," *Shirim* ("Poems"), (Tel Aviv: Devir, 1926)), p. 156.

8. F. Lakhover, *Toledot ha-Sifrut ha-Ivrit ha-Hadashah*, vol. 2, bk. 3, pp. 140–69.

The Khmelnitzki massacres of Jewish communities in the Ukraine were perpetrated by the Cossacks, headed by Bogdan Khmelnitzki, during their rebellion against their Polish landlords in 1648 and 1649. See *Yeven-Metzulah*, by Rabbi Nathan Hanover, an eye witness of the massacres. (Translated into English by Rabbi Abraham Mesh [New York: Bloch Publishing Co., 1950].) See also I. S. Hertz, *Di Yidn in Ukraine* (New York, 1949).

9. See Rabbi Leib Soré's in Biographical Notes, pp. 267–68.

10. M. Z. Feierberg, *Sippurim* (Warsaw: Ahiasaf, n.d.), "Ha-Tselalim."

11. *Ibid.*

12. Feierberg's letters, among them those to Berdichevsky and Ahad ha-Am, were published in *Gilyonot*, nos. 19–22 (1929).

13. F. Lakhover, *Toledot ha-Sifrut ha-Ivrit ha-Hadashah,* vol. 2, bk. 3, p. 144.

14. I. L. Peretz, *Hasidut ("Hasidism"),* (Tel Aviv: Devir, 1925); *Kol Ketavé Yehudah Steinberg* (Tel Aviv: Devir, 1959), "Sippuré Hasidim," pp. 285–313, "Sihot Hasidim," pp. 314–51.

15. F. Lakhover, *Toledot ha-Sifrut ha-Ivrit ha-Hadashah,* vol. 2, p. 157.

16. *Ibid.*

17. *Sippurim,* "Ha-Tzelalim," p. 40.

18. See Joseph Klausner's Introduction to Feierberg's *Sippurim.*

19. *Sippurim,* "Ha-Tzelalim," p. 40.

20. Uri Nissan Gnessin, *Ha-Tziddah* (Tel Aviv: Sifriyat Po'alim, 1946), pp. 87–115. On Gnessin see the collection also entitled *Ha-Tziddah* (Jerusalem, 1904), which contains articles evaluating his works, biographical notes and reminscences by various Hebrew writers, and his youthful poems, as well as sixty of his letters. In English see Joseph Rider, *Negative Tendencies in Modern Hebrew Literature* (Cincinnati: Hebrew Union College, 1925), pp. 465–66.

21. *Ha-Tziddah,* p. 87.

22. *Ibid.,* p. 89.

23. *Ibid.,* p. 93.

24. *Ibid.,* p. 106.

25. *Ibid., Beinatayim,* p. 117.

26. *Ibid.,* p. 136.

27. *Ibid., Be-Terem,* pp. 145–238.

28. *Ibid.,* p. 146.

29. *Ibid.,* pp. 152–53.

30. *Ibid.,* p. 158.

31. *Ibid.,* p. 167.

32. *Ibid.,* p. 174.

33. *Ibid.,* pp. 188–89.

34. *Ibid., Etsel,* pp. 239 ff.

35. *Ibid., Be-Terem,* p. 192.

36. *Ibid..* p. 210.

37. *Ibid.,* p. 237.

38. *Ibid., Etsel,* p. 239.

39. *Ibid.,* p. 240.

40. *Ibid.,* p. 247.

41. *Ibid.,* p. 252.

42. *Ibid.,* p. 255.

43. *Ibid.,* p. 259.

44. *Mi-Saviv La-Nekuddah* ("Around the Point"), (Tel Aviv: Am Oved, 1953), vol. 1, pp. 8–156. On Brenner see: Ja'ari Poleskin, *Me-*

Haiyé J. H. Brenner (Tel Aviv, 1922); Alexander S. Rabinovich, *Haiyé Brenner* (Tel Aviv, 1922); Jacob Rabinovich, *Hedim,* no. 10 (1927), 51 f., and *Ha-Tekufah,* 10 (1921): 463 f.; Simon Halkin, *Modern Hebrew Literature,* p. 116 f.

45. *Mi-Saviv La-Nekuddah,* p. 5.
46. *Ibid.,* p. 10.
47. *Ibid.,* p. 99 f.
48. *Ibid.,* p. 23 f.
49. *Ibid.,* p. 19.
50. *Ibid.,* p. 15.
51. *Ibid.*
52. *Ibid.,* p. 107.
53. *Ibid.,* p. 58.
54. *Ibid.*
55. *Ibid.,* p. 47.
56. *Ibid.,* p. 119.
57. *Ibid.*
58. *Ibid.,* p. 149.
59. *Ibid.,* p. 156.
60. Jacob Rabinovich, *Ha-Tekufah,* 10 (1921): 463 f.
61. J. H. Brenner, *Shekhol Ve-Khishalon* (Tel Aviv: Am Oved, 1953), p. 288.
62. D. A. Friedman, *I. H. Brenner, Ishiyuto Vizirato* ("I. H. Brenner, His Personality and Works"), (Berlin: Yiddisher Farlag, 1923), p. 91. (The Brenner quote is taken from his *Shekhol Ve-Khishalon,* p. 290.)
63. Isaiah Wolfsberg, "Demuto ha-Ruhanit ve-Olamo ha-Mahshavti" ("His Spiritual Personality and His Intellectual World"), *Sefer Zeitlin* (a collection of articles dedicated to the memory of H. Zeitlin), (Jerusalem, 1948), p. 71 f.
64. Hillel Zeitlin, *Mahshava ve-Shirah* ("Intellect and Poetry", Warsaw, 1911).
65. See pp. 124–44.
66. *Mahshava ve-Shirah,* "Mi-Ketavé Ahad ha-Tse'irim" ("Letters by One of the Young Followers of Berdichevsky"), p. 43 f.
67. *Ibid.,* vol. 1, pt. 1, p. 133 f.
68. *Ibid.,* p. 60.
69. *Ibid.,* pt. 2, pp. 83–88.
70. *Ibid.,* pt. 1, p. 129.
71. Hillel Zeitlin, *Ha-Tekufah* (Berlin, Stiebel), vol. 20, "Mi-Tehomot ha-Sefek veha-Yeush," pp. 425–44; vol. 21, pp. 369–79.
72. *Mahshava ve-Shirah,* vol. 1, pt. 2, pp. 100–16.
73. *Ibid.,* p. 111.
74. *Ibid.,* p. 115. See also Rabbi Nathan, *Haiyé Moharan* (Lublin, 1922).

75. Rabbi Nahman, *Ma'aseh Meha-Zain Betlers,* ed. S. H. Horodetsky (Berlin, 1923); Martin Buber, *Die Chassidischen Bücher* (Helleran: Hegner, 1928); Martin Buber, *Die Geschichte des R. Nahman* (Frankfurt am Main, 1906); S. Z. Zetzer, *Ma'aseh Meha-Zain Betlers* (New York, 1929).

76. Hillel Zeitlin, *Mahshavah ve-Shirah,* vol. 2, p. 165.

77. For biographical information on Shoffman see "Le-Yovel Shoffman," *Moznaim,* no. 22–23 (1930) and Fischel Lakhover, *Rishonim ve-Aharonim* (Tel Aviv, 1934), pp. 133–35.

78. *Kol Ketavé* (Tel Aviv: Am Oved, 1960), vol. 1.

79. *Ibid.,* "Ha-Mehitzah," pp. 38–44.

80. *Ibid.,* pp. 38, 40.

81. *Ibid.,* "Le-Yad ha-Derekh," p. 111.

82. *Ibid.,* "Ha-Taluy," p. 148.

83. *Ibid.,* "Lo," p. 159.

84. *Ibid.,* "Ahavah," p. 221.

85. *Ibid.,* p. 229.

86. *Ibid.,* p. 230.

87. *Ibid.,* "Bitti ha-Ketannah," vol. 2, p. 184.

88. *Ibid.,* "Kartis ha-Nesi'ah," p. 195.

89. *Ibid.,* "Sof," p. 198.

90. *Ibid.,* vol. 3, p. 207.

91. *Ibid.,* "Ha-Nesi'ah," pp. 111 ff.

NOTES TO CHAPTER 3

1. On Berdichevsky see Fischel Lakhover, *Toledot ha-Sifrut ha-Ivrit ha-Hadashah,* 12th ed., 2 vols. (Tel Aviv: Devir, 1954), 2:71–139; David Neumark, "Die Juedische Moderne," *Allgemeine Zeitung des Judentums,* LXIV (1900), no. 45, pp. 34–42; Hugo Bergmann, *Yavneh und Jerusalem* (Berlin, 1919), pp. 34–42; Joseph Rieder, "Negative Tendencies in Modern Hebrew Literature," *Hebrew Union College Jubilee Volume* (Cincinnati, 1925), pp. 451–53, 472–73; S. Spiegel, *Two Heretics: Hebrew Reborn* (Philadelphia: Jewish Publication Society, 1962), pp. 332–70.

2. H. N. Bialik and I. H. Ravnitsky, *Sefer ha-Aggadah,* 2 vols. (Tel Aviv: Devir, 1920), vol. 1, sec. 216, p. 101. See also M. Y. Berdichevsky, *Tzefunot va-Aggadot* (Tel Aviv: Am Oved, 1951), "Koveshe ha-Yetzer" ("The Conquerors of Lust"), pp. 196–75.

3. M. Y. Berdichevsky, *Tzefunot va-Aggadot,* "Al ha-Mashiah" ("On the Messiah"), pp. 290–306.

4. See Harry Sackler, ed., *Sefer ha-Mahazot* (New York: Ogen, 1944), *Yosi Min Yokrat,* pp. 9–61; *Ketoret be-Af ha-Satan,* pp. 331–81; *Ha-*

Hozeh roeh et Kallato, pp. 382–416. See also Aaron Zeitlin's poem, "Joseph Dela Reina," *Shirim u-Poemot* (Jerusalem: Mosad Bialik, 1949), pp. 165–210.

5. F. Lakhover, *Toledot ha-Sifrut ha-Ivrit ha-Hadashah,* vol. 2, bk. 3, p. 79.

6. Ahad ha-Am, *Al Parashat Derakhim,* 4 vols. (Berlin, 1921), vol. 1, "Shilton ha-Sekhel," pp. 1–36. See also M. Y. Berdichevsky, *Kol Maamaré* (Tel Aviv: Am Oved, 1951), "Mi-Shené Avarim," pp. 63–115.

7. Jacob Rabinovich on Ahad ha-Am and A. D. Gordon, *Hedim* (1923).

8. "Megillat ha-Esh," *Shirim* (Tel Aviv: Devir, 1926), pp. 347–58.

9. M. Y. Bin Gorion, *Kol Maamaré,* "Al Harhavat ha-Sifrut," pp. 153–77.

10. H. N. Bialik and I. H Ravnitsky, *Sefer ha-Aggadah,* vol. 1, sec. 181, p. 162.

11. M. Y. Bin Gorion (Berdichevsky), *Kol Sippuré* (Tel Aviv: Devir, 1959), "Me-Arpillé ha-Noar," pp. 3–7; "Mi-Huts li-Tehum," pp. 50–51; "Me-Ever la-Nahar," pp. 8–11.

12. *Ibid.,* "Pat Lehem," p. 74; "Zo be-Tzad Zo," p. 58.

13. *Ibid.,* "Kalonimos ve-Naomi," pp. 157–205; "Parah Adummah," pp. 181–84.

14. *Ibid.,* "Ha-Yetziah," pp. 147–51.

15. *Kol Maamaré,* "Mishnat Hasidim, Histaklut," p. 4.

16. *Ibid.,* "Rikkudim," p. 6.

17. *Kol Sippuré,* "Ha-Hafsakah," pp. 154–57.

18. *Ibid.,* p. 156.

19. Martin Buber, "Die Geschichten des Rabbi Nahman," *Die Chassidischen Bücher* (Helleran: Hegner, 1928).

20. *Kol Sippuré,* "Bayit Tivneh," pp. 250–60; "Be-Seter Raam," pp. 235–50; "Miriam," pp. 271–317.

21. H. N. Bialik and I. H. Ravnitsky, *Sefer ha-Aggadah,* vol. 1, secs. 22–23, p. 8.

22. *Tsefunot va-Aggadot.*

23. *Ibid.,* "Yosi demin Yokrat," p. 162.

24. *Ibid.,* "Nathan Zuzita," p. 169.

25. *Kol Sippuré,* "Et Korbani," p. 232.

26. *Ibid., Miriam,* pp. 271–317.

27. *Ibid.*

28. *Ibid.*

29. *Ibid.*

30. *Kol Maamaré,* "Diverei Sifrut," p. 153.

31. See Berdichevsky on Ahad ha-Am's concept of literature, *ibid.,* pp. 147–53; see also Berdichevsky on Reuben Brainin, *ibid.,* pp. 200–22.

32. On the realistic tendencies of the "New Trend" see *ibid.,* p. 153 f.

33. On Ben-Avigdor see F. Lakhover, *Toledot ha-Sifrut ha-Ivrit ha-Hadashah*, vol. 2, bk 1., pp. 14–21.

34. *Ibid.*, p. 30

35. Buki ben Yogli (I. L. Katznelson), *Shirat ha-Zamir* (Warsaw, 1904), and *Aggadot ve-Sippurim* (New York, 1917). On I. L. Katznelson see Joseph Klausner, *Yotzerim u-Vonim* (Tel Aviv: Devir, 1925), pp. 293–97.

36. *Ketavé*, 5 vols. (Tel Aviv: Devir, 1950–53), vol. 2, "Yom ha-Din Shel Feivké," pp. 51–71; "Karet," pp. 184–202, vol. 1, "Talush," pp. 102–30.

37. *Ibid.*, "Yom ha-Din Shel Feivké," p. 51.

38. *Ibid.*, p. 54.

39. *Ibid.*, p. 63.

40. *Ibid.*

41. *Ibid.*

42. *Ibid.*, "Karet," pp. 184–85.

43. *Ibid.*, "Talush," pp. 102–30.

44. *Ibid.*, p. 103.

45. *Ibid.*, p. 120.

46. "Be-Ir ha-Haregah," *Shirim* (Tel Aviv, 1925), p. 321.

47. *Ketavé*, "Talush," p. 121.

48. *Ibid.*, p. 110.

49. *Ibid.*, p. 124.

50. *Ibid.*, p. 110.

51. *Ibid.*, p. 129.

NOTES TO CHAPTER 4

1. Mosheh Ben-Eliezer, *Olam Over (Temunot ve-Tziurim)*, (Tel Aviv: Devir, 1927).

2. Simhah Ben-Zion, *Kol Ketavé* (Tel Aviv: Devir, 1948).

3. *Second Aliyah* (New York: He-Halutz Organization of America, n.d.).

4. Devorah Baron, *Mah she-Hayah* (Tel Aviv: Davar, 1939); Shelomo Tzemach, *Shiv'ah Asar Sippur* (Tel Aviv: Devir, 1930); Mosheh Stavsky, *Sefer ha-Behemot* (Tel Aviv: Omanut, 1930); Aaron Reuveni, *Sippurim* (Jerusalem: Ahiever, 1928); Dov Kimhi, *Tziurim me-Olam she-Nishkah* (Jerusalem: 1943); Asher Barash, *Temunot mi-Bet Mivshal ha-Shekhar* (Jerusalem: Mitzpah, 1929); M. Siko, *Even Tiz'ak* (Jerusalem: Devir, 1945).

5. Aaron Kabak, *Shelomo Molkho* (London: Ha-Olam, 1928–29).

6. Aaron Kabak, *Ba-Mish'ol ha-Tzar* (Tel Aviv: Am Oved, 1937).

7. Aaron Kabak, *Be-Halal ha-Rek* (Tel Aviv: Am Oved, 1943).

8. Haiyim Hazaz, *Sippurim Nivharim*, 12th printing (Tel Aviv: Devir La-Am, 1952), pp. 133–48.

9. Haiyim Hazaz, *Be-Ketz ha-Yamim* (Tel Aviv: Am Oved, 1950); *Sippurim Nivharim*, "Ha-Derashah," pp. 184–202.

10. *Hagorat Mazalot* (Tel Aviv: Am Oved, 1958), pp. 164–259.

11. *Ibid.*, pp. 7–259.

12. *Be-Kolar Ehad* (Tel Aviv: Am Oved, 1963).

13. S. J. Agnon, "Ha-Mitpahat" ("The Kerchief"), *The Jewish Caravan*, trans. Leo W. Schwartz (New York: Rinehart, 1935).

14. S. J. Agnon, *Hakhnasat Kallah* (Jerusalem: Schocken Books, 1939); *Oreah Natah la-Lun* (Jerusalem: Schocken Books, 1939); *Samukh ve-Nir'eh/Sefer ha-Ma'asim* (Jerusalem: Schocken Books, 1950), pp. 103–249; *Temol Shilshom* (Jerusalem: Schocken Books, 1950).

15. See Murray Krieger, *The New Apologists for Poetry* (Bloomington, Ind.: Indiana University Press, 1963), especially pp. 140–55. See also René Wellek, *Concepts of Criticism* (New Haven, Conn., and London: Yale University Press, 1963), especially pp. 54–68.

16. *Hakhnasat Kallah,* p. 8.

17. Maqama: "An Arabic term meaning a meeting place, a meeting, an exposition. It was especially used as a designation for stories written in flowery and rhymed language, including metric poems" (Haiyim Shirman, *Ha-Shirah ha-Ivrit bi-Sefarad u-Provence* [Jerusalem and Tel Aviv: Mosad Bialik and Devir, 1956], pp. 97–169, 710). The Hebrew poet Yehudah Al Harizi, who was born in Spain in the second half of the twelfth century, and later lived in Provence, Egypt, and elsewhere, developed the Hebrew maqama in his *Sefer Tahkemoni.*

18. Moshkheni and Narutza are humorous names meaning "Draw-Me" and "We-Will-Run." These two words are found in the Song of Songs 1:4.

19. A Jewish liturgical song.

20. *Hakhnasat Kallah,* p. 8.

21. *Ibid.*, pp. 468–70.

22. *Oreah Natah la-Lun.*

23. A prayer of supplication recited by Jews on weekdays.

24. *Oreah Natah la-Lun,* p. 14

25. D. Bergelson, *Nokh Alemen* (Berlin: Vostok, 1921).

26. *Oreah Natah la-Lun,* p. 63

27. *Ibid.*, p. 71.

28. *Ibid.*, p. 109.

29. *Ibid.*, "Rachel," pp. 87–97; "Ha-Tinok ha-Holeh," pp. 188–91; "Etzel ha-Tinok ha-Holeh," pp. 296–306.

30. *Ibid.*, pp. 26–27.

31. Souls that wander naked about the universe is a concept of the Kabbalah. See Isaiah Tishbi, *Torat ha-Ra veha-Klippah be-Kabbalat ha-Ari* (Jerusalem: Mosad Bialik, 1924).

32. *Oreah Natah la-Lun*, p. 119.
33. *Ibid.*, p. 120.
34. *Ibid.*, p. 571.
35. *Ibid.*, p. 572.
36. S. J. Agnon, *Temol Shilshom*. See also note 3.
37. *Sefer ha-Ma'asim*, p. 105.
38. *Ibid.*, pp. 122–23.
39. Kinneret and Deganiah were the first small communes ("Kevutzot") founded by the pioneers of the Second Aliyah.
40. *Temol Shilshom*, pp. 168–69.
41. A. D. Gordon, *Selected Essays*, trans. Frances Burnce (New York, 1938), especially the biographical sketch by I. Silberschlag. On Y. H. Brenner see chapter 2 of the above and the Biographical Notes, pp. 264–65 of this book.
42. *Temol Shilshom*, pp. 168–69.
43. *Ibid.*, p. 313.
44. *Ibid.*, p. 312.
45. *Ibid.*, p. 399.
46. *Ibid.*, p. 544.
47. The Hebrew word is "tikkun," which Gershom Scholem defines as "salvation, restitution of the ideal order which forms the original aim of creative re-integration of the original whole" (*Major Trends in Jewish Mysticism* [New York: Schocken Books, 1941], p. 233).
48. *Temol Shilshom*, p. 604.
49. *Ibid.*, p. 306 ff.
50. *Ibid.*, pp. 606–7.

NOTES TO THE APPENDIX

1. H. N. Bialik, *Diveré Sifrut* (Tel Aviv: Devir, 1925), pp. 217–32.
2. *Ibid.*, pp. 233–37.
3. *Ha-Tekufah* (Moscow: Stiebel, 1918).
4. Isaiah Rabinovich, *Shorashim u-Megamot* (Jerusalem: Mosad Bialik, 1967), pp. 10–109.
5. Shaul Tchernikhovsky, "Hatunatah shel Elkah," *Shirim Hadashim* (Leipzig: Stiebel, 1924), pp. 87–134.
6. David Frishman, Introduction to *Kol Ketavé Mendelé Mokher Sefarim*, ed. Joseph Klausner, 4 vols. (Jerusalem, Berlin, and Odessa: Moriah, 1921), vol. 1, bk. 1, pp. i–xxix.

Biographical Notes

SHMUEL YOSEF AGNON

S. Y. Agnon (Literary name of S. Y. Czaczkes) was born in 1888, in Buczacz, East Galicia. There he was steeped in Jewish religious life, in talmudic, midrashic, and hasidic learning, and in the folklore of his people. At the age of sixteen he began reading non-Jewish literature, especially German. A year later he began to write poems, stories, and essays in Hebrew and Yiddish. In 1913 he went to Palestine and settled for a time in Jaffa, where he associated with the pioneers of the Second Aliyah—an association that was brought to fruition in his later stories and novels. In Jaffa Agnon published his story "Agunot" (about women whose husbands have deserted them without freeing them from the bonds of marriage), which evoked great praise from the literary critics of the country. It is from this story that the pseudonym Agnon is derived.

In Jaffa Agnon also published his remarkable story *Ve-Hayah he-Akov le-Mishor*. This story, which was a fusion of fantasy and reality, served as a forerunner of Agnon's epic works; it was enthusiastically received by critics and readers and was later translated into several languages.

In 1919 Agnon went to Berlin. He also lived in Hamburg, where he helped Martin Buber prepare his collection of hasidic stories. In 1922 he returned to Israel and settled permanently with his family in Jerusalem. There he wrote his best short stories and novels.

Agnon is one of the most esteemed authors in Israel. In 1966 he was awarded the Nobel Prize for literature. He has also received the most coveted literary award in Israel, the Bialik Prize for Hebrew Literature, and the highest award of honor given by the Israeli government, the Israel Prize.

259

AHAD HA-AM
(*Literary name of Asher Ginzberg*)

Ahad ha-Am was born in the Ukraine in 1856. He received a traditional Jewish education, but he early immersed himself in studies of languages, sociology, and philosophy. He studied at the universities of Vienna, Berlin, and Breslau (1882–84). Settling in Odessa in 1886, he joined the Hovevé Zion ("Lovers of Zion," who established a few settlements in Palestine), while he criticized their policies in his essays. In 1896 he founded the monthly *Ha-Shilloah*. He lived in London from 1908 to 1922, when he moved to Israel and settled in Tel Aviv, where he published his correspondence and memoirs. Ahad ha-Am's essays and theories were mainly concentrated on his idea that the Land of Israel should become the spiritual center of the Jewish Diaspora. He thus opposed the mainly political character of Dr. Theodor Herzl's activities. He died in Tel Aviv in 1937.

SHOLEM ASH

Sholem Ash was born in 1880 in Kutna, Poland, where he received a Jewish education. In 1900 he left his home town for Warsaw, where he spent much time with I. L. Peretz. It was under Peretz's influence that Ash began to write his Yiddish stories. His first literary steps, however, were made in Hebrew. He continued writing in Hebrew for a number of years and contibuted to many Hebrew periodicals in Europe and the United States.

Ash quickly won a high rank among the younger writers in Poland with the publication of his impressionistic short novel *Dos Shtetl* ("The Small Town"). Then followed an array of brilliant epic and dramatic works that have made him preeminent in modern Yiddish literature. Many of his novels have been translated into a number of European languages, and several of his plays have been successfully presented in major European cities.

The stormiest period of his life was that of his christological trilogy: *The Nazarene* (1939), *Apostle Paul* (1943), and *Mary* (1949), as well as of his novels *Moses* (1951) and *The Prophet* (1916).

Biographical Notes

All his life Ash had wandered over Europe and America. He also visited Israel several times. In 1954, while visiting Israel, Ash finally decided to settle there and built a house for himself and his wife in Bat-Yam. He died in London, in 1957.

RABBI ISRAEL BAAL-SHEM-TOV

Rabbi Israel Baal-Shem-Tov (1700–60) was the founder of the great hasidic movement in the eighteenth century. His life is shrouded in many legends of the supernatural. His movement, however, rejuvenated the depressed Jewish communities in Eastern Europe after the massacres in the Ukraine by the Cossacks and the dismal messianic failure of Sabbatai Tzevi. The Baal-Shem-Tov ("Man of the Good Name") was a holy teacher, a healer of the body and of the spirit, a destroyer of evil, and a comforter of the afflicted. His religious teaching (see notes on Hasidism in the Preface, pp. vii–ix) attracted to him the great masses of Jewish people in Eastern Europe as well as many intellectual rabbis. His personality dominated the religious hasidic literature and indirectly contributed to the renaissance of modern Hebrew literature.

MIKHA YOSEF BERDICHEVSKY
(M. Y. Bin Gorion)

M. Y. Berdichevsky (1865–1921) was born in Mezhibuzh, Poland, in 1865. There his life was governed by the strict piety of his father and by the hasidic atmosphere of the town. He attended the famous Yeshivah of Volozhin, where he dedicated himself to intensive talmudic studies. Like many of his peers he began early to contribute essays and stories to the Hebrew periodicals of the time, and later he also wrote in Yiddish and German.

The impact of European literature on Berdichevsky, especially the aesthetic individualism of Nietzsche, brought about a radical change in his attitude toward the national and social ideologies that permeated both Jewish society and Hebrew and Yiddish literature in the last two decades of the nineteenth century and the first decade of the twentieth century. He rebelled against utili-

261

tarianism in literature and questioned Ahad ha-Am's interpretations of Jewish history. Hence his struggle against crystallized "history" (the "book," the "script"), which, according to him, represents an accumulation of strictures crushing the individuality of the Jewish personality. Only aesthetic literature, which intuitively gives expression to man's deepest yearnings, is the real characteristic of the people. Because of this extreme individualism and aestheticism, the Hebrew critics of the time attached to him the name "Aher" ("the alien," "the apostate"), which underlines the loneliness of the great author.

The latter part of Berdichevsky's life was spent in Berlin and Breslau, where he became completely absorbed in philosophy and aesthetics, and where he also wrote his stories, which drew their subject matter from the Jewish past in the small towns of the Ukraine. He imbued the dormant milieu of the towns with deeply running intuitive and instinctive undercurrents of yearnings and struggles that had seemed to be long forgotten. By the same token Berdichevsky began to reinterpret the talmudic and midrashic aggadah in his *Sefer Hasidim* ("Book of Hasidim") and his *Mishnat Hasidim* ("The Teaching of Hasidim").

His collected works were published several times, and recently interest in his literary work has considerably revived in Israel.

ITZHAK DOV BERKOVITZ

Itzhak Dov Berkovitz (1885–1967) was born in Slutsk, White Russia. His early education was strictly religious; at the age of fourteen, however, he became interested in the Haskalah literature and turned also to secular studies. His first, youthful stories appeared in a stenciled "periodical" that he and his friends published. Later he came to Lodz, Poland, where he met the Hebrew poet Itzhak Katznelson (murdered in the Lodz Ghetto by the Nazis in 1944), who greatly encouraged him in his literary work. He wandered about for some time until he settled in 1905 in Vilna as the literary editor of the daily *Ha-Zeman* ("The Time"), in the meantime contributing stories to the most important Hebrew periodicals of the day and growing in stature as an author of epic prose.

Biographical Notes

In 1906 Berkovitz married Esther, the daughter of the renowned Shalom Aleikhem. Due to his various literary activities, both of them wandered about Europe until the end of 1913. At the beginning of World War I he emigrated to the United States. There he lived for a number of years, serving as the editor of the periodical *Ha-Toren* ("The Mast"). In 1928 he settled in Israel, where he was very active in writing, as well as in editing and translating Shalom Aleikhem's works into Hebrew, and also pioneering a Hebrew repertoire for the theaters of the country.

In his old age Berkovitz was one of the greatest prose writers in Hebrew literature and a most honored citizen of the state of Israel.

HAIYIM NAHMAN BIALIK

Haiyim Nahman Bialik was born in 1873 to a very poor family in the Ukraine. His father died while he was still a very young child, and he went to live with his strictly religious and kindhearted grandfather, who gave him a traditional Jewish education. At the age of sixteen Bialik began his studies at the great Yeshivah of Volozhin, where he spent several years, living in hardship and yearning for his family and for the "great world." At Volozhin he became intensely interested in the Haskalah literature and also began to study Russian literature. There, too, he wrote his first poem, which greatly impressed Hebrew readers.

Returning home, he became a teacher, and devoted much of his time to writing Hebrew poetry. In 1901 he settled in Odessa, one of the great centers of Hebrew culture. There he published his first volume of poems and also became the literary editor of the very important Hebrew monthly *Ha-Shilloah*. He also occupied himself, in collaboration with his friend Ravnitsky, with publishing a collection of modern, medieval, and aggadic literature. The people, as well as Hebrew criticism of the time, saw in him their greatest Hebrew poet.

In 1924, Bialik settled in Palestine and very soon became the most dynamic force in the cultural life of the country. He also went on many missions to the Jewish communities of Eastern Europe and America.

Besides poetry, Bialik also wrote stories and translated Cervantes' *Don Quixote,* Schiller's *Wilhelm Tell,* and Anski's *Der Dibbuk.* His poems are available in various English translations. He died in 1934, after a prolonged illness.

YOSEF HAIYIM BRENNER

Y. H. Brenner was born in the Ukraine in 1881. He was killed by an Arab sniper in the spring of 1921, not far from Tel Aviv.

Brenner was a wanderer for most of his life. In his youth he studied for a while at the Yeshivah in Pochep, White Russia, where he met his future intimate friend Uri Nissan Gnessin, the son of the head of the school. In 1897 Brenner went to Homel, where he was active in the life of the Jewish community. In Homel he joined the Jewish Socialist Party Bund, which he later left. While still young he began writing short stories in Hebrew, and his first story, "Pat Lehem" ("A Piece of Bread"), was published in 1900, in the then-influential journal *Ha-Melitz.* In the same year Ben-Avigdor's publishing company, Tushiyah, in Warsaw, published Brenner's first collection of stories, *Me-Emek Akhor* ("From the Valley of Gloom"), describing the poverty and hopeless desolation of Jewish life in the Pale of Settlement.

Brenner served as a private in the Russian army. The deep misery of his life there motivated his book, *Me-Alef ad Mem* ("From A to M"). From 1904 to 1908 he lived in London, where he worked as a publisher and a typesetter. In addition, he sold copies of his literary journal, *Ha-Meorer* ("The Awakener"), to which he had drawn the most important Hebrew writers of the time. In London he also published his long stories, *Ba-Horef* ("In the Winter"), and *Mi-Saviv la-Nekuddah* ("Around the Point"). He then went to Lemberg, in Galicia, where he met his friend Gershon Shoffman, with whose assistance he published his literary collection *Revivim* ("Showers").

Early in 1909, Brenner joined the pioneers of the Second Aliyah in Palestine. There he lived in various settlements and was regarded by the laborers as their comrade and teacher, as was his friend Aaron David Gordon. He contributed mostly controversial

Biographical Notes

critical essays on the new Hebrew literature to a variety of literary magazines, as well as articles on various social, political, and cultural problems of the time. His novel, *Shekhol ve-Khishalon* ("Misfortune and Failure"), was also published in Israel. Hope and despair, a keen sense of pity and justice, and an everlasting struggle for human decency were the traits of Brenner's dynamic personality.

MORDEKHAI ZE'EV FEIERBERG

See chaper 3, pp. 43–55.

DAVID FRISHMAN

David Frishman (1863–1922) was most of all an ardent pioneer of modern Hebrew literary criticism. He was born in Sgierz, Poland, and most of his adult life was dedicated to what he called the Europeanization of Hebrew literature. He scornfully rejected the flowery language of the Haskalah literature and mocked its lack of literary taste. He constantly advocated the expression of "beauty" as the ultimate aim of creative literature.

Frishman wrote some collections of short stories and poems. Besides his work as a literary critic, he is known as one of the greatest translators in Hebrew literature. He knew European languages and translated works of Goethe, Byron, Tagore, Nietzsche, Wilde, and many others into a beautiful Hebrew. He also did excellent work as an editor.

URI NISSAN GNESSIN

Uri Nissan Gnessin was born in 1879 in White Russia. He received an extensive education in the talmudic institute headed by his father, where he also met his life-long friend Yosef Haiyim Brenner. In 1900 he went to Warsaw and worked on a newspaper, *Ha-Tzefirah* ("The Hebrew Daily"), in which he published his youthful poems.

Gnessin traveled about Russia, Poland, and elsewhere, driven by his changing moods and looking for some source of livelihood. At the invitation of Brenner, he settled for a few years in London, and then he visited Palestine. The first collection of his stories, *Tzilelé ha-Haiyim* ("The Shadows of Life"), was published in 1909.

As Gnessin went on writing his stories, he became more and more introspective, withdrawn, and given to pessimistic fatalism. His expression of these moods is unique in its originality of language and style.

Gnessin died in 1913, at the age of 34. Interest in Gnessin's works has recently been greatly revived among Hebrew critics in Israel and America.

AARON DAVID GORDON

Aaron David Gordon was born in 1856, in Troyanov, Russia, and died in Deganiah, a settlement in Israel, in 1922. In his youth he received a Jewish religious education. He served for a time as a minor official for Baron Guenzburg, but in 1904, at the age of forty-eight, he left for Palestine. There he became a manual worker among the men and women of the Second Aliyah.

Gordon soon became a leader and teacher of the Jewish workers in Palestine. By his writings and living example he developed the idea of the return of the Jew to his own soil in the land of Israel. Thus, he may be regarded as the father of Halutzism, or pioneering, in Israel.

For Gordon, work was based on a cosmic idea, binding mankind not only to nature, but also to the entire universe. This doctrine was not unlike that of Tolstoy, who greatly influenced Gordon, and his philosophy thus acquired a religious nature. But above all, he taught that work binds man to the soil of his own community and of his own country, so that a people can take root in its own land only by means of work, especially farming.

HAIYIM HAZAZ

Haiyim Hazaz was born in 1898 in the Ukraine. The beautiful countryside surrounding his small town had impressed him deeply in his childhood and later served as background for one of his first novels. His writings, however, soon underwent a drastic change, for the October Revolution and its aftermath of civil wars completely uprooted the Jewish communities in the Ukraine, and this uprootedness became the main theme of Hazaz's stories.

He left Russia for Paris and elsewhere in Europe in the early years of the Revolution. There his stories drew their material from the life of the Jewish communities in European capitals, a Jewry whose foundations had already been undermined by the cruicial changes that shook the world.

In 1921 Hazaz settled in Israel. There he became intensely interested in the life of the Yemenite Jews and devoted much of his time to closely observing their family and individual life, studying their customs and their manner of speech. He then wrote a series of stories based on his observations of the Yemenite Jews and of other oriental Jews, including *Ya'ish,* in four parts, *Mori Sa'id,* translated into English by Ben Halpern, *Rahamim the Porter,* translated into English by I. M. Lask, and a number of others.

With the establishment of the state of Israel, Hazaz has turned to the various oriental and non-oriental Jewish settlements in the Negev and in the Lakhish district, observing their problems of adaptation to their new surroundings, their economic, social, and cultural difficulties, their worries and aspirations. His stories have assumed a specific quality that expresses the historic destiny of Kibbuz Galuyot ("the ingathering of the exiles"). His Hebrew is based on the idioms of countless Jewish generations, a very flexible language and one capable of delving into the depths.

Today Hazaz is ranked among the greatest Hebrew authors and is a highly honored citizen of Israel.

RABBI LEIB SORÉ'S

Rabbi Leib Soré's was one of the most heroic figures in eighteenth-century Hasidism. There is very little authentic biographical information about him, for his personality seems to be completely enveloped in hasidic fantasy and folklore. He always lived among the plain people, wandering from place to place in the disguise of the simpleton, the ignorant, the lowly. Yet "in reality," according to legend, he was one of the very few holy men for whose sake the world can still exist. Tradition always portrays him as struggling against Satan and evil doers, and their deeds, thus bringing solace to the poor, the afflicted, and the despairing.

MENDELÉ MOKHER SEFARIM
(Literary name of Shalom Jacob Abramovich)

Mendelé Mokher Sefarim was born in Lithuania in 1836 and died in 1917. He received an extensive religious education, and, after the death of his father, he also studied at a Yeshivah. His mother's second husband was a mill owner in the village of Mel- niki, in Lithuania, and the young Shalom came to live with them. The quiet Lithuanian countryside later provided him with ma- terial for the landscapes in his various novels, especially in *Sefer ha-Kabtzanim* ("The Book of the Beggars").

Much of Mendelé's writing still belonged to the type of the Haskalah, having as its aim the struggle for changes in the life of the Jewish community. His stories and novels, however, finally assumed the character of great creative writing. It was only then that he changed his name to the folkish pseudonym Mendelé Mokher Sefarim ("Mendelé the Wandering Bookseller").

Mendelé first wrote his novels in Yiddish, and later rewrote them in Hebrew, opening the new era of modern Jewish litera- ture in both languages. His stark literary naturalism reflects much of the actual Jewish life of his time—a life of poverty, misery, and social injustice. Most of all, however, Mendelé's writings serve to satisfy the creative urges of the author in search of an adequate expression in Yiddish and in Hebrew.

His flexible Hebrew style, which made use of mishnaic and midrashic idiom, opened great potentialities for the development of modern Hebrew literature in all its variations and phases.

RABBI NAHMAN OF BRASLAV

Rabbi Nahman of Braslav was born in 1772 in Medzhibozh, in the Ukraine. Being the great-grandson of Rabbi Eliezer Baal- Shem-Tov, the founder of the hasidic movement, Nahman was raised in an intensively hasidic environment. He was deeply immersed in studies of the Talmud and the Kabbalah, and had an everlasting desire to commune with his Creator through prayer, singing, and dancing, in which the whole universe would participate. His doctrine stressed the idea that all things in nature, whether animate or inanimate, possess an inner "mind," an internal light constantly waiting for man to recognize it and awaken the worship of God.

Man, however, is usually in deep spiritual slumber and is in constant need of being awakened. For his prayers can rise to the Almighty himself only by means of the hidden light of the soul, a light of great charm and beauty that serves as the greatest means of true worship. This doctrine was a result of torturous efforts and deeply conflicting moods—great elation on one hand and dark melancholy and despair on the other. Rabbi Nahman seemed to have overcome them in the end by the attainment of "dibbur" ("speech"), which manifested itself in his talks with his most ardent follower, recorder, and editor, Rabbi Nathan of Nemirov, and in his stories, which he would periodically tell his hasidim. His doctrine was written down in his book *Likkuté Moharan,* and an analytical biography of him, *Haiyé Moharan,* was written by Rabbi Nathan of Nemirov.

Rabbi Nahman's doctrines and ways of prayer were bitterly opposed by many hasidic centers and aroused against him the animosity of certain famous hasidic rabbis. In 1798 he visited Palestine, hoping to be inspired by the sight of the Holy Land. On his return he became ill and had to leave the town of Medvekova, where he had moved earlier and attracted many followers, for the town of Uman. He died there in 1811.

JOSEPH OPATOSHU

Joseph Opatoshu was born in 1889 in Mlawa, Poland, where he received a very good Jewish education. He participated in the Russian Revolution of 1905, and after its failure he left for France, where he studied engineering. In 1907 he emigrated to the United States. There he worked as a newsboy, a factory laborer, and a teacher in a Hebrew school in New York.

In 1914 Opatoshu decided on a literary career. His main writings were in Yiddish; his short stories and novels drew most of their subject matter from various generations in Jewish history. He also wrote in Hebrew and contributed stories to various Hebrew periodicals in Europe and in the United States. Many of his books have been translated into Hebrew and other languages, among them the novel *In the Forests of Poland,* a work of great epic quality.

Opatoshu died in New York in 1954.

ITZHAK LEIB PERETZ

Itzhak Leib Peretz (1852–1915) was born in Zamocz, Poland. He received a thorough religious education and also studied Hebrew language and literature, as well as European languages. He was greatly influenced by the new "schools" of European literature, which profoundly stimulated his efforts to modernize literary creativity in Yiddish. He thus came to be considered the father of modern Jewish literature.

Peretz's occupations were many, but he is primarily remembered as the great master of the short story and as the guide of a younger generation of writers in their search for new forms of expression in poetry, fiction, and drama. His was a dynamic personality, and he dedicated all his creative efforts to extricating himself and the younger Jewish writers from the moralistic utilitarianism of the Haskalah period.

A number of Peretz's stories were written in an impressionistic vein, while his hasidic stories and his most important play, *Di Goldené Keyt,* utilize a symbolic mysticism not unlike the Polish and French symbolism he adored. One of his plays even adopted the expressionism that was very characteristic of some European literature of the time.

Peretz had always been alert to his Jewish environment and to the social, economic, and cultural problems of the Jewish community in Poland and Eastern Europe. His essays on those problems are marked by profundity of thinking and creative lucidity of expression.

Biographical Notes

SHALOM ALEIKHEM
(Literary name of Shalom Rabinovich)

Shalom Aleikhem, a pen name which is a specific Jewish greeting meaning "peace be with you," was born in Pereyaslav, Russia, in 1859. He began his literary career in Hebrew, but very soon he turned to Yiddish, the language of the Jewish masses in Eastern Europe. With Mendelé Mokher Sefarim and I. L. Peretz he became one of the three master builders of Yiddish literature (and of Hebrew literature as well, due to the excellent translations of his works by his son-in-law, Itzhak Dov Berkovitz).

Shalom Aleikhem has endeared himself to generations of Jewish readers by the great humor that permeates his writings. His humor was profoundly humane, a mixture of light and shadows reflecting the tragedy of the Jewish individual caught in the social, economic, and religious changes characteristic of that period in Jewish history.

Shalom Aleikhem had ups and downs in his many business affairs, but whenever he could he helped financially and otherwise in furthering the development of modern Yiddish literature, whether by publishing periodicals, anthologies, and literary collections, or by advancing honorariums to participating authors.

In the later years of his life, Shalom Aleikhem was ill for long periods and visited many of the healing centers of Europe in search of some alleviation of his pain. When World War I broke out he came to the United States. He died in New York in 1916.

GERSHON SHOFFMAN

Gershon Shoffman was born in 1880 in Orsha, White Russia. His education was religious; he studied in several "small yeshivot." In 1901 he came to Warsaw, where a collection of his stories was published; it was well received by the reviewers. He served for three years in the Russian army at Homel, where he was befriended by Uri Nissan Gnessin and a number of other young Hebrew authors. During the Russo-Japanese War, he lived in Galicia, writing his short stories and teaching. In the city of

271

Lemberg he met Y. H. Brenner and became one of his best friends, assisting him in the publication of the literary collection *Revivim* ("Showers"). In 1914 a collection of his short stories was published in Odessa. Shoffman later moved to Vienna and contributed stories to the most important Hebrew periodicals of the time. Four volumes of his stories were published during the years 1926 to 1937.

Shoffman lived about eight years in the village of Gratz, Austria. When the Nazis crushed Austria, Shoffman and his family went to Israel. He now lives in the beautiful city of Haifa.

HILLEL ZEITLIN

Hillel Zeitlin was born in 1872 in Russia, in a deeply religious and hasidic environment that left an indelible mark on him throughout his life. He did not, however, remain isolated within the walls of the Bet ha-Midrash or Yeshivah for long. He became enchanted by European literature, especially by the aesthetic pessimism of Schopenhauer, Hartman, Nietzsche, Shestov, and by the depths of Spinoza. His first published work was *Ha-Tov veha-Ra* ("The Good and the Evil"), published in 1898; it was followed by two monographs on Spinoza and Nietzsche in 1900.

Zeitlin regarded himself as a Hebrew thinker whose greatest task was to prove the philosophic and religious relationship between the Kabbalah and Hasidut on one hand, and Zarathustra, Spinoza, Schopenhauer, and Nietzsche on the other. He thought of his efforts as a change of values and a new solution for mankind.

Zeitlin, however, could not detach himself from the actualities of the Jewish life of his time. His urge to react to the various social, political, and cultural problems of East European Jewry drew him to journalistic work in Yiddish dailies. From 1916 he was one of the most fruitful Yiddish journalists, writing for *Der Heint* and later for *Der Moment*.

In the last years of his life Zeitlin became more and more steeped in religious mysticism and orthodoxy. The Nazis murdered him in the Warsaw Ghetto.

Glossary

Aggadah: the legends of the Talmud and the Midrash; the homiletical sections of rabbinic literature.

Azazel and Shemhazai: two heavenly beings who, according to legend, descended from heaven and married "the Daughters of Men."

Balak: the king of Moab who sent Balaam to curse the Hebrews in the desert.

Batalon: see *Kabtziel.*

Bet ha-Midrash: house of religious learning and prayer.

Chariot mysticism: speculation about the divine chariot, "God's preexisting throne, which embodies and exemplifies all forms of creation" (Gershom Scholem, *Major Trends in Jewish Mysticism* [New York: Schocken Books, 1941], p. 44), arising from the description of Ezekiel and from other sources of mysticism.

Deganiah: see *Kinneret.*

Diaspora: "dispersion"; the Jews living outside Israel.

Etsel: ultra-nationalist Jewish military organization that fought against the British mandatory government.

Gaberdine: a long garment worn by orthodox Jews.

Garden of Eden: Paradise; home of righteous men after death.

Gehinom: hell; the place where wicked men are punished after death.

Gemara: "compilation"; the second and supplementary part of the Talmud that interprets the first part, the Mishnah.

Halakhah: the legal part of the Talmud and rabbinic literature.

Hasid: pious follower of the hasidic movement.

Hasidut: the hasidic movement.

Haskalah: "enlightenment"; term designating a rationalist period in Hebrew literature.

Havdalah: the benediction over the cup of wine at the conclusion of the Sabbath and the festivals.

Heder: religious elementary school.

Herut: ultra-nationalist political party in Israel.

Hoshanot: "hosannas"; set of prayers recited in the synagogue at the Feast of Tabernacles; willow twigs used in a liturgical ceremony while the prayers are recited.

Hovot ha-Levavot: "Duties of the Heart"; a morality book written by a medieval Jewish philosopher, Rabbi Bahya ibn Pakuda, who lived in the eleventh century.

Japheth: youngest son of Noah; the ancestor of the white non-Semitic races.

273

GLOSSARY

Kabbalah: Jewish mysticism and its literature.

Kabtziel, Kissalon, Batalon, Madmenah: names of towns in the novels of Mendelé Mokher Sefarim ("the town of beggars," "the town of fools," "the town of idlers," "the town of mud").

Kegavna: a mystic description of the "the Queen Sabbath," taken from the Zohar and included in the liturgy on the eve of the Sabbath.

Kelippah: an evil spirit in the Kabbalah.

Kimhi, David (1160–1235): a medieval commentator on the Bible and Hebrew grammarian.

Kinneret, Deganiah: two communes founded in Palestine by Jewish pioneers who immigrated there during the first decade of the twentieth century.

Kissalon: see *Kabtziel.*

Kol Nidré: the solemn chant at the beginning of the service on the eve of the Day of Atonement (Yom Kippur).

Lekhu Neranenah: Psalm 95, which serves as the beginning of the service on the eve of the Sabbath.

Lurianic Kabbalah: the mysticism that Rabbi Isaac Luria introduced into the teachings of the Kabbalah in the sixteenth century.

Breaking of the Vessels: term denoting the idea that the endless divine light that filled all space before creation was broken by the creation of finite beings and forms.

Sparks: the sparks of this broken light wander throughout the universe, and only when they return (after the breakdown of the evil forces in man and in the world) to their original source in heaven will man and the universe be redeemed.

Husks or Shells: the forces of evil.

The Right Side: the realm of light and holiness.

The Other Side: the realm of evil, of Satan.

Madmenah: see *Kabtziel.*

Maidanék and *Treblinka:* places in Poland where the Nazis established extermination centers for European Jews.

Malbim (1809–79): commentator on the Bible.

Maskil: follower of the Jewish Enlightenment. An enlightened man.

Midrash: homiletical commentary on the Scriptures.

Minyan: ten adult Jews, the minimum for congregational prayers.

Musar: instruction in moral behavior; a specific school of piety.

Nebuchadnezzar: the Babylonian military commander who exiled the Jews in Babylon.

Rebbe: Yiddish word for rabbi, hasidic leader, religious teacher.

Sabbatai Tzevi (1625–76): the leader of a false messianic movement.

Second Aliyah: the second immigration to Palestine, 1904–14.

Selihot: special prayers for forgiveness.

274

Glossary

Seventeenth of Tammuz: the day of fasting and mourning for the breaking of the wall of Jerusalem by the Babylonians. Tammuz is the month approximating June to July.

Shaar ha-Hamishim: "the Fiftieth Gate"; the ultimate mystery of the universe.

Shaharit: morning prayers.

Shekhinah: the mystical feminine element of God's glory.

Shem: oldest son of Noah; the ancestor of the Semitic peoples.

Shema Israel: "Hear, O Israel"; the confession of the unity of God.

Shtetl: small Jewish town in Eastern Europe.

Shofar: the ram's horn blown at the synagogue on the High Holy Days.

Shohet: ritual slaughterer.

Tah and Tat: the massacre of the Jews by the Cossacks of Khmelnitski (1648–49).

Talmud: Jewish "oral law" based on the "written law" of the Scripture.

Tallit: prayer shawl.

Tefilin: phylacteries.

Torah: the literature of the Jewish law; the Pentateuch.

Tzaddik: a great hasidic rabbi.

Tzenah Ure-enah: a Yiddish collection of biblical stories, midrashim, aggadot, and commentaries read by pious Jewish women, especially in the Eastern European countries, on Sabbath afternoons.

Yeshivah: a school of higher talmudic learning.

Yom Kippur: the tenth day of Tishri, the month corresponding to September-October; "Day of Atonement," a day of fasting and prayer for forgiveness, the holiest day of the Jewish calendar.

Zohar: the book of the Kabbalah presumed to have been written in the thirteenth century.

Index

Abramowitch, Shalom Ya'akov, 4, 267; *see also* Mendelé Mokher Sefarim

Aestheticism: of Peretz, 29, 30, 38, 44; of Gnessin, 70; of Baum, 81; of Brenner, 91; of Zeitlin, 102, 103–5, 110; German aesthetes, 104; of Berdichevsky, 126, 127, 128, 131, 133–34, 144; new, 129–30; of Agnon, 217, 220, 227, 230

Aggadah, 204, 206; dynamic force of, 208, 213, 220, 221, 222, 262

Agnon, Shmuel Yosef, viii, 9, 52, 169; realism, 177, 185, 189, 192, 196, 202, 208, 210, 219, 221; *The Bridal Canopy*, 178–92; epic quality of works, 178, 180, 202, 204, 205, 206, 209, 210, 211, 214, 220; sense of unity, 178, 181, 185, 188, 189; technique, 178, 179, 181, 184, 185, 187, 191, 196, 214–15; dialectic element, 179; dialogue, 179, 185; loquacity, 179; Messiah, 179, 180, 203, 213; folkloristic and religious sources, 179, 180, 181, 185, 187, 191, 197, 204–5; omniscient author/narrator, 180, 192, 211; redemption, 180, 185, 201, 218; style, 180, 187, 201, 222; symbolism, 181, 185, 193, 196, 208, 202–9; characters, 182, 187, 192, 211–13, 226; modernism, 183, 188, 202, 205, 209; satire, humor, and irony, 183, 188, 211–12, 224, 228, 229, 231; rhythm of prose, 184, 216; ambivalence, 185, 196; organization of works, 186; artistic purpose, 189, 205, 209, 211–12, 223–24; language, 190, 196, 204, 210, 216; and Mendelé, 190; *A Wayfarer Tarries the Night*, 192–209; "crises," 192; illusion, 192, 193, 195, 196; nightmare, 196, 199, 206; children, 200–201; *The Crooked Shall Be Made Straight*, 202; demonology, 213, 224; trilogy, 213, 218; *The Book of Deeds*, 214–18; expressionism, 214, 226; surrealism, 214; and Kafka, 216; *A Day Before Yesterday*, 218–32; fantasy, 219; naturalism, 224; madness, 230; prizes, 259

Ahad ha-Am: essays of, 2, 15; humanist philosophy of, 45, 48; secular nationalism of, 49; and *Ha-Shilloah*, 49, 130; intellectualism of, 50, 55, 104; school of, 124; historical teaching of, 125; "historical account" of, 126, 127; concept of "spiritual center" of, 128; influence of European philosophy on, 128, 130, 131, 136; national intellect in writings of, 137, 144, 260; interpretation of, 262

Aher, 262

Aliyah: Second, 15, 97, 99, 123, 166, 167, 173, 209, 212, 219, 220, 222, 224, 259, 264; Third, 172; *see also* Brenner, Yosef Haiyim

Altenberg, Peter, 242

Anski, Solomon: and Jewish folklore, 11; *The Dibbuk*, 40, 204, 239, 264

Ash, Shalom: first novels, 24, 43; "The Country Tzaddik," 151–53, 155, 260, 261

Autobiography, 66, 87; elements

277

Index

Brainin, Reuben, 144, 145, 146
Brenner, Yosef Haiyim, 46, 55, 56, 63, 73, 74, 80, 81; stories, 81; *Around the Point*, 81–100; meaning of personal life, 82; psychological and ideological searching, 82, 85, 89; messianic role, 83; "point," 84, 98; ambivalence, 84; tragic quality, 84; contradictions and struggles, 84, 85, 86; satire, 85, 86; style, 86; and Baum, 87; pessimism, 87; depths, 87; artistic longing, 87; levels of meaning, 88, 90; inner world, 88; language, 89; sadness, 89; tragedy of, 90; realism, 91; and Abramson, 92; social aspects of works, 93; primitive force, 93; messianic echoes, 94; expressionistic naturalism, 94–95; immediacy of expression, 96; existential basis of stories, 98, 99; and Second Aliyah, 99, 265; with pioneers in Israel, 100, 104, 107, 111, 112, 114, 116, 119, 121, 124, 149, 150, 158; and expressionism, 160, 162, 169, 171, 190, 205, 218, 219, 223, 240, 264; and *Ha-Meorer* and *Revivim*, 264; personality, 265, 272
Briand, Aristide, 236
Brod, Max, 242
Broides, Reuben Asher, 148
Brooks, Cleanth, ix
Bruriah (wife of Rabbi Meir), 4
Buber, Martin, 259
Buffoonery, 64
Bund, socialist, 25, 264
Byron, George Gordon, Lord, 243, 265

Cecil, Robert, Lord, 236
Cervantes, Miguel de, 264
Chariot mysticism, 33
Chekhov, Anton Pavlovich, 242

Cohen, Ya'akov, 239
Collection of Hebrew literature, 233–36
Comic: quality, 8, 9, 10, 13, 170; vein, 175; demonological purpose, 226
Communities, Jewish: in Eastern Europe, 1, 2; in Poland, 25; in Poland, Lithuania, and the Ukraine, 46, 85; in America, 263; *see also* Bialik, Haiyim Nahman
"Confusion of the Domains," 45
Congress of Hebrew Literature and Culture, 233–35
Cossacks, 25, 261
Crisis: European, 233; of art forms, 234
Criticism, literary, 174; new, viii, 84; modern, 52
Czaczkes, Shmuel Yosef, 259; *see also* Agnon, Shmuel Yosef
Czernowitz Conference, 45

Dante, 88, 240
Decadent movement, 80, 144, 196
Deganiah, 99, 219, 223, 232, 265
Dela Reina, Joseph, 4
Dialectic element, 179
Diaspora, 1, 10, 11, 52, 94, 167, 168, 174, 177, 260
Dichotomy. *See* Brenner, Yosef Haiyim
Dickens, Charles, 10, 242
Didacticism: social, 6; intellectual, 40, 45; rational, 49; of satire, 95; moral, 130, 145, 204
Diesendruck, Tzevi, 239
Dostoevsky, Feodor Mikhailovich, 107, 240, 241
Dyboski, R., 249

Ein Ganim, 167, 221–23, 226, 232
Elegiacs, Latin, 239
Eliot, T. S., ix, 173, 236

279

Index

Index

Kabak, Aaron, 168
Kabbalah: mystic symbolism, vii; popular Kabbalah, 4, 5, 33, 34, 180; symbolic and allegorical categories of, 4; demonic dualism, 5; "practical" Kabbalists, 34; folklore of, 35, 47, 136, 142, 145, 479; "orchards" of, 108, 109, 110, 125, 132, 133; literature in, 139; visions from, 142; sayings of, 187; philosophy of, 207, 234, 238, 239, 240, 242, 269, 272
Kafka: *The Castle*, 71, 79; style of, 73, 80; universe of, 207; world of, 216, 218
Kariv, Abraham, 8
Katznelson, Itzhak, 262
Katznelson, Yehudah Leib, 148
Kegavna, 135
Khmelnitski, Bogdan, massacres of, 47, 261
Kibbutz, 122, 123, 173
Kibbutz Galuyot, 267
Kiev, 66; intelligentsia of, 77, 78
Kimhi, Rabbi David, 136
Kimhi, Dov, 168
Kinneret, 99, 219, 223, 232
Klatzkin, Ya'akov, 240
Klausner, Joseph, 7, 13
Kossover, Rabbi Baruch, *The Book of Faith*, 49
Kotzk: Rabbi of, 5; hasidim of, 43
Krokhmal, Nahman, *Guide for the Perplexed of the Time*, 49

Lakhish, 267
Lakhover, Fischel: on Feierberg, 47, 49, 51, 52, 53; on Berdichevsky, 127, 147
Landau, Zisho, 44
Language: musicality of, 62; simplicity of, 94, 119, 120, 135, 164, conciseness of, 138; Berdichevsky's, 141; Berkovitz', 149; per-

ceptiveness, 163–64; expressing future, 175; abstract, 177; inner dimensions of, 190; richness and immediacy of, 190; of complex dialogue, 195; and demonic impulses, 213; sensitive, 216; intensity of, 224, 226; grotesque undercurrents in, 225; European languages, 260
Lask, I. M., 267
Leib, Mané, 44
Leib Soré's, Rabbi, 47, 51, 267
Lekhu Neranena, 135
Levontin, Itzhak, 148
Literature: Yiddish, 22, 25, 43, 44, 45, 158; European, 25, 181, 218, 270, 272; Polish, 26, 240; Russian, 26, 69, 83, 147, 263; aesthetic movement of, 45; Western European, 69, 131; of nostalgia, 166; realistic, 169; world, 222; humanistic, 235, 236; Western, 240, 243, 261
Lithuania, yeshivah in, 268
Lodz, ghetto of, 262
Loss and Failure, 93, 99, 100; *see also* Brenner, Yosef Haiyim
Lublin, 28
Ludwig, Emil, 242
Luria, Rabbi Isaac, 33, 139; Lurianic Kabbalah, 4; and "breaking of the vessels," 33; and "Right Side" and "Other Side," 33; messianism of, 204
Lyricism, 78, 79, 118, 123; delicate, 155; pleasant, 167

Maeterlinck, Maurice: symbolism of, 30; symbolist works of, 36, 38, 39, 241; *Pelléas et Mélisande* and *Les Aveugles*, 38; responsiveness to a world beyond the physical, 39
Maidanék, 105, 240

283

Index

Rabinowitz, Alexander Siskind, 147, 148
Rabinowitz, Shalom Nahum, 14; *see also* Shalom Aleikhem
Ravnitski, Yosef Haiyim, 137, 233, 263
Realism: static, 9, 10, 11; and humanism, 14–24, 237; literary, 32, 46, 52, 59, 127, 130–31, 148–49, 165, 190, 219; historical, 53; rejected, 55; blurred, 56, 192; in setting, 58, 150–51; and isolation, 67; and description, 68, 74, 134; intense, 69, 91; concrete, 75; new, 77; psychological, 77; ultimate, 79; surface, 82, 214; and truth, 82; deeply rooted, 87; as veil, 89; direct, 93, 101; middle way of, 104, 111; vivid, 112; immediacy of, 121; startling, 123; primitive, 126, 196; and illusions, 129; weakened, 131; of the Jewish scene, 150, 151; mundane, 153, 154, 202; full, 156; level of, 163; toned down, 166; bent toward, 167, 175; messianism and, 180; and fantasy, 182; realm of, 185; visionary, 195; nightmarish, 204; architectonic, 210; and fulfillment, 219; and portrayal, 221; and atmosphere, 224
Renaissance, Hebrew, viii; poetry of, 2, 15, 261
Reuveni, Aaron, 168
Revivim, 264, 272
Rhythm, 57, 61, 68; special, 61
Rolland, Romain, 236, 237, 241
Russian Revolution: October, 44, 121, 166, 169, 170, 171, 172, 175, 176, 194, 267; of 1905, 269

Sabbatai Tzevi. *See* Tzevi, Sabbatai
Samael, 5; as Satan, 48, 51, 54; satanic intent of, 228; and comedy, 231
Sarcasm, 78, 79
Satan, 268
Satire: 7, 11, 94, 224; intellectual, 45; vein of, 85, 86; and intent, 95; and irony, 183, 185, 186, 188; *see also* Mendelé Mokher Sefarim
Schiller, Friedrich, 242, 264
Schopenhauer, Arthur: pessimistic fatalism of, 81, 102, 103; inspiration of, 103, 104; noble pessimism of, 106; ideas of, 128, 130, 233, 272
Scriptures, 3; contradictions in, 102
Secularism, 89; and stories, 173; studies in, 262
Shakespeare, William, 11, 242
Shalom Aleikhem (pseudonym of Shalom Nahum Rabinowitz), viii, 14; humanism and realism in writings of, 14–24, 32, 148, 151, 154, 156; interest in writings of, 15; historic and artistic undercurrent, 16; tragic depth and humorous redemption, 16, 17, 19; world of, 16; characters, 17, 20, 23; epic quality in writings, 18; existential meaning, 18; and haskalah writing, 19; irony and humor, 20, 163, 183, 184, 263, 271; and monologue, 20–22
Shekhinah, 142
Shemhazai, 140, 142
Shestov, Lev: philosophy of, 107, 110, 111, 239, 272; and despair, 110
Shimonovitz, David, 240
Shneour, Zalman, 14
Shneour Zalman of Lyady, Rabbi, 109
Shofar, 232

Due